Ruth McClendon
Leslie B. Kadis

Reconciling Relationships and Preserving the Family Business
Tools for Success

Pre-publication
REVIEWS,
COMMENTARIES,
EVALUATIONS . . .

"*Reconciling Relationships and Preserving the Family Business* is a practical survival guide that should be required reading for anyone thinking of creating or currently involved in a family business, whether they be family members, professional advisors, or nonfamily member managers. Ruth McClendon and Les Kadis, a licensed clinical social worker and a psychiatrist, have applied their internationally recognized expertise in couple and family therapy to help families cope successfully with the myriad challenges encountered in running their own businesses. These prominent clinicians and educators have developed a unique intervention called the Reconciliation Model. This approach can assist families in sustaining healthy relationships during both good and bad economic times. This outstanding book, written for non–mental health professionals, introduces basic psychotherapeutic concepts and assessment tools frequently used by therapists in a jargon-free style that should prove informative and refreshing to the general reader. McClendon and Kadis, who operate their own family-run business, the Carmel Institute for Family Business, draw on their own experience as well as expertise to provide insights into the psychological sequelae of business decisions. I highly recommend this excellent book, written by well-respected mental health professionals, for anyone involved in family businesses anywhere in the world."

Robert E. Hales, MD, MBA
Joe P. Tupin Professor and Chair,
Department of Psychiatry
and Behavioral Sciences,
Davis School of Medicine,
University of California,
Sacramento

More pre-publication
REVIEWS, COMMENTARIES, EVALUATIONS . . .

"When you enter the world of secrets, hidden agendas, power plays, and revenge, you have entered the realm of family business. You will need trusty guides and effective tools. This book is it. The authors thoroughly understand the complexities, joys, and struggles of melding family and business concerns. Your clients will be grateful you took the effort to read this book."

Peter Pearson, PhD
Co-Director, The Couples Institute,
Menlo Park, California

"Open your mind and your heart and allow Ruth McClendon and Les Kadis to courageously guide you along the previously uncharted path of reconciliation in family business. With wisdom, clarity, and enlightenment, they tackle the daunting task of bringing about lasting change and reconciliation in damaged or traumatized relationships in family businesses. After reading this book, you will understand the complexity of the obligations, loyalties, and responsibilities each family business member faces; how to define the necessary characteristics of future leaders for the business rather than selecting favored children; and how to tackle thorny boundary issues of who is in and who is out (in-laws/stepchildren). You will never look at a family business the same way after reading this extraordinary book!"

Ellyn Bader, PhD
Co-Director, The Couples Institute,
Menlo Park, California

"This book is an in-depth exploration of relationships in family businesses. It comes at a critical moment due to the enormous pressures to succeed in a rapidly changing world. As experienced practitioners, the authors bring profound insights into the intricacies of one of the most rewarding and challenging of human enterprises—the family business. Through the application of powerful tools, this book will help families in business together understand and master the complexity of their relationships. Families working together constantly face the potential for hidden as well as explosive conflict. Within the framework of the Reconciliation Model, the authors offer a highly effective method for resolving the wounds of the past and rebuilding trust for the future. The reader will discover how separation and broken bonds can be handled successfully, and how this is at the heart of success in personal and business relationships. This is a must-read book for anyone operating in a family-run business, or for any organizational leader wishing to understand the role of reconciliation in keeping people motivated and inspired. It is rare that a book can translate so directly into practical application with a direct and immediate result on the botton line."

George A. Kohlrieser, PhD
Professor of Leadership
and Organizational Behavior,
International Institute
for Management Development,
Lausanne, Switzerland

Reconciling Relationships and Preserving the Family Business
Tools for Success

THE HAWORTH PRESS
Titles of Related Interest

Reconciling Relationships and Preserving the Family Business
Tools for Success

Ruth McClendon
Leslie B. Kadis

The Haworth Press®
New York • London • Oxford

The Haworth Press, Inc., 10 Alice Street, Binghamton, NY 13904-1580.

PUBLISHER'S NOTE
Identities and circumstances of individuals discussed in this book have been changed to protect confidentiality. Any resemblance to actual persons, living or dead, is entirely coincidental.

Material adapted from NO EXCUSES MANAGEMENT by T. J. Rodgers, William Taylor, and Rick Foreman, copyright © 1993 by T. J. Rodgers, William Taylor, and Rick Foreman. Used by permission of Doubleday, a division of Random House, Inc.

Cover design by Jennifer M. Gaska.

Library of Congress Cataloging-in-Publication Data

McClendon, Ruth.
    Reconciling relationships and preserving the family business : tools for success / Ruth McClendon, Leslie B. Kadis.
        p. cm.
    Includes bibliographical references and index.
    ISBN 0-7890-1799-7 (alk. paper) — ISBN 0-7890-1800-4 (pbk. : alk. paper)
    1. Family-owned business enterprises. 2. Family corporations. 3. Family—Economic aspects. 4. Reconciliation. 5. Family psychotherapy. 6. Communication in the family. I. Kadis, Leslie B. II. Title.

HD62.25.M39 2003
658'.04—dc21
                                                                                  2003001810

This book is dedicated to our three daughters, Lee Beer and Cheryl Kadis, who after years in Silicon Valley have just started their own family business, and Julie McClendon-Kadis, a recent graduate in business, whose financial and marketing skills have already helped her sisters.

May you use your experiences to strengthen your relationship.

ABOUT THE AUTHORS

Ruth McClendon, MSW, and **Leslie B. Kadis, MD,** are co-founders of the Carmel Institute for Family Business, a consulting organization offering services to family firms across the United States and around the world. They have co-written two books on family therapy—*Chocolate Pudding and Other Approaches to Intensive Multiple Family Therapy* and *Concise Guide to Marital and Family Therapy*—and developed the Reconciliation Model for resolving relational conflicts. Ms. McClendon is a psychotherapist working in private practice and is a founding board member and fellow of the Family Firm Institute, a national forum for business practitioners. Dr. Kadis is a former editorial board member of The Family Business Review and has been honored as a Fellow by the American Psychiatric Association for his professional and community work.

CONTENTS

Foreword

In the past two decades myriad books have been published on assorted topics revolving around family businesses and family business consultation/advising. Yet none fill the same niche that McClendon and Kadis so candidly and compassionately address in *Reconciling Relationships and Preserving the Family Business: Tools for Success.* Their writing is lucid and succinct, yet descriptive and analytic. The book is refreshingly free of professional jargon, yet it is clear that they are deeply steeped in the lure, drama, and day-to-day functioning of a multiplicity of kinds and sizes of family firms.

Most remarkable is the outstanding ability of these two clinicians, both of whom have vast experience as individual, family, and group therapists as well as family-business consultants, separately and as a team, to transform the concepts and techniques of what they developed and designated Redecision Relationship Therapy (RRT) from the therapeutic arena to the family business consultation arena. What emerges is the Reconciliation Model, a superb model for helping families who are in business together to deal with the real and imagined hurts, insults, schisms, and disagreements that have transpired and existed between them so that they are able to heal the wounds and resolve the deep-seated hostilities that plague their personal and business relationships. As a family business consultant who shares their background as an individual, family, and group psychologist/therapist, I have found their model absolutely brilliant and compelling since I was first introduced to it several years ago. Their careful, precise yet still flexible delineation of the Reconciliation Model is presented in such a way that it is understandable to the diverse audience to whom it should have appeal and applicability: family business owners and their relatives, nonfamily-member managers and supervisors, shareholders interested in knowing more about the company in which they have invested, and consultants ranging from novices to sophisticated, longtime family business advisors. Particularly noteworthy is how they balance their sensitivity to individual feelings and needs, the relational dynamics, and the reality of business demands and pressures. The authors know the heartbreak of rifts and cutoffs in family systems and how costly and devastating this can be to everyone who falls within the purview of what they call the "family community," a wonderfully useful conceptualization of the gestalt. They also know and convey the exhilaration that occurs and the momentum that can be achieved when apologies are made, forgiveness bestowed, and reconciliation achieved. This is essential for the business to thrive to the mutual benefit of all.

The authors' concepts and strategies are related descriptively and also clearly exemplified in the four "interludes" in which they chronicle an in-depth study of the conflicted multigenerational Sampson family and their company, Sampson Seeds. Obviously, their underlying philosophic stance is a highly ethical one, with great care given to protecting privacy and confidentiality and to not engaging in unnecessary dual relationships. They respect and honor the people they consult with in complex family businesses and their tremendous knowledge, skill, diagnostic acumen, and sensitivity to their clients and colleagues radiates in every page. In this book, McClendon and Kadis have achieved a thorough tour de force that is enlightening, informative, and a pleasure to read.

Florence W. Kaslow, PhD
Director, Florida Couples and Family Institute
Visiting Professor of Medical Psychology
in Psychiatry at Duke University Medical Center

Acknowledgments

As is usual with any book, we have many people to both acknowledge and appreciate. The idea to write a book about relationships in family business grew out of a series of workshops we—the authors—led conjointly with our colleague Marta Vago. Thank you for your enthusiasm, Marta. Florence Kaslow was central to moving our idea to the next step — Florrie, without your support and encouragement this book would not have gotten beyond the first stage. To Mary Goulding, our teacher, mentor, and dear friend, thank you for, among many other things, teaching us the power of an affirming environment. Muriel James, author, teacher, innovator in psychotherapy, and great friend, listened to our ideas, helped us frame them, and constantly spurred us on. Robert E. Hales first encouraged us to write a chapter in his *Textbook of Psychiatry,* and then our own book, *Concise Guide to Marital and Family Therapy.* Thank you, Bob. A very special thanks is due to Barbara Marinacci, our editor. As we went back and forth between different parts of our Reconciliation Model, Barbara, your unerring sense of order and your "fiddling" helped make this a more readable book.

Throughout the course of this book we note and reflect on the courage of our clients who trusted us and trusted the reconciliation process. So, even though you remain anonymous, to us you are very real. Thank you.

We also have a new appreciation for each other. Authoring conjointly can tax a relationship and writing this book was like building a house with each of us making room for the other's ideas while letting go of some of our own. We have grown through the process and are stronger for it.

Introduction

As longtime consultants to family-owned businesses, we always keep in mind a useful maxim:

> Good relationships are the foundation for the survival and ultimate success of all business enterprises undertaken by families. When a family maintains mutual respect and repairs the inevitable rifts among its members, it will flourish—and the family business itself will prosper. When family members are unwilling or unable to reconcile and reestablish trust, their enterprise is highly vulnerable and may even fail—unless or until changes are made to ameliorate relationship ruptures.

Reconciling Relationships and Preserving the Family Business: Tools for Success will serve as a practical and concise guide to relationship success of the family community within the diverse world of family business. What distinguishes family business from the rest of all other business-organization forms? It is the community of family and the interdependence of goal-sharing people who have lifetimes of knowing one another and working together. The relationships within the family community therefore can make or break the family firm because they provide the foundation for either its survival and success or its destruction and death.

Because we have worked with many family businesses of all sizes and types, we can say with confidence that relationship problems are more often than not at the root of failure within a family business, since its very success depends on shared goals and harmonious action. Just as some relationships within families inevitably falter, so do some family workplace relationships. Thus, with families who work together, personal issues, along with financial interdependencies and work grievances, tend to get ensnarled, amplify, and never let up. If allowed to persist, if never properly addressed and resolved, in time they can deal deadly blows to a family enterprise.

What Makes Family Businesses Desirable?

Families who are in business together are special people who have made, and continue to make, important and sometimes extraordinary contributions in our rapidly changing world. They offer a strong and stable link to our human past, to the long tradition of doing business in ways that are personal, meaningful, ethical—and pleasing to both provider and customer. Family-owned businesses are a wonderful natural resource within today's complex modern society. In this uncertain and perilous period of time, these beginning years of a new century marred by rampant terrorist acts and mounting warfare among nations and between ethnic or religious groups, the family community can function as a safety zone, a haven. It can also offer a satisfying way to make a good living. A family-owned business is a challenging alternative to working for someone else.

In a family-owned business, putting energy, effort, imagination, and dedication into doing a job well will benefit oneself, one's loved ones, one's community, and even the wider world. People can choose to work with clear consciences and also bring their family's values with them as they grow and compete in the world of global business.

Why This Book?

The need for *Reconciling Relationships and Preserving the Family Business* is clear. A surprising number—about 90 percent—of the United States' and the world's business establishments are essentially owned and often run by families. Though we may be unaware of it, each of us, daily, probably has contact with the products and services of numerous family businesses.

Statistics also show that a large percentage of family-owned businesses will not survive the transition from the first to the second generation and even fewer survive into the third generation. This is both alarming and disheartening. Because these failures often occur independently of market segment and market conditions, it is hard to attribute them solely to business circumstances. Roy Menninger of the Menninger Clinic was reportedly fond of saying to high-powered CEOs: "You don't have business problems; you have people problems." In family business we amplify that to include: "You don't have business problems; you have relationship problems."

If the issues leading to failure are not business-connected ones, they must then be personal and this leads directly to the need for our book. We believe in making every effort to protect the family-owned business from the form of self-destruction inherent in failing to safeguard the relationships that nurture both the family and the nonfamily employees.

Family businesses come in many different sizes and kinds, from small, couple-owned ones (sometimes of the "Mom and Pop" variety) to large multinational corporations. They are of widely varying ages, from a recently founded restaurant to a large clothing design and manufacturing firm in its fifth generation. Family businesses vary, too, in the nature of their enterprises and the numbers of people they employ. Some create or obtain raw materials, while others transport or transform them, or sell the finished goods. Some provide services while others provide products. Some deal in real estate properties; others function only with paper or electronic communication devices. Some are storage facilities; others supply security systems. Some have many hundreds of employees (few of whom are family-connected), whereas others consist of only several unsalaried family members who perform a variety of as-needed jobs.

Family businesses also differ greatly in their experience, outlook, and energy level. Some very new firms are filled with entrepreneurial zeal but may be inept at handling problems that arise among recruited family members. Others—middle-aged, with reduced stamina and possibly getting hidebound—can be reluctant to grant important decision-making roles to a successor generation that offers new energy, ideas, and flexibility. Still other businesses are approaching the mortal end of the evolutionary cycle—which sooner or later all must do if they cannot adapt to the new environments surrounding them as culture and technology continuously change in the ever-accelerating pace of the modern world.

The families themselves who operate businesses together are greatly varied, too: in their structures and beliefs; in their processes and rules; in their values and goals. Individual family members, moreover, can be quite different from one another in innate abilities and acquired skills and knowledge, in dreams and values, in memories and perceptions, and in enthusiasm and energy. Some family members participate daily in conducting their family's business, while others take an interest from the sidelines.

A successful family business, whatever its size, age, or focus, has many aspects to it. It is about relationships and community: about developing, honoring, and respecting the different people of the same family. Family business is about security: providing material, economic, and psychological resources for loved ones. Family business is about generosity in both the sanctuary of home and the greater community, and about highly functioning teams of parents and children, siblings, and cousins. Family business is about excellence and caring ... and about the past, the present, and the future.

This book presents information on how relationships work within a business-owning family and why they may not be working well. If a family business is to endure, family relationships will always need care and attention. Therefore, we suggest in detail various methods for addressing and resolving difficult or ruptured family relationships. Above all, we give explicit guidance in ways to help people alter patterns of interaction so as to achieve success in the close relationships so important in family life—and especially crucial in families who work together. Our perspective comes from understanding that achieving success in family business takes patience, persistence, and a commitment to the ones you love.

Who Will Benefit

This book focuses on the relationships and family community within an operating business that contains at least several family members. *Reconciling Relationships and Preserving the Family Business* is a survival guide for people involved in family businesses, for both family members and those serving as their advisors. The information and guidance provided is based on many years of experience and will be helpful to family members who are current or prospective shareholders, owner-managers, or otherwise have a stake in the business. People in any of these family groups will gain valuable insights into ways to avoid or heal relationship problems that undermine the success of a family business.

Many professional advisors, such as lawyers, accountants, and business consultants, lack expertise in handling interpersonal problems in family businesses they deal with on a regular or occasional basis, though they may be keenly aware of entrenched troubled situations. In contrast, most marital and family therapists, whose training and practice focus on resolving relationship issues, have no background in counseling family members within a business setting. Both groups of professionals will find specific guidelines in this book.

Another group who will find this book useful are managers in a family-owned business who are not family members themselves yet have become enmeshed in difficult family conflicts that adversely affect the operation of the business. It is unlikely that most have been trained or positioned to resolve personal disputes or tension. However, by using this book's information, they may persuade family principals to seek help from those who specialize in this field.

This book, therefore, is written for different readerships. It is written for our colleagues—the field of excellent advisors to family businesses around the world. It is written as well for the owners and members of family businesses everywhere: for the present but also for the benefit of the upcoming generations—family members who are children and students now. It is written for all who are ready to learn about relationships in the family business setting—healthy relationships that determine success and ruptured relationships in dire need of repair. It will be useful to everyone who wants to learn about achieving reconciliation to assure a more productive present and the best possible future in a family enterprise.

Because we know that many readers will not be mental health professionals, we introduce and explain some basic concepts that are well-known to other psychotherapists. Likewise, we mention certain assessment tools already familiar to therapists. These terms and tools are useful only as they can ultimately help people understand and empower themselves so as to contribute, perhaps significantly, to the happiness and well-being of the family and to the success of the family's business.

Who We Are

The difficult dynamics of relationships within family-owned businesses are well-known to us. So are their innumerable ramifications and complications in the workplace, on the family business's board of directors, and around the holiday table.

For many years we have practiced psychotherapy with individuals, couples, and families—one of us as a licensed clinical social worker, the other as a psychiatrist. Initially, both of us helped to resolve conflicted relationships in individuals' personal lives: with family members, with spouses and significant others, with friends, with strangers, with fellow workers and supervisors, and within individuals.

Separately and together, when working with clients we developed and then successfully applied the concept and techniques of Redecision Relationship Therapy (RRT), which empowers clients to build mutual empathy, respect, and caring while growing in self-understanding and self-esteem. We have presented this therapeutic approach in-depth in many articles and in our previous books, *Chocolate Pudding and Other Approaches to Intensive Multiple Family Therapy* (McClendon and Kadis, 1983) and *Concise Guide to Marital and Family Therapy* (Kadis and McClendon, 1998).

While conducting our private practice and intensive workshops for family groups over weekends, sometimes even over a week's time, we often found ourselves dealing with a special complex of problems experienced by family members who were in business together. We then adapted, to excellent effect, the theories of RRT to work with members of family enterprises and to reconcile relationship difficulties that endangered business viability and success. From this base we created the Reconciliation Model, which occupies the central place in this book because it has proven to be highly successful in its application to resolving relationship problems in family businesses.

Eventually, we became a family business ourselves, as founders and codirectors of the Carmel Institute for Family Business. It was started in 1983 (formerly as the Institute for Family Business) when we realized that a near void existed in developing and applying a coherent approach to resolving relationship problems in family businesses. Likewise, few programs were available anywhere at the time to train therapists and other professionals in working as advisors and counselors to family businesses. Today, of course, that situation has changed. There are several large membership organizations, notably the Family Firm Institute (of which Ruth was a founding member) for advisors and educators, and the Family Business Network for families themselves. In addition, many university-based programs and private endeavors focus on family business issues.

Because we have frequently taught our methods in both theory and practice to family business consultants in seminars, workshops, and internships, we are well equipped to prepare a guidebook that will help many more people than we could possibly assist as individual practitioners.

In addition, because of our long experience in treating families with a wide variety of relationship problems, either within a therapeutic context in our private offices or in business consultations, we are qualified to write a book that addresses the many relationship concerns of business-involved families. We empathize with their often elusive dream of mutuality in interests and accomplishments, which goes on even while they are dealing on a daily basis with difficult relationship realities. Among daily realities are overt or covert conflicts between family members: deep-seated and long-standing rivalries, resentments, frustrations, and disappointments. Many of these enduring feelings originated in childhood; others are embedded in stressful marriages, unrealistic or overbearing parental expectations, mismatched personality styles and values, and business roles and responsibilities.

Topics

This book has two main parts and a concluding chapter for advisors and families utilizing advisors. Part I focuses on the basic principles underlying relationships in business-owning families. Chapter 1 first introduces the ideology which frames the Reconciliation Model for relationship repair, presented in Part II, and then presents in detail our understanding of the individual dynamics underlying the human dilemmas in family business. We provide a virtual "road map" to the complex forces that fashion the individual actors in a family business—some with distinctive roles and personalities, and even hidden agendas or unfilled emotional needs that work counter to the family's best business interests.

The theoretical underpinnings of family relationship systems are outlined in Chapter 2: what they are, how they originate, and how they often interfere with both family accord and with successful business operations. Following this discussion, clear steps and practical tools are provided to aid advisors and families in moving the multiple relationships of family business toward healing, health, and hope.

Chapters 3 and 4 address the two key relationship problems most often seen in family business: "power over" or oppression, and family disengagement and fragmentation. The multiple and complex issues and psychic wounds created by oppression and fragmentation are considered, including the tendency to pass them along through the family tree. This section offers readers various case examples of prevalent, interrelated relationship problems involving oppression and fragmentation that we have encountered in our practice, leading the reader to clear definitions and definite strategies for resolution.

Part II, the heart of the book, describes our Reconciliation Model. Chapter 5 provides an overview of our comprehensive method for attaining reconciliation when family relationships in business are ruptured and probably in urgent need of repair. When a family's livelihood and well-being are threatened, it becomes crucial for its members to acknowledge that what unites them is far more important to heed and honor than any grievances that divide them. The specific steps in the model are individually highlighted in Chapters 6, 7, and 8. These chapters show how to intervene effectively in troubled relationships that are harming the family business's operation. These chapters also help families understand how the healing of rifts within their ranks can take place so that members are more willing to participate in open dialogue and make changes in their attitudes and behaviors.

The model emphasizes the importance of assessing family relationship patterns in the present, designing ways to reconsider feelings and attitudes of the past that inevitably have invaded the workplace, and rebuilding trust for the future. Thus, family members learn how to apply, in an ongoing way, new relating skills to achieve the desired mutuality of interests crucial to the synergy that attracts people to founding family businesses to begin with.

In the epilogue, we take a practical, experience-based look at the roles, responsibilities, and ethics of advisors who work with relationship-based businesses, which sometimes have controversial aspects and are always challenging.

A glance at the table of contents shows the presence of four special units that are called "Interludes." These are inserted in appropriate places within the text to serve as segments in an in-depth study of the Sampson family and their company, Sampson Seeds. In these interludes we detail our intensive relationship-repair efforts, which took place over many months, within this conflict-ridden three-generation family and the business it owns. This story is intended to show how our Reconciliation Model works, stage by stage, in an actual (though disguised) family business situation.

Finally, a note about the various vignettes and stories in this book. Confidentiality is central to building and maintaining trust while the need to tell stories is essential to showing others what we do so they can judge its validity for themselves. Reconciling the two, confidentiality and telling stories, is a challenge for all who write about their work. Although the stories in this book are mostly drawn from our own experiences in advising family-owned businesses we have worked with over the years, they have all been disguised in both names and types of business to retain confidentiality. Some of the stories are a composite of several families. When we have used this latter approach we have tried to remain as true to the facts and spirit of the people and situations as we could. If some stories seem familiar, it is because the range of human dilemmas is actually quite small and common themes abound. The uniqueness of family businesses comes from the family itself and from the uniqueness of the individuals involved.

Working with Families in Business

Just as patience, persistence, and commitment are required to successfully run a family business, these qualities are also needed when advising a family business. We hold fast to the belief that the solution to most family business problems involves repairing relationship problems in the family community.

When family members work consciously and conscientiously together to resolve their conflicts, they will be able to figure out whatever is needed to "fix" the problems in the business. Moreover, this process may be speeded up or indeed may only be made possible by bringing in an experienced advisor to guide the reconciliation process. An objective outsider can assist in identifying the real sources of perceived problems, and in enabling family members to feel safe enough to communicate openly and honestly with one another, especially those with whom there are deep conflicts. Such a consultant also helps bring about important decisions and changes in attitudes and behaviors.

We have written *Reconciling Relationships and Preserving the Family Business* because we admire and care deeply about the existence of family businesses. By working directly with family businesses themselves, and indirectly by training other professionals to work in a similar mode, we know we have already helped many family people stay in business together by empowering them to navigate safely through the natural perils of their world. We trust that our book will now amplify this assistance, so that many family members, now and in the future, will weave the tapestry of continuation and continuity in the mutual business occupying so much of their time, devotion, and lives.

We hope that this book, as well as our work with clients and advisors over the years, contributes to the continued or ultimate success of many firms in the wide world of family business—including those waiting in the wings, or yet to be born.

Each time we begin our work with a new family business we start with the following message. It is delivered to the entire family community and to every individual family member present, regardless of age, education, gender, or role in the family, or of the nature of the business itself:

> You hold in your hands a family and a company of great importance and potential. Will they become just another part of the archives of a dying world, or will they weave real magic for all? The choice and the power belong to you.

PART I:
RELATIONSHIPS
IN BUSINESS-OWNING FAMILIES

Family life is too intimate to be preserved by the spirit of justice. It can be sustained by the spirit of love which goes beyond justice.

Reinhold Niebuhr

Chapter 1

The Past and the Present Merge

As a member of the fifth generation, I often wonder how my family has made it through the challenges of family business. I believe it is because everybody's voice counted. My great-grandfather and his father before him always said that the key to success was to talk, talk, talk . . . and keep it positive.

A client

All relationships need repair at some time or another—especially in the complex family business relational environment where there can be a strong pull toward regression, emotionality, and internecine warfare. Both individual problems and interpersonal conflicts easily find breeding places within family businesses, which are extremely fertile fields for inhibiting individual freedom and developing hostile-dependent systems.

In a nutshell, we maintain that positive and enduring change will occur when the relational difficulties in the present—the observable here and now—are reconciled. The focus of the reconciliation effort is to take what *is,* to consider rather than forget what *has been,* and to use the family's resources to seek out internal strengths that can be highlighted and developed for what *will be:* the future good of both the family and its business. Thus, an improved understanding of the past when combined with both acceptance and a willingness to change, promises a beneficent and collaborative future among discordant family members.

Our Reconciliation Model offers an additional way of thinking about the individuals and relationships in business-owning families. The model is firmly grounded in established theory regarding both individual development and systems operations. It acknowledges and respects reciprocity: how each individual impacts and shapes the family and how the family impacts and shapes each individual. Our emphasis is on providing a clear, coherent theory along with practical application techniques that are particularly suited to the unique circumstance of families in family business together.

THE PAST: INDIVIDUAL DEVELOPMENT

Understanding the particularities of relationships is the key to comprehending the dynamics of any family in business. Life is begun and lived in relationships, and in family businesses that condition is more intensified and complicated than in any other circumstance. The quality of family business relationships has a great deal to do with how life for the family and the health of its joint enterprise turn out. Disputes, especially among key family members in a business, inevitably create and sustain stress, and can even trigger depression and self-destructive maneuvers in individuals, while for the business itself disputes can cause failure if allowed to go on without resolution.

The road to reconciling troubled or ruptured relationships within a family-owned business often involves a long and arduous journey. Many families have struggled to come to terms with their past, and have then proceeded with their current and future agendas. Many others, however, have chosen to avoid, ignore, or even deny this shared past. All have found that, in the long run, it is not possible simply to discount or forget whatever happened that has caused deeply held resentment, hurts, and anger among family members—people who ideally love, trust, and support one another throughout their lifetimes, come what may.

The extraordinary work of South Africa's Truth and Reconciliation Commission (TRC, 1998) has helped us learn this lesson. It is necessary to turn the page of history and move on, but first we need to read that page and learn from it. The reform process in South Africa stressed that the past could not be ignored, and that accountability was a prerequisite for establishing trust. The questions then became what form that accountability should take, and whether the elusive search for reconciliation could ever be ended. Of course, if a country is to be whole and healthy rather than divided against itself, the process that seeks truth and reconciliation must be ongoing; it can never really stop being vigilant.

The situation in a family-owned business in turmoil can be strikingly similar to a nation wracked by internal strife. In family business the past, present, and future intersect and are mutually interdependent. Both a nation and a business-owning family have a primary commitment to the welfare of the upcoming generations, so that great attention is usually given to offspring—to the children and grandchildren who embody great hope for biological, cultural, and economic continuance over time.

Similar to a nation consisting of diverse groups of people, the family enterprise may be extremely and perpetually vulnerable to divisions among its participants. As with a beleaguered nation, families can and will become split into warring factions. Ultimately, only a rational approach and a patient, conciliatory attitude cultivated consciously and carefully among family members can resolve intense interpersonal problems that have invaded and infected both home and workplace.

In working with troubled relationships in family business, our focus is on meeting the challenges of the present by finding ways whereby relationships can heal. We strive to discover how family members came to be the way they are in the present. We then work with people to alert them to their prescribed roles in the family discord, roles which usually have roots in past traumas and misunderstandings. Through understanding the past, the present and future can be changed.

In past years, when considering the psychology of the family and its individual members, the field of family business has largely relied on the family-of-origin approach of Murray Bowen (Bowen, 1978; Friedman, 1991). This approach, which focuses on the developmental processes of separation and individuation and the nature of transgenerational patterns and bonds, has proven extremely useful. Yet it still leaves some seeking additional ways of understanding current relationship problems and interventions, additional ways that will lead more directly to effective and concrete change in the present.

In this section we briefly describe the theoretical underpinnings which support the reconciliation approach. We want to point out, however, that the particular choice of a theory is not as important to successful change as is a solid grounding and belief in some coherent theory. A theory both prescribes and proscribes the way advisors see things, say things, and structure interventions. It therefore can offer both advisors and clients a stable and dependable framework for positive change.

Back in the early 1960s, Eric Berne (1964) developed a theory of human personality and social behavior called Transactional Analysis. In the following years Bob and Mary Goulding developed redecision therapy as an outgrowth of Transactional Analysis (Goulding and Goulding, 1995). Underlying both Berne's theory and the Gouldings' work is the concept that individuals start off in an autonomous state. In this view, each child has the power to make unique choices about himself or herself, and about how to think, feel, and *be* in the world. Over time and through the constant repetition of the parent-child-family interaction, these choices become what are called early decisions. This concept of *early decisions* has profound implications for those of us who work with family business relationships.

To be more specific, various key factors create the environment to which the child must adapt: the young child's inner needs and the intensity with which they are experienced; the availability of the parents and family to respond to the child, along with the quality and consistency (or unpredictability) of this response; and the time period over which the responses are made. Parents, the world in which a child grows up, and his or her own inner processes deliver messages to that child about how to think, feel, and behave. Many of these messages, hopefully, are caring and nurturing, instructive, and supportive. Inevitably, of course, constricting or negative messages are also given.

At the most basic level, the child must adapt to the family environment in order to survive; at the next level, to feel the least pain; and at the highest level, to feel actual pleasure. Through this process of adapting, individuals build an internal model of the self that is based on relationships with parents or parenting persons, and later with people in the outside world. The early established model is then carried by each person throughout life—into every room, every experience, and every relationship, unless, of course, some intervention occurs and there is a need to alter one's way of thinking of self and others, and therefore one's behavior.

Furthermore, when parents are raising a family, the messages given to their children about how to think, feel, and behave are both congruent with their own early decisions—and therefore, aimed toward continuing to make life predictable for them—and also related to their current circumstances and emotional well-being. The negative messages that constrain children, and sometimes result in their need to confine or hide who they really are, arise when a seemingly well-functioning and caring but susceptible adult is plummeted emotionally back into a distant past by some shock or stressful period in the here and now.

To understand the power of negative messages it is essential to understand something about "shame affect." As used by Nathanson (1992), shame affect is a primitive reflex that makes us feel as if the floor is falling out from under us. When the negative messages are paired with a child's naturally wired shame affect, the child's attentions are so focused on the parent and the particular "don't" message that he or she is driven to decide to change themselves. In other words, the young child has two tasks: he or she must learn to minimize the impact of the shame affect in order to continue functioning, yet at the same time learn to avoid or minimize the painful parental or environmental consequences of the "don't" prohibitions. With time and repetition, the child's defensive maneuvers against both the shame affect and parental injunctions become ingrained and reified as early decisions.

For a moment now, let's turn to a brief example. Jenny and Connie are co-owners and comanagers of a local market and deli founded some years earlier by their parents. They were recently thrust into these positions when their widowed mother was diagnosed with cancer and decided to turn everything over to her girls. Jenny saw herself as "just like her mother"; she was highly visible within the store and aggressive about getting things done her way. As the oldest daughter she had always believed herself responsible for taking care of her family's domestic needs and that she would never receive any help because her parents always seemed to be away, working at their store. Connie, in contrast, was someone who accommodates—always willing to adjust her views; so whenever she tried to assert herself, Jenny argued her down. Now, more than ever, Connie felt like an outsider and thought there was no place or use for her in the business. This relationship pattern—assert and accommodate—between the two sisters had been playing out for years, almost since Connie was born. However, the quiet conflict had escalated now with the stress of their mother's illness and taking over the business.

Our job as advisors was to help both Jenny and Connie identify their own particular parts in the relationship problem; recognize their early decisions; and understand that their beliefs and behaviors, important in childhood, were no longer necessary for their present adult family and business situations, and in fact were impediments. Through choosing to change their early decisions, which were driving their current relationship patterns, Jenny and Connie were able to mutually support each other in both their grief and the new challenge of running the family business.

Two more important points should be made about early decisions as the basis for the plan of how adults manage both their internal and external environments:

- All early decisions are made as a result of the child's perception of the best way to manage or survive in the here and now.
- All early decisions are individual and unique productions of the person making them.

We can reasonably conclude that current behavior observed in patterns of interaction and personal history in the form of early decisions operate in a reciprocal relationship. Problems are apt to occur whenever two discordant behavior styles, based on early decisions, collide. They are apt to worsen if there is already an unhappy relational history involved. This information has an enormous implication for our work with families who manage and own businesses together. It gives advisors a direction for change, and it gives family members the power to change.

The theory of early decisions and early decision making, grounded in self-preservation and manifested in self-presentation, is closely akin to many other current psychological theories based on the idea of the creation of core beliefs about the self and others. An individual's core beliefs act as a template for the perception of the rest of life's decisions and interactions. Early decisions serve as templates, too.

Since in this conceptual framework people are considered to be actually in charge of making their own early decisions in life, they are also perceived as capable of making redecisions for themselves in the present. Redecisions are revised beliefs about the self. They occur with the here-and-now incorporation of updated and current information about one's self and circumstances. Jenny redecided that she did not always have to go it alone, while her sister Connie redecided that there was a place for her in the business and she could speak up for herself. Through redeciding Jenny and Connie took steps to free themselves to think, feel, and behave differently in their current lives: in other words, to make free choices in the present rather than to react with the resounding echoes of the past.

Since people can redecide and change certain entrenched attitudes and behaviors, they are positioned to reconcile conflicted relationships. The implications and applications of this redecision capability to family business environments are profound, because daily family interactions often replicate negative situations and scenarios of the past.

RELATIONSHIPS: MAKING THE PAST PRESENT

Definitions are important. *Webster's Dictionary* records seventeen uses for the word "relationship." Most commonly, it refers to a connection between people. However, even "connection" doesn't fully express why the relationship concept is so important to thinking about family business dynamics. To understand the heart of the matter, we need only to observe the interactions between a mother and her newborn child. As infant and mother focus on each other, their facial expressions change to match each other's. The close interplay does not allow an observer to know for certain where one identity begins and the other leaves off.

This attachment/bonding cycle is a chief element in human development. This experience of bonding with another person is a primary motivation in all human relationships, regardless of the context, because this bond affirms one's very existence. It begins with the mother-child bond, which serves as an experiential model for all future bonding. That does not mean we all are still looking for our mother. What it does mean is that we all seek the recognition and security implicit in that first secure relationship.

Many theorists have suggested that this primal bonding of mother and baby is the essential transaction in human interaction: the recognition of the self by the other. Martin Buber (1974) speaks of the space between two intimately connected persons, calling it the "I-Thou." Eric Berne (1964) addresses the need for "strokes" and the efforts humans will make to be acknowledged, to be recognized as worthy, by a fellow being. These relationship factors that foster bonding and self-acceptance are as follows:

- Each person is recognized as an individual.
- Their unique contributions are acknowledged and valued, even when there may be some disagreement about them.
- Each person accepts the obligation to listen to the others, to be patient, attentive, and sensitive to gradual revelations of whatever deep feelings and hidden truths may lie beneath the surface of others' words and actions, in both the present and the past.

This ideal bonding state, however, is just that: ideal. This earliest of bonds will inevitably be broken and mothers are never perfect. Though useful as a goal, ideal bonding is never, of course, always achieved. Later, mentors may fail us in many ways, management is not primarily concerned about our well-being, and the business-owning parent who must choose and anoint a successor may pass over us.

In many circumstances, obviously, it is neither necessary nor appropriate to take the time and energy to listen that intently to persons with whom one is connected in some way. One should be aware, though, that the failure to pay respectful attention may create a small rupture in the relationship, which sooner or later will need repair, particularly when an ignoring response is a regular occurrence.

When two or more people come together for any length of time, they form a relationship unit. Depending on how long they are together, the commonality of their interests, and the strength of their bond, each unit develops a specific character of its own, or a *system*. Each family is a unique system unto itself, and a basic understanding of how the relationship system works is shared, though not usually articulated, by each of the family's members.

When the family environment is primarily affirming in nature, this shared understanding can provide comfort and security, a sense of inclusion and belonging. On the other hand, there are many nonaffirming family environments that are detrimental to some or all of its members creating deep relationship and individual problems. In the nonaffirming family, powerful early decisions inevitably clash, eliciting correspondingly negative responses in other members of the family system.

In family businesses, sibling relationships are especially vulnerable since behavior patterns established in childhood experiences and reinforced throughout life are frequently and instantly brought into play. Brothers and sisters are reminded daily of their earlier competition for naturally sought-after affection, approval, and validation from their parents—or parental representatives, such as the business itself.

When children become adults, they most often choose marital and life partners whose early models of themselves and the world interface with their own in a way that not only allows but actually encourages the continuation of their early beliefs or decisions. In other words, when selecting a partner, a person may try to make life as predictable and secure as possible by enlisting as a mate someone whose background, style, and early decisions will allow the patterns of interaction in the marriage to reinforce his or her early decisions. In this way the past and the present always merge.

Once established, relationships go through relatively universal stages of development. However, each relationship moves through the stages in its own way (Bader and Pearson, 1988). Initially Bader and Pearson called the first stage of a relationship the "symbiotic stage" because of its similarity to the earliest stage of infant development. In a later work they referred to this stage as the "honeymoon stage" in which each partner in a couple sees the other as an extension of himself or herself, and, as such, perfect (Bader and Pearson, 2000). Family business relationships begin with a similar honeymoon stage in that there are strong attachments, great fantasies and hopes, unspoken expectations, and plans for the ideal and profitable future. Few families are able to look ahead and see any difficulties: "After all, he's my brother . . . and things are going to be just great for us."

However, just as in the course of human development itself, differences eventually emerge during a relationship that must be acknowledged. Whether it is the toddler asserting himself or herself by saying "No!" or "I do it!" or the lover preferring to go to a different restaurant or movie, or the next generation wanting to do it their own way, these expressions of individuality are experienced as differences and must be accounted for. Allowing for emerging differences and making room for individuality is the second stage of relationship development and requires the active participation of everyone involved— a couple, parents and children, siblings, cousins, and any other family members. All too often individual differences in style and divergent opinions regarding the business are experienced as violations of the original relationship or considered defects in the other person. It is here that many relationship ruptures arise.

It is not just the toddler who must find better ways of expressing herself or himself; it is also the parent who must learn age-appropriate parenting skills. Similarly, not only the current and controlling generation in a family business must learn to be more flexible and willing to compromise, but the next generation as well. This stage of accommodating individual differences and separate identifications— the third stage in the development of a relationship—foreshadows the fourth stage, in which each person recognizes and values the other person for who they are. In this final stage of the relationship the substance in the relationship itself brings life to the systems perspective on the family in family business, a topic to be taken up in the next chapter.

Since relationship ruptures are so common, and even everyday experiences, we are all lucky that, as it turns out, the rupture is actually less important to the maintenance of human relationships than its repair (Lewis, 2000). This normal relationship cycle when ruptures are automatically repaired is central to building and maintaining relationships (see Figure 1.1). Our Reconciliation Model, detailed in Part II, takes up the particulars of the relationship-repair process when a reconciliation effort is needed to bring about restorative justice.

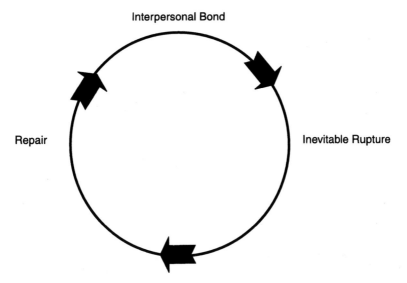

FIGURE 1.1. Relationship Cycle—Normal Rupture and Repair (Based on Lewis, 2000)

CHOOSING TO CHANGE

Because people originally make their own choices of how to be with themselves and others, they are likewise able to change those choices when their circumstances of life become different—as in adulthood. Since core beliefs drive people and their interactions with others, and since one's interpersonal behaviors are reciprocal with other family members' behaviors, then an individual can make a difference by choosing not only how to relate, but also how to relate differently than before. Just as important is the knowledge that one person does not make all of the difference in how things are; others also choose how to relate.

What bearing do these insights have on resolving troubled relationships in a family business? Real autonomy is achieved by knowing and believing that each one of us utilized our power and freedom to make early decisions, and can therefore change in desired directions. In other words, people do not have to consider themselves as bound by being members of the business-owning family. Instead, they can function as separate and equal selves who possess the power to make a difference and to initiate necessary changes, which hopefully will in turn precipitate other positive changes around them.

The early *decision/redecision* process carries two benefits: it offers advisors a basic and concrete framework for understanding the roots of the current family problems; and it grants family business members the power to self-govern.

As advisors we can guide the various participants involved toward resolving their enmeshed relationship problems and directing their behaviors and even their lives differently. This can be done by enabling everyone to see themselves as autonomous from the very beginning of their lives as persons who made early decisions and choices for themselves, and therefore capable now of making new decisions. Family members empowered through the reconciliation process to view themselves as accountable, responsible, and self-directed are better able to navigate through whatever challenges, obstacles, and adversities life may throw at them. In all the ways we know, we encourage family members to take charge of their behavior, to own their own thoughts, and to manage their feelings.

When people realize the power and the importance of early decisions, it is an easy step to convince them that within themselves they still hold that power and can therefore redecide for themselves. Redecisions, as mentioned before, are revised beliefs about the self, others, and the current world; they are the building blocks necessary for reestablishing trust and building collaboration with others.

When updated information about oneself, others, and circumstances is incorporated, early beliefs and responses can be changed. Through the concurrent reconciliation process, individuals take the steps to understand themselves and the others around them differently in the framework of their current lives, and to make autonomous choices in the present.

IDEOLOGY UNDERLYING
THE RECONCILIATION APPROACH

Underlying the reconciliation-effecting approach are five fundamental principles. Outlined as follows are the most important tenets that provide the foundation for decreasing family vulnerability, increasing probability of successful reconciliation of troubled relationships, and augmenting family business success over the generations.

Clear, Positive Direction

The reconciliation approach keeps a positive direction by giving advisors and family members alike a plan for caring and for talking even when the conversations become most difficult and involve honest self-revelations, attentive listening, and confrontations. Since relationship problems will always occur, the model provides a flexible process that constantly moves toward creating new and healthy relationship dynamics—a most critical factor for the longevity of a family enterprise.

A clear, positive direction defines the tone of a successful family business and the environment that advisors aim to create when utilizing reconciliation processes: safe, involved, caring, respectful, interactive, and even fun. Success in family business occurs when its members share a common vision of themselves as a family, of the business and its place within the owning family, and of the relationship between the family and those managers, family members or not, who actually run the company on a day-to-day basis.

Keeping a clear, positive direction encourages family members to participate, to be honest, and to reveal themselves, even though this is a most difficult thing for many people particularly within the family context. It motivates family teams to learn and change together and is critical in the move toward mutual empathy and mutual empowerment.

Self-Determination

Each person has the power to make unique choices about how to think, feel, and behave in his or her world. Who we are is not predetermined alone by our biology, our history, our parents, or our current circumstances; these are contributing but not defining factors. The reconciliation approach honors the idea that "We are what we make of and for ourselves."

A person is not simply an object that can be perpetually acted upon. Certainly in family business situations, as in all of life, there are victims of unjust acts, as well as perpetrators and rescuers. However, each person has choices for the future and can summon up the insight and power to make them. Everyone, no matter what they have been programmed to believe about themselves or where they live or work, is actually in charge of their own plan for the future. Although they can do nothing about the past except accept it for what it was, they still can move away from it, and even move out of a present situation if it is unacceptable to them.

This concept of self-determination is essential in the world of family business relationships where so many generations, so many people, and so many roles interface, not always harmoniously. The basic position—that no matter what the circumstances, there is always a choice to be made—opens up multiple options for reconciling ruptures caused by multifaceted differences and innumerable divisions seemingly inherent within business-owning families' relationships.

Personal Responsibility

Our model is built also on the principle that every person can and must assume personal responsibility for the wide-reaching consequences of his or her choices and behaviors. All of our relationships are impacted by the decisions that we make for ourselves. In family business our choices, whether personal or professional, will cause repercussions that affect parents, children, siblings, and others associated with the family enterprise. Unfortunately, sometimes, individual choices have enormous negative and even devastating impact on others, and, all too often it is too late to reverse course when the dire consequences of someone's particular choice are realized.

Astute advisors often play a crucial role in averting future problems that may result from someone's unilateral and uninformed decision. For example, in a recent consulting assignment we learned that Marshall had partially distributed ownership interest in his cosmetics firm to his three children as part of his estate planning. His oldest daughter, Jill, was currently managing the business and Marshall had assumed an advisory position. His youngest daughter, Barbara, was established in her life as a wife and mother and had no particular interest in the family business other than as part of her inheritance. George, the middle child, had worked in the business alongside his father for five years but left to build his accounting practice after Jill finished graduate school and came on board. Struggling in both his personal and professional life, George frequently complained about the lack of cash distributions, as Jill and Marshall reinvested profits in the business. He often alluded to his desire to be bought out by the family.

Marshall asked for our help because he was uncomfortable with his relationship with his son and had recognized that George's attitudes could cause problems for future generations. He also knew that distributing shares equally—his original plan—might create problems for his other two children, particularly Jill, who would ultimately have the total responsibility of running the family business. After some initial investigation we suggested that Marshall and George, in conjunction with Marshall's attorney, consider a way that George would receive his inheritance from nonbusiness-related assets plus a gradual buyout of his current shares, hopefully averting a potential disaster for both the family and the business.

Direct Action

Survival in the world of business requires a family enterprise to compete actively in a dynamic and fast-moving business environment. In today's highly competitive business world, the enterprising companies that move quickly gain the market share. To succeed or to retain success, family businesses must have both achievable business strategies and achievable family strategies that reflect the family's ever-evolving situation, and can operate in accordance with the current economy. Families constantly confront decisions about operations and about what is the right thing to do. Competing in the swiftly moving and changing marketplace demands an active, on-target, and collaborative approach in which family teams can act quickly, competently, and creatively.

Like a family operating successfully in the world of competitive business, as relationship advisors to businesses we take a direct approach to reconciling the ruptured relationships that are interfering with the family's business operations. We face issues head-on and move quickly to facilitate changes. Clients are confronted and asked to make clear behavioral changes—changes that can have a cumulative effect, beginning with small steps that combine and then lead to overall family change. In this way we are always introducing small relationship changes that will have larger systemic consequences.

We also hold to the idea that *not* to act is itself a direct choice; in other words, inaction is an action in itself. However, in the pressure cooker of a fast-paced business it is prudent to combine quick action and forward movement to get the task done or the problem resolved.

Family As an Affirming Community

Families involved in family businesses have enormous power to either help or interfere with the well-being of one another, of the business, and of other individuals who work in the business. The family community has a history, a present, and a future together, all of which can be either bound by caring, respect, and strong loyalties or else riddled with resentments, attempted sabotages, and hidden or open dislikes.

The reconciliation model emphasizes the importance of conducting a healing dialogue within families and of ultimately developing collaborative teams. Our model facilitates family members working together on their relationships in a constructive manner. It confronts the competitive stance that results when family members vie for power, prestige, and money within the family business—a high-risk war game apt to result in business stagnation and failure, or relationship fragmentation.

Considering the family as a network, the model focuses on constantly working toward utilizing the entire family community as a positive resource. Family networks can be organized, consciously or unconsciously, either to help or to interfere, to empower and nurture, or else to destroy.

As advisors to family businesses, we think in terms of self-help within this small community and therefore look for problem-solving resources within the family. These resources may be hierarchical, involving the people at the top mentoring the next generations; they may be lateral, involving peers helping one another; or they may even be bottom up (Madanes, 1995), in which, for example, grandchildren have the most influence on their elders. We are also always searching to identify those in the family who can initiate positive change, and then maintain it. This resource quest usually yields good choices in ensuring success.

AIMING FOR RECONCILIATION

In our work with families who own and/or operate businesses together, when moving from relationship rupture and even estrangement to the reconciliation of damaged relationships we keep in mind the following guiding principles:

- Every family member is equal in importance and influence in family relationships. This may not be so within the management of the business itself, but within the interpersonal environment of the family all people are equal and deserve to be attended to with care and respect.
- Every person is valuable, with special capabilities and interests that have been predetermined by biology, physical condition, and a unique set of life experiences. Each unique and autonomous person needs to be acknowledged, appreciated, accepted, and honored as an individual.
- People have the power to choose, and they have decided for themselves how to view themselves and others, and how to relate to the world they live in.
- Since people choose how to relate to themselves and others, individuals are responsible for their own behaviors and accountable for their interactions.
- The personal prerequisites necessary for achieving reconciliation in family relationships are courage, an ability to be positively self-critical, and compassion for other family members.

We strongly believe that effective action can always be taken to resolve relationship problems in a business-owning family whenever the people who are shareholders and perhaps work together—and are expected to love one another because they are all "family"—are in fact experiencing strained, distant, or even fractured relationships. For both the sake of preserving the business and reinstating family unity it is highly desirable to make a strong and concerted effort to settle the divisive issues. Reconciliation leads to restoring trust and creating or strengthening bonds among warring or alienated relatives.

In the following chapters it will become even clearer how these underlying concepts bring hope and healing to estranged or ruptured relationships that threaten the well-being of a family business.

Our reconciliation journey taken with the Sampson family, delineated in the book's four Interludes, will show in some detail how the overall procedure and its several stages worked out with an actual case.

Chapter 2

Family and Family Business Systems

I'm a very competent businessperson, I'm well-educated and I've accomplished a lot. But every time I'm around my parents I feel like a little boy. And my parents treat me like a little boy. I don't know if it's them or if it's me, but it's driving me crazy.

A client

In the previous chapter we introduced the ideology underlying our Reconciliation Model with its promise of resolving family relationship problems that are interfering with successful operations of the family enterprise itself. We then considered the evolution of individuals: how each person's sense of himself or herself develops during childhood and how that emerging identity manifests itself in early decisions. From there we focused on how, through redecisions, all of us, as adults, can become accountable for our actions and how this pertains to family business operations. In addition, we considered important factors in the development of relationships.

In this chapter, we further pursue the subject of human relationship systems, their power to facilitate or impede individual growth, and their power to make or break both the family and its business enterprise. Then in the following two chapters we explore how to recognize and intervene when family systems—the patterns of interaction that define the family—support oppressive behaviors and contribute to disengagement, thereby bringing harm to both people and the businesses they conduct as a family unit.

WHY CONSIDER A SYSTEMS PERSPECTIVE?

When looking carefully at the way people relate to one another, patterns of interaction become apparent, which then repeat themselves as if they had a life of their own. Whenever people are together with others, whether socially, in the workplace, or in a variety of other settings, we observe that a "dance" goes on continuously among them which revolves around an intense human need for recognition and acknowledgment by others. As with any dance, a ritual or repetitive pattern develops based on each person's expectations of what is to happen, the circumstances surrounding the event—a family gathering, say, at the holiday dinner—and, most important, the responses of the other participants. When dancing partners anticipate each other's moves, their steps are coordinated and their product, "the dance," flows easily. But ill-matched partners misinterpret each other's signals or are unhappy to be dancing at all, thus negativity escalates and calamities occur.

The observable collection of patterns that emerge from the interactions in any relationship is called a system. Said differently, "system" is the word descriptor used to describe the constellation of patterns of interaction in relationships—patterns that usually operate outside of conscious awareness, unless one develops the habit of looking for them. In all family businesses multiple systems interface and impact one another; even though there is a similarity in patterns, individual family businesses are also unique unto themselves.

A family business exists externally within the much larger world of family business in general, which itself is but a part of the greater universe of all forms of organizations and business enterprises. Family business is also composed internally of a series of smaller units involving unique relationships. The nature and quality of these special relationships between and among particular members of the family, which have been shaped by distinctive experiences, are extremely important matters. By becoming aware of the different relationship systems operating in the personal and working lives of families who own businesses together, advisors open up opportunities to intervene and consciously help restructure family interactions. Successfully targeted systems interventions have an immediate power to change family relationships so that they move in the direction necessary, and therefore desirable, for business success.

A systems approach to anything addresses this crucial issue: How to make sense of complex phenomena and complicated dynamics for which there are multiple explanations that fit the facts. Also, because the systems perspective is neutral with regard to individual causality when applied to human affairs, it disregards people's vexing tendency to place blame on others when things are not working well.

Systems that operate effectively, as well as individual success-attaining actions based upon one's role in the system, lie at the foundation of every highly successful business team such as couples-in-partnership teams, intergenerational teams, and sibling teams. Sports teams are no exception to this rule. For instance, when the highly touted Los Angeles Lakers were trounced in the fourth game of the 2000 NBA championship series, the media were poised to pounce on two of the basketball players for their less-than-stellar performances. However, Coach Phil Jackson would have none of that. Focusing instead on the team's failure to operate as a team, in the practice sessions that followed he reinforced the collaborative aspects of his team's play. Coach Jackson thought and acted in terms of systems. Because he understood both the nature of systems and the importance of collaboration, after carefully observing his players' patterns of interaction, he intervened at a critical point and achieved the desired outcome. His team went on to win the final game and the championship.

What useful tip might both families and business advisors glean from a systems perspective? Never believe that you have the key to resolving relational problems until you have considered each of the players' viewpoints and then stepped back to witness the interactions that repeat themselves in the moment and over time. *In family business, as with any other team, we must always consider the system.*

UNDERSTANDING SYSTEMS: A PRACTICAL APPROACH

The critical tenet of general systems theory, that the whole is a separate and different entity than the sum of its parts, is the overriding key to understanding human relational systems. Thus a family business is different from what might be envisaged from knowing the individual persons who make up the family.

To illustrate this concept further, when describing a machine—or a government, a single-cell organism, a family—as a system, the description is made from the perspective of how the various parts interact. Systems thinking recognizes that a car engine is a very different entity than what might be expected from just seeing the components laid out on a table. Although a car engine contains cylinders and pistons and many other parts, moving or immobile, the engine is considered as a totality; it is described from the perspective of how all the parts interact to enable the mechanism to work.

As with a car engine, the success of any family business and the smoothness with which it operates depends on the way all of the separate parts interact and relate to one another over time. Each successful family business has its own structure, its own process, and a unique context within which it has survived and even thrived through the ups and downs of its life. Success depends on these organizational and relational elements functioning well together. If in a business one or more of these key elements are not functioning properly and are never corrected, the business itself eventually is apt to fail.

In addition to the fact that each human system is a separate and distinct entity, different from any of its separate parts or combinations of parts, awareness of several other systems factors will aid both advisors and families in their search for success. So let us now consider the context in which the family business operates, plus the separate but always intertwined elements of structure and process in the family business.

CONTEXT

Context refers to both the environment in which the family business operates and the particular circumstances of the family at any given moment in time. Context includes all of the factors that surround and impact the business, therefore both defining and clarifying the family business system. Thus, it is extremely important to both the family's and its advisors' understanding of the relational patterns within the family, because context provides a perspective on the many obligations, loyalties, and responsibilities that family members have toward one another.

Multiple Operating Environments

Context recognizes that while the family functions as a unit, individual family members also interact with the entire family as a system as well as individually with one another. Context furthermore recognizes that a family business itself operates, as mentioned earlier, in both the wider worlds of family business and of business enterprise in general. Advisors must always recognize the multiplicity and complexity of obligations and responsibilities that each family business has to follow, which arise from this much larger arrangement. The various and different settings in which the family firm is operating, such as the macro- and microeconomic climates; the legal system; the tax laws; the distinctive cultures within the company itself, of the business-owning family, and of the society in which the business is functioning all influence the tone and form of the family relationships. Thus it is important for advisors to pay attention to the arrangements, accommodations, compromises, and bargains that a family business must make to function successfully in this wider world and how such transactions can affect and even define family relationship patterns.

Culture

Various cultural elements, such as ethnic or national background, can matter to a great degree because they are likely to influence the way behaviors manifest themselves. For example, even though it is both unfair and a gross oversimplification to refer to stereotypes, there is validity in the observation that wide differences exist in cultural expectations. Some groups value overt expression of emotion, while others abhor it. Some revere age, whereas others—youth-oriented cultures—do not. Some present themselves much as they conduct their business, through aggression and sharp bargaining; others, appearing "laid back" and almost timid, wait for others' actions. Some focus on the worth of each individual, while others see a group as the important entity. Some, especially traditional cultures, regard males as the only gender qualified for leadership roles, whether in government, business, or the family itself, whereas many modern societies are moving toward full gender equality. These values, which reflect significant differences among people's attitudes and behavior, are bound to affect the way a family organizes its management and conducts its business.

Developmental Cycles

The next contextual ingredient to be considered is the interrelatedness of *developmental life cycles*. The idea that systems change with the passage of time is particularly true for family relationships in the context of the family business since participants respond to the effects of distinct but overlapping life cycles. The work of Gersick and his colleagues (1997, 1999) in this area has contributed greatly to our understanding of the life cycles of the family business and therefore to our ability to effect caring and sensitive change within the family business system.

Three different developmental cycles intersect over the life of the family business—the family, the business, and ownership. The traditional family life cycle is punctuated by the life events of birth, starting school, graduating, launching a career, finding a partner, possibly raising children, and reaching full maturity, which culminates finally in death. Then there is the traditional cycle of the business itself, which sometimes parallels the life stages of the family, and sometimes contradicts, such as when a need is evident for business growth just at the time the managing generation is ready to retire. Finally, there is the cycle of ownership development as it moves from the controlling owner to the sibling partnership to a cousin consortium.

Considering the different developmental forces that impact the business-owning family directs us to inherent relationship ruptures that may develop when vastly different needs and tasks must all be accomplished simultaneously. The needs and properties of the business are different in the entrepreneurial stage as compared to the mature stage of its development. So too, the needs of the family and the individuals are different when the founder, or the currently owning generation, is a relatively young person with younger children, than when they are at a later stage in the life cycle.

At any time, life-cycle issues can add enormous complexity to the ways in which the family and its business are seen and see themselves. During difficult times especially, understanding the strong impact of interacting life-cycle issues can help the family feel less embattled and more normal. If we can normalize what is happening, we thereby remove the stigma and support the family in resolving their relational issues.

Let's consider an example of how life-cycle considerations impact the business-owning family. Boyd, the founder of a medium-sized, extremely successful manufacturing company, which produced bindings for belts, was well past the age of retirement. His son, Bob, who had already assumed many of the functions of CEO and president, felt more than ready to take complete control of the business. In fact, various advisors had recommended to Boyd that he step aside. Boyd was reluctant to do so, as he recalled the pain of how his own father had withered and died shortly after retiring, as if his father had lost any reason to remain alive. Resolution occurred when Bob was able to respond to his father's concerns by completing agreements regarding finances and giving him a role within the future business. Boyd also worked toward forgiving himself for how he had treated his own father when the baton was passed to him.

FAMILY STRUCTURE

The structure of the family business in large part defines the process of family business relationships—therefore, one of the focuses of many advisors is to help the family inject appropriately designed structure into their family enterprise. Our interest here is in the general elements of structure that advisors using a family systems approach can employ to aid them along their journey—their road-to-reconciliation practices and collaborative relationships over the generations.

Structure organizes and frames the family, giving it form and shaping the family processes. Structure is best considered by looking at the boundaries between different individuals, between different generations, and between family and nonfamily. We typically think of boundaries as divisions between parcels of land or other physical entities. When applied to human interactions it is somewhat similar. Boundaries are a set of invisible characteristics by which individuals and groups distinguish themselves from one another. With their multiplicity of relationships, functions, obligations, and loyalties, business-owning families have the greatest opportunity for success when relationship boundaries are clear.

Many years ago Eric Berne (1963) presented a way of looking at the relevant boundary configurations of a group. This scheme, also relevant to business-owning families, included the minor internal boundary, the major internal boundary, and the major external boundary (Figure 2.1).

The *minor internal* boundary is the boundary between people; it is how individuals distinguish themselves from each other. What does this actually mean? The minor internal boundary defines how individuals know themselves, how they know others, and how they think others know them.

People need to know themselves in a physical sense: how they look, what physical efforts they are capable of, and what physical stresses they are able to tolerate. People also need to know themselves in an emotional sense including how they feel and how they react in various situations; and in an intellectual sense, too: how they think, the strength of their judgment, their competencies, and their

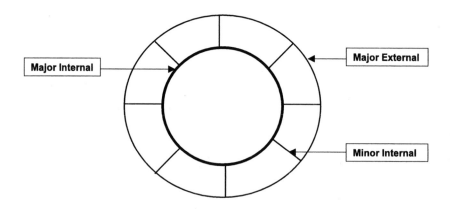

FIGURE 2.1. Boundaries (Adapted from Berne, 1963)

weaknesses. Similarly, people need to know themselves in the context of their relationships: how they accept responsibility and if they feel compassion for others.

Relationships work best and are most easily repaired when the way people see themselves corresponds with the way others see them and the way they see others seeing them. Since human beings and relationships are always changing, each of us needs to be able to compare the personal information coming into us from others with what we actually know about ourselves. When balance is achieved, a secure identity and positive self-image are created and a collaborative team member is born. On the other hand, when dissonance reigns, individuals, relationships, and families are wounded—sometimes beyond repair.

The *major internal boundary* distinguishes leadership from non-leadership. It establishes hierarchies. Sometimes the hierarchy is easy to understand: children report to parents, and managers report to vice presidents or the CEO. Even within the couple relationship there are various hierarchies. Typically, one partner is the acknowledged leader in some areas and the other partner in other areas. Other hierarchies are less clear, and the rules that govern them can be difficult to understand. For example, when some parents constantly give in to their child's demands and desires, the boundary between parents and child becomes unclear, so that the chain of command gets inverted. When children *act as if* they are the parents, even though, underneath, they feel unsure of themselves, the family can be unsafe for all, including the parents. When these children grow up, this prior experience may predispose them to becoming tyrants when they are parents, managers, and owners. They still act as if they are absolutely sure of what they're doing and that they are right. Chaos and oppression reign in systems that lack recognizable, caring, and qualified leadership.

Family members and business advisors alike need to pay special attention when establishing or reinforcing family business hierarchies. Too often, family politics can dictate the selection of a business's future leadership that is misguided, wholly inappropriate, and even harmful to business success. Conscious, thoughtful decisions about ownership and leadership need to be made—in a timely manner, before it is too late to avert disaster.

Parents have the original power to define the major internal boundary of their business. Following are a few important things to consider when choosing the leaders of the future:

- There is no direct relationship between birth order and competency as a leader.
- There is no direct relationship between gender and competency as a leader.
- Leader credibility, one of the prime components of leadership, contributes significantly to improved business performance (Kouzes and Posner, 1993).
- The most important components of leader credibility are: honesty, vision, inspiration, competency, and fair-mindedness.
- Consider carefully the extent to which each person's behavior is consistent with his or her position in the hierarchy and the components of success for that position.
- Only offer positions of leadership to persons who are continuously able to take and accept a critical look at themselves plus show compassion for others.
- Always remember that intentions don't count; actions do.

Hierarchies exist; they're neither good nor bad. They either promote the well-being of relationships in a family business, or they don't. When they don't, change is essential: families need to shift the hierarchical structure aimed at altering the patterns of behavior and improving the nature of the relationships.

The last important element of structure to be considered is the *major external boundary*—the boundary that distinguishes family from nonfamily. This boundary has immediate implications for family business advisors, since the advisor is always a family outsider. Stepping inside sensitive family territory, albeit with both respect and expertise, involves crossing a family boundary. The issue of how to enter the family comes up constantly for advisors, mostly under the heading of trust. To avoid the risk of being considered an unwelcome trespasser, each new entry must be handled with care, respect, and consideration.

The subject of boundaries also brings up important family business questions. Prominent among them are: Who is allowed or qualified to own shares? (What about stepchildren and adopted children?) What kinds of employment opportunities do in-laws have; are they considered insiders or outsiders? How can anyone get out of the family business yet still be included and respected within the family? How does the family present itself to the outside world? What happens when a family member rebels against the family's public face and its public values? Where do family loyalties lie?

The inside reality of any family is different than the outside face of the family. In some families this difference is small and in others it is enormous. The closer the internal and external realities, the healthier the family.

One final note on structure. Structure provides safety when there is a solid internal framework and an outer protective layer. However, family structure must be flexible and open enough to accommodate the various circumstances of the family and the business over the passage of time and as changes occur.

FAMILY PROCESS

Systems thinking directs us toward looking for patterns of interaction among family members rather than looking for a direct cause-and-effect relationship between happenings. It also provides us with the perspective of the whole being more than the sum of its parts. A systems perspective dictates that there is not necessarily a direct relationship in time between an event in the present and any response to that event. Finally, systems thinking reminds us that a change in any part of the system will always create a change in other parts.

The process of the family, the step-by-step unfolding of interactions, is governed by these principles: circularity, the uncanny relationship between time and events, and concurrent change.

Circularity

Human beings tend to think linearly. The opening lines of the Book of Genesis, "In the beginning . . ." is the defining paradigm of Western civilization, attesting to how strongly the idea of cause and effect is ingrained. The world in reality, however, is more complex, and understanding that complexity requires a different outlook.

The systems approach requires us to shift from cause-and-effect to circular thinking. In systems terms, A does not cause B; instead, A and B reciprocally interact and impact each other. Intuitively, this is known to be true since each one of us has heard the typical dialogue, A: "I wouldn't yell if he listened to me," followed by B: "I can't listen when she yells."

As the noted author, politician, and U.S. Treasurer Ivy Baker Priest reminded us: "The world is round and the place which may seem like the end, may also be only the beginning" (cited in Maggio, 1992, p. 28). She pointed out, as others have too, that how any interaction is seen is the result of how the viewer chooses to punctuate the sequence of events or placements.

Here is another example of circularity. A story common to many cultures aptly describes the dilemma of understanding the inner dynamics of the family-owned business. In one version two brothers are asking the advice of their father, the senior member of the family business. Each one presents his own version of the issues at hand. At the end of the first presentation the father acknowledges the first brother's position saying, "You're right." After the second presentation he acknowledges the second brother's position and again says, "You are right." A sister who has been listening to this interchange looks confused. She asks her father, "How can they both be right?" The father turns to her saying, "You are right, too."

Everybody is right, including the father, because everybody describes the situation from his or her own perspective. But if that is the case and everybody's perspective is correct, how can this family, or by extension any group, ever achieve a common goal? More to the point, could they ever learn to collaborate so as to sustain a successful enterprise?

This story is linear; the children ask and the father does not take a position that would choose one over the other. But how might this story be understood by proponents of the systems perspective? The answer, of course, is "in many different ways" because taking a systemic perspective means looking for the patterns that recur and then generating hypotheses about those patterns.

One way of restating the situation from the perspective of patterns considers two children asking their father to solve problems that he simply refers back to each of them. From this we would then generate some hypotheses. For instance: (1) Perhaps the father believes that his children need to be solving these issues between themselves; or (2) Perhaps the children sense that their father needs to stay involved in the business, so the questions they are asking help this to happen; or (3) Maybe this family cannot tolerate discord, and the father steps into the picture at the slightest provocation to smooth everything over. Each hypothesis takes us along a different path and thus directs us toward taking different next steps.

In this oversimplified illustration, regardless of the specific viewpoint taken, the family business advisor needs to describe the pattern of interactions and design appropriate interventions leading to positive change. For example, the advisor might help the advice seekers find ways to solve the problem themselves, while their father looks on.

Just interrupting a recurring pattern will often change the interpersonal dynamics and even allow for personal growth. Simple interventions can also help participants recognize that there are at least as many different valid views of the situation as there are people involved in the conversation.

Before concluding our discussion on the principle of circularity in systems thinking, it is important to mention the idea of *triangulation,* a special relationship pattern that can be extremely useful in understanding family business systems. Triangulation, first observed and reported by Murray Bowen (1978), refers to a process in which two people in conflict reduce the relationship tension by incorporating a third person into the relationship. Extramarital affairs in couple relationships are one possible result of this dynamic. Another is the standard internecine sibling war that brings in the parents to mediate, or usually take sides—a common occurrence with siblings at the helm of a business. Still another is when a parent avoids spousal relationship problems by creating special emotional ties with one of the children—a maneuver that frequently upsets the balance of power in the business.

One strategy for managing triangulation uses the genogram, developed by Bowen and elaborated on by McGoldrick and Gerson (1985), to aid individuals in separating from their family of origin. When constructing the genogram an individual is guided to draw his or her family tree going back at least two generations and forward as many generations as there are. This visual representation of the family tree helps put the entire family and particularly the family of origin in both historical and emotional perspective.

The act of constructing a genogram provided a new emotional perspective to our client quoted at the beginning of this chapter, who had said, "Every time I'm around my parents I feel like a little boy." It allowed him finally to experience himself and his parents as separate individuals.

Time and Events Factor

The second important concept of systemic process is that particular events or actions may not be, or appear to be, related in terms of time (Senge, 1990). This principle points out that emotionally charged current events can easily trigger related events from the distant past, resulting in responses in the present that actually carry the weight and intensity of past emotions with them.

Cause and effect are not necessarily related in time. Systems thinking considers what effects a decision will have in the long term as well as what it will bring in the immediate future. Incorporating the capacity for change has the slow, evolving caliber of time-lapse photography rather than the relatively instantaneous quality of taking a snapshot.

Time is also an important consideration in evaluating systems in general and family systems in particular, because over time systems tend to evolve and become more complex (Gulbenkian Commission, 1996). In families, relationships are not static. Their cycles and rhythms change whenever the nature of the connection between the people themselves changes. Change happens because people change over time and with different circumstances. People change with respect to one another as they mature and gain their adult identity; as they age and lose their potency; or as they feel more or less secure within themselves and their life situation.

The point here is that relationships in family business go through many natural changes that present practical family business problems, and are therefore likely to require attention. Many problems arise that relate to where individuals or the family are in the developmental cycle. People in the midst of a personal crisis can be difficult to deal with or help; they get touchy, impatient, or depressed, and may act in ways that are hurtful to themselves or others. In family business the potential for adverse personal moods and reactions to interfere with managing the business and ownership responsibilities is extremely high. Since relationships extend beyond the boundaries of the workplace or normal business hours, there is a greater chance for interpersonal slights to happen or disagreements to develop. In addition, when trust is taken for granted, as it is within most families, betrayals of trust are harder to withstand. Solutions to these problems can be simple when the relationship ruptures are attended to early on and not allowed to escalate and compound.

Family relationships are also driven by external circumstances. It may become necessary to replace a brother or cousin when economic times require downsizing, or when one sibling will not stop harassing another. These sometimes-necessary decisions can cause deep-seated hurt and anger, which have the potential to undermine family relationships and affect business obligations.

Concurrent Change

A change in one part of the system has a wide-ranging impact and will effect changes in all other parts of the system. If an individual family member changes, particularly someone in a position of power in the business, the complex pattern of interactions within the family will necessarily change in some way.

This principle of concurrent change is what allows, and what demands, family members and advisors alike to "think family" (Kadis and McClendon, 1998). This allows us to approach any given problem in such a way that it will have the most impact on the family, and, as a result, change will be more significant and lasting. In family-owned businesses, thinking family is essential because of the complexity and depth of familial interactions over time and their connections with the business operation. Although all advisors may not have access to everyone in the family, working effectively with several key players can effect strategic changes that will resonate throughout all parts of the family business. It is important to respect the power one individual has to impact the entire family unit.

Family relationships also change as positions in the company hierarchy change. For instance, when one sibling is promoted his or her position in the family does not change. She or he is still a sister or brother. But as a result of his or her change in the business hierarchy, relationships are necessarily different—the people he or she reports to change, meetings are different, and peers change. All these changes require some adjustment in the sibling relationship, particularly if his or her status is higher than before. Similarly, when shares in the family business are distributed, the nature of the relationships within the family is likely to change because those newly received shares represent a much stronger influence within the business.

As an example, when John and Nancy started their restaurant, they were relatively young and had no children. Both were fully committed to making a success of the business and even dreamed of growing it so that eventually they would expand by selling franchises. They had a clear contract and a clear direction. However, when their children began to arrive and Nancy started splitting her time between home and the business, problems began to arise. Nancy's expectations changed; the restaurant greatly missed her talents and began to falter; John was angry and disillusioned—after all, he was just doing what he and Nancy had agreed to do at the beginning.

It was at this point that John and Nancy asked for our help in sorting out their priorities and making plans for the future. Addressing their concerns from a systems perspective that used a developmental paradigm allowed the couple to depersonalize the issues, reorder their current priorities, and design a clear and positive direction for themselves, their grown children, and their beloved restaurant.

UNSPOKEN ISSUES IN FAMILY SYSTEMS: EMOTION AND NORMALITY

Feelings are rarely far from the surface in a family business. Anyone who has sat through a board meeting in which there is a contentious issue on the table or in which there are strong feelings among various family board members is aware that emotions are important factors in the actual operation of family business systems.

Advisors who have watched the pain of a family trying to deal with the death of a leader know, for instance, how the emotions of shock, loss, and confusion can have adverse impacts on running the business. Also emotionally devastating, of course, are the instances when a family discovers that the heir apparent is strung out on drugs, or that a senior family member has misused the family trust.

In each of these examples familiar to us the interactions between people are ordered and modulated by their emotions (Johnson, 1998). As advisors we need a plan, a map, to direct our professionally appropriate responses to enable family members to contain their emotions, employ their thinking, and utilize their problem-solving skills. This map will emerge and be our focus in the following chapters.

Furthermore, as advisors we must continuously ask ourselves: What is normal? What does a healthy family and family business actually look like? Strictly from a business perspective the answer is simple: What is normal and healthy is what *works*. From a family and a family-business perspective, however, the answer is less clear because evaluating what works depends on what aspect of functioning we are looking at. What works for the family may not work for the family business, and vice versa. What works for some individuals within the family may not work for others. Because owners' goals are typically different from those of management, what works for one group may not work for the other group.

Fortunately, we do have good ideas of what works for most families, ideas that derive from our observations of optimally functioning families, families that function in midrange, and families that barely function at all. We know that the families which are cohesive, adaptable, can solve problems, are organizationally stable, and have effective leadership and open communication are the same families that deal with the problems of life effectively and provide stable homes. We can measure these variables and use the results to help families in business improve the way they function (Olson, 1993; Walsh, 1994; Lewis, 1998).

As we continue, much more will be said about how to help members of family businesses manage emotions and build healthy, functioning families.

GATHERING INITIAL INFORMATION

Given the complexity of the family business, advisors need some way to create order—to make sense of their observations, their hunches, and the information available and not available to them. Have a schema for determining which information to pay attention to and include, and which to discard; which issues to explore further and which ones to file away, possibly to be pursued and considered at a later time.

The following brief overview will introduce this vital and complex subject of information gathering, which begins with the first contact. Later, when discussing our model, we expand this schema and go into greater depth.

The Individual Players

A complete list of all participants in the family business is essential, along with their ages and their role in each of the several subsystems—parent or child and from which generation; owner, manager, or family, or any combination of the latter three. This information helps fix a point in the life cycle of the family and order family priorities. It also provides a clue to understanding influence and the distribution of power. All too often people behind the scenes actually have as much or more influence than do the people who appear to have the power. Advisors therefore must ask themselves the question: "Who is in charge of the one who appears to be in charge?" This dislocation often explains why succession plans either may not get consummated or else have gone awry.

The System

One way to begin to understand the family system is to observe it in action in as many circumstances as possible over time: in the boardroom, at dinner, during a retreat when significant others are present, in small work-group settings, and wherever else the family will allow the advisor to be present. Since it is not usually possible to have all of these observation opportunities, especially early on, another way is to ask questions that elicit relationship-based information. In either case we both look and listen for the patterns that are either congruent or incongruent with what has already been learned about the family in the business and the family with the family. When we observe particular sequences of interactions—boundary crossings, triangulation, abusive behaviors, connections that do not occur and should—we take note and look for the sequence to repeat itself in other settings, thus forming a pattern. When we see it a second or third time, we know it is important, and begin to consider ways that this pattern impacts the entire family and the business system.

SYSTEMS THINKING: A REVIEW OF PRINCIPLES

The principles involved in *systems thinking* are straightforward:

- Remember that every family and every family business exists in a context much larger than is readily apparent. Ask questions about and respect the multiple environments that a family business operates in including family culture, current interfacing developmental cycles, and the wider business system.
- Consider the family structure and changes needed to achieve success.
- Keep in mind the complex web of interactions that characterize systems, even when working with a single individual.
- Focus on the patterns of interaction that will provide the greatest leverage, remembering that a change in one part of the system will impact all other parts of the system.
- Remember that it is essential to change patterns rather than fix the problem. The problem will reappear in another form if the patterns of interaction continue.
- Keep the time and events factor in mind. As Peter Senge (1990, p. 63) said: "There is a fundamental mismatch between the nature of reality in complex systems and our predominant ways of thinking about that reality. The first step in correcting that mismatch is to let go of the notion that cause and effect are close in time and space."

In Chapters 3 and 4 two significant and all-too-prevalent family patterns will be reviewed: oppressive systems and disengaged systems. Highly detrimental to family members and to the businesses they own and operate, these patterns usually cause relationship schisms that make healing wounds impossible unless and until successful reconciliation can be achieved.

Chapter 3

Oppression in Business-Owning Families

"My brother has a softer relationship with me as long as I show him submission. He has even told my sister how he is going to get rid of me. She said she would never say so in front of him or she too would have to go."

A client

Oppression is one of the most destructive forces in family life. It robs individuals of their dignity, denies and negates their abilities, encourages obedience rather than participation, and creates a sense of insecurity and personal vulnerability. Oppression is often identified as a major player in problems within business-owning families. Thus its active presence is likely to damage any family business's viability. Within a family, oppression is a violation of kinship rights. But more to the point: oppression produces the antithesis of the very kind of person you want parenting a child, sitting on a board of directors, or holding a senior management position.

Oppression is the pattern that results from acts of sustained imposition of unreasonable burdens on others. Its various behaviors are designed to keep others in subservience through the cruel or overbearing use of power or authority and the absolute suppression of dissent. Oppression results from a history of aggressive or demeaning acts against people, acts that are covert or overt attempts to control others' lives, thinking, and relationships. Generally, when we think of oppression we think of an overwhelming physical force. More recently we have come to realize that an unjust use of the emotional bond, verbal and emotional abuse, taking advantage of a person's trust, and other forms of coercion and intimidation can be every bit as oppressive as physical force. In our experience, a persistent use of power over others is oppressive, not simply unjust and cruel. As a pervasive pattern of abuse, oppression adversely affects all aspects of an individual's and a family's existence.

For good reason, then, we pay considerable attention to oppression—both in this book and certainly in our work with client families who are in business together. In this chapter we look at the systemic factors that create and continue oppression generally, especially in families. We furthermore consider some of the personal and environmental roots of the roles people play in oppressive systems. Finally, we suggest some ways to stop oppression and change systems that are oppressive. As professionals who are ever alert to the possible presence of oppression in families that own businesses, we work diligently with family members to reduce and hopefully even eliminate this entrenched and destructive problem that is so prevalent in business-owning families in a variety of forms.

OPPRESSIVE SYSTEMS

A broad spectrum of factors interact to create oppression in business-owning family systems. Societal, cultural, and business norms, elements in the family environment, and individual attitudes and behavior all cooperate to varying degrees to create oppression rather than systems of caring, respectful, and responsible patterns of interaction.

The family is inherently a political association. Like nations and other hierarchical organizations, families must have a mechanism to govern, so as to administer and control their internal and external affairs. Equally or even more important, however, is the fact that the family as a unit relies on exchange principles to manage its internal relationships (Jacobson and Margolin, 1979). By this we mean that the family is a storehouse for both material and immaterial resources such as love, money, food, protection, access to opportunities, and other comforts, and that family members regularly negotiate with one another to obtain or maintain these resources—the possession of which is equated, in everyone's eyes, with power.

At the simplest or material level, parents exchange money in the form of an allowance for chores completed by their children, or else desired playthings or articles of clothing for some special achievement. More complex exchanges include approval and recognition, or permission and special privileges, which can be given or withheld depending on the nature or outcome of the exchange arrangement, such as the child's obedience or good behavior.

Resources typically available for exchange can be almost anything from money to sexual availability between husband and wife, to respect or deference between parents and children or siblings. Family members who lack resources—notably children, aging family members, women, and even minority shareholders—are seen, and often experience themselves, as having much less power than family members who possess all or most of the desired resources. In business-owning families the available resources are frequently unequally proportioned and "lesser" family members, perhaps women, younger siblings, in-laws, family members who aren't part of management, and management persons who are not part of the family, to name a few, typically lack both positional power and relationship influence.

Negotiating the material and immaterial exchanges for resources important to family members requires bargaining skills. Although we would expect that family people who love and care about one another would manage these resource exchanges through thoughtful negotiation, this is not always the case. Children, for example, will at first simply try to negotiate with their parents to obtain something they want. However, if that fails, they may wheedle or whine, stage an angry sulk or tantrum, or resort to bullying. Some other children's successes are due to skillfully charming parents and others to get what they want. When successful these tactics reinforce an adult tendency to manipulate people with the wanted resources.

Although adults generally prefer to negotiate in order to resolve differences or get something they want, that doesn't always happen. When thwarted adults may regress, reverting back to coercive and harassing strategies from childhood times, such as bullying, threatening, and intimidating other workers (Laursen et al., 2001). In the business world one can expect to see many forms of human behavior intended to manipulate others and to gain, retain, and display both resources and power. Family businesses are no exception.

In all business-owning families the forces of personality, competition, need for favor, recognition, and money continuously collide, making the family business extremely vulnerable to becoming an agent of oppression. Some people who crave power may abuse it if they ever attain it—as when becoming the CEO. Other family members, who need or seek material or immaterial resources from those who have them and are powerful, behave in a variety of ways that reflect earlier decisions.

Oppressive systems develop when some family members seize or receive the opportunity to have power over others; when other family members cooperate with oppressors and submit to their demands, out of fear of personal harm, isolation, abandonment, or conflict; and when still others contribute by keeping silent so as to avoid becoming involved in the problems themselves.

Thus it is often easy in the environment of family business for some family members to gain and maintain power over other family members—and even to get rid of those who don't cater to them or who appear to question their qualifications or authority. It is easy also for others to fall short in the power game because they were shunted aside by factors such as gender, birth order, favoritism, special abilities, or fierce ambition. It is also understandable why some of the family members simply avoid or withdraw entirely from the problems engendered by the presence of oppression in the family business.

In a family-owned business, control over the resources of money, position, approval, status, and relationships traditionally lies in the hands of only a few people, or even a single person. When such persons are unwilling to fairly exchange resources, oppression can easily rule. The abuse of power on a daily basis can ultimately have a devastating impact. When oppression reveals itself as a pattern of unjust and even cruel acts intended to suppress or eliminate other family members, it is a compelling force that affects everyone. Although abuse of power can be a single act, oppression is a pervasive pattern that invariably affects and infects both the family and its business.

THE MAIN ROLES IN SYSTEMS OF OPPRESSION

Oppressive systems are composed of three major interacting parts: the role of the oppressor, the role of the oppressed, and the role of the beneficiary (or those who stand by). By its very nature oppression is relational. For every oppressor there is an oppressed person, who is often called a "victim" and in every system of oppression there are beneficiaries.

In working with family systems where oppression can be identified as a dominant relational issue it is necessary to understand the relationship between the oppressed and the oppressor, and also to understand the separate relationships of the beneficiaries to the oppressed and to the oppressor. In the following section we will consider the roles of oppressor, oppressed, and beneficiary. People can perform different roles especially when the generations change.

The Oppressor

As was previously noted, oppression in families is a pattern, rather than an event or series of events, that can be traced not only to childhood but also through several generations. Physical and emotional abuse and their more subtle form, neglect, deprive the child of his or her sense of self and the ability to live and enjoy life. Such a pattern of abuse has been aptly called soul murder because it results in loss of identity, spiritual annihilation, and emotional bondage to the abuser (Schatzman, 1976; Shengold, 1999). Oppressors are soul murderers.

Some people become oppressors because they themselves have been either victims of or witnesses to serious abuse, usually within their birth families. Considerable evidence suggests that the origins of abusive patterns in adults can be traced back to the "combination of witnessing or directly experiencing violence, shaming, and insecure attachment" in early childhood (Lawson, 2001, p. 506). The weight of evidence and experience indicates that such oppressed children may become oppressors as adults unless they learn to limit their own oppressive tendencies.

The role of oppressor is also taken by some because it has been granted by birthright, such as being the eldest brother, or in many cultures and households simply by being born a male. Others achieve positional power because of favoritism, special advantages, manipulative talents, brutal behavior, or intense ambition.

Misusing and abusing power is easy to do if people don't have what Bandura (1999) called the "moral agency" to control themselves—to put limits on their own actions when they hurt other people and to consciously treat other people well. He reminded us that moral agency is not automatically engaged; it takes an act of will.

Oppressors proclaim by their words and actions: "No matter what you do or think, I am right. . . . No matter what I do or think, I am right." So how do some people come to believe that they are always right? The answer lies in their inability to tolerate themselves if they are shown to be wrong or inadequate in any way. Oppressors define themselves on the basis of strength, power, ability, intelligence, and skill. Shunning intimacy and informality, when they might show a more humane and even vulnerable side of themselves, they avoid close contact with other family members—and, by the way, almost always try to avoid participating in a reconciliation process.

When oppressors feel threatened their chosen defense is to attack others. Usually they focus on particular individuals whom they suspect might actually have more strength, wisdom, ability, or other personal asset than they have. Frequent targets in family businesses are siblings, since many have been competing with one another in these areas since birth.

Actually, oppressors often see themselves, and portray themselves to others, as the real family victim, because they maintain that they are contributing far more and working far harder than anyone else. This approach typically presents as, "No one can do as good a job as I can, and I am the only one in the family who has held things together so far."

Moreover, oppressors are actually quite often correct in saying that they work harder and hold things together; they rarely delegate authority and important responsibilities to others because that would mean sharing power and credit. They maintain, of course, that all others are too incompetent, lazy, or uncommitted to do their jobs, therefore, they have to work harder to do what needs to be done to keep the business profitable. When this is the case others who do not share in positional power, decision making, and accomplishment are apt to support the oppressor by slacking off or giving up. It is, after all, futile to do your best when no acknowledgment or credit is given, and when there is always criticism and interference for doing the job. In this way family members cooperate and the oppressor remains a martyr, sacrificing himself or herself for "the good of the family." Furthermore, everyone is supposed to be grateful.

Oppressors have a hard time tolerating any confrontation from others, and are usually totally blind to their own part in any difficulty. After all, who would admit to be occupying the oppressor role?

The Oppressed

The oppressed say to oppressors: "No matter what you do or think, you are right and I am confused. . . . No matter what I do or think, you are right and I am inadequate."

Oppressed family members gradually lose their confidence, their self-esteem, and their spirit. In an effort to avoid their feelings of helplessness in the face of problems, they turn against themselves to fix it, thinking to themselves, "After all, if I am to blame, then I can fix myself and there is some chance of resolution of the problem and the relationship."

Oppressed persons respond with deference and conformity so that oppressors will feel better about themselves and then the threat they embody will go away. Having become masters at keeping themselves down, they have internal conversations with themselves, which are self-oppressive.

Persons predisposed to this role have frequently witnessed or experienced abuse somewhere in their childhood and have managed their own pain and weakness through accommodation. From the beginning they have received messages that say "don't be yourself, because you are inadequate in some way, or you remind me of. . . ." Oppressed persons decide early that they are not good enough or not right enough. They are sensitive and generally overidentify with others in distress. Sometimes they have even been asked to move aside or take care of siblings or parents who are having difficulties.

Looking at the oppressive system from the standpoint of the oppressed, we see discomfort, frustration, feelings of helplessness, and self-questioning, such as, "Am I crazy, stupid, and worthless?" When this pattern develops, people do things to make themselves be even more inadequate, unworthy, unable to ever measure up, and even dumb. They feel bad about themselves, hold others in higher esteem, and tend not to do their best in their jobs and family business positions. The results, of course, confirm their negative self-image, making it even less possible to ever challenge any of their own or others' assumptions about them.

If and when persons exit an oppressive system, each must take responsibility for having participated in it. This is not to say that the oppressed are to blame; we simply mean that everyone must take responsibility for themselves—for their own actions and inaction. In our experience, whenever we successfully help individuals extricate themselves from an oppressive situation they invariably ask, "Why did I wait so long to leave?"

The Beneficiaries

Beneficiaries are family members who just stand by and do nothing. They say to themselves: "Yes, I see what is going on but there really is no problem here."

If they are aware of the problems, they gain something for themselves by not protesting the existence, importance, or the destructive intent of the ongoing oppression. People in this position tell themselves and others that there really isn't anything to worry about, or actually the problem is caused by the victim's ineptitude (as oppressors assert), and therefore there really isn't anything different for them to do. In this way beneficiaries can justify their passive participation. Others in the beneficiary position simply don't allow themselves to know that any problem exists.

Beneficiaries pretend not to see, hear, or know the truth of the oppression. As a way of defending themselves they attempt to avoid, disguise, circumvent, or diminish the problem. They don't want to face up to others and endanger themselves; therefore, they persist in their own self-protective stance and avoid challenging and confronting oppression. Beneficiaries compromise others, frequently sacrifice their own values, and make poor choices based on self-interest.

Beneficiaries make excuses whenever problems are brought to their attention, especially if they might be traced to them in some way: for example, "My son really isn't doing that," or, "He'll get over it," or, "It's really her fault, anyway," or, "I promised him when he was just a baby and now I have to follow through."

Beneficiaries choose to do nothing—which is, in effect, choosing to support oppression. As a result, they are a key part of the problem. In family business, for example, parents frequently gain status and feel included when they must continuously fix up or clean up problems that occur when one or more of their offspring are oppressing others. Their constant involvement tells them and others, "I am still important and needed."

Underneath, though, beneficiaries feel that they are powerless to do anything. If beneficiaries actually involve themselves, it is usually through "help that is not help" to either the oppressor or the oppressed. Challenging the oppressor is avoided—perhaps justified by saying that he or she "couldn't stand the stress if confronted, and it's really not so bad, anyway." They see the oppressed as responsible for their own plight. They think, "Since they won't help themselves, why should I bother to do anything?"

THE IMPACT OF OPPRESSION ON FAMILY BUSINESSES

When persons predisposed to be oppressors control the power and resources in a family or family business, oppression inevitably reigns. Interpersonal interactions are characterized by devaluing others, and blaming. Strong business control is exercised and it is easy for those in control to move strategically to denigrate and even eliminate all those who are seen as threats.

A few behaviors are definite markers for the existence of oppression in the business-owning family. These include threatening statements, accusations, name-calling, fits of fury, frigid or angry sulking, and withholding resources from others. Discounting, another behavior, usually takes the form of inviting ideas and then rejecting them out of hand. Suggestions are either trivialized or undermined, and rewards are withheld. When oppressors are confronted, however gently, the confrontation is most often met with denial or an escalation of the abusive behavior. When the pattern of response holds true, the challenging family member backs off, saying, "I must have been wrong."

In an oppressive system many of these behaviors occur in a constellation. In other words, when one or several behaviors are present, more are apt to appear; soon the pattern of oppression becomes clear. Oppression sustained in childhood and then continued in the workplace over the years as continuous or intermittent disparagement, invalidation, and distrust eventually destroys everyone involved as in the following tale of the decline and near-certain demise of a family business.

Donald Manweather is ninety-four years old and his wife Sally is eighty-seven. Since neither of them is in good health and they are both of advanced age, their prognosis for long-term survival is poor indeed. Their sons, John and Matt, are in their sixties. Kept "waiting in the wings" for years, they were denied both management and ownership of the family's multimillion-dollar real estate empire. John and Matt were constantly belittled and criticized for their stupidity and ineptitude—their parents' rationalizations for not transferring management and assets to them. Matt handled this maltreatment by disappearing from the family's midst, whereas his brother stayed on, trying ever harder to please his parents.

The Manweather Company assets are now in a state of disrepair, seven lawsuits against the family are pending, and the estate taxes eventually due will leave little for the next generations. John still does whatever he can for his folks, but he has become a broken man, collapsing under the weight of the oppression. His parents' unwillingness to let go and their relentless disparaging of their two sons has ruined their business assets, alienated and/or destroyed their sons, and undermined any sense of family cohesion.

Oppression in families and in family businesses also has a way of continuing on into the next generation. Roles in oppression do not remain static; they tend to rotate, especially with the generations. As mentioned, the abused have a high potential for becoming the abusers, and beneficiaries in one generation, using the original oppressor as a model, may themselves become oppressors.

As an example, let's look at the Brown Public Relations Firm. Rochelle Brown, forty-three years old, is co-owner, with her younger sister, of the firm founded by their father. In addition, Rochelle is currently CEO. Shortly after finishing college Rochelle entered the business, taking it over five years later following her father's sudden death. She called us for several reasons: her sister was not carrying any responsibility for the business; she was having difficulty keeping good managers; and she knew that morale was poor among her twenty-two employees.

We could see that Rochelle, bright and hardworking, who labeled herself as "your typical Type-A personality," was extremely demanding of herself, and of others as well. But in talking to her senior managers we found that the problems went deeper. Although the employees—men and women alike—respected her commitment and expertise, they experienced her as aloof and always felt personally judged and put down by her. Their jobs paid well, but it was an uncomfortable and unhappy place to work. Several employees had actually sought help by contacting her sister, Marianne, who had refused to even give an opinion.

It was not difficult for us to get to the root of her interpersonal behaviors. Rochelle had assumed the role of oppressor. During our talks she quickly became aware that she was using, in what was essentially now *her* PR agency, the same coercive tactics her father had used with her and her sister throughout their early years. Her father even continued his abuse later in the girls' lives. When Rochelle came home from college he would put down her efforts as worthless and stupid. She dreaded coming home, where she invariably felt defensive, withdrawn, and fearful of his criticism. Later, when she worked under him at the agency, he was almost always condescending, demeaning, and dismissive of her work.

Since her father was so successful, Rochelle couldn't help but think that his judgments of her were correct. So, as owner-manager she vacillated between being critical of others and being worried that her staff would judge her ineffectual as a manager. Not surprisingly, she was the most critical of others at the times when she felt most unsure of herself.

Helping Rochelle was intense because her considerable insecurity frequently triggered defensiveness and ingrained attack on others' behavior. But we made good progress because she was quick to learn, insightful, and determined to make things work better. Once she fully understood what provoked her condescension toward others, our coaching helped her learn to manage herself differently. Rochelle and Marianne, understanding more about their mutual history and the oppressive system of their family of origin, soon reconciled and Marianne became an active and enthusiastic supporter of the firm and its future direction.

The case of Rochelle is an example of one of the many middle-of-the-road types of family oppression. In its more extreme forms, oppression results in either annihilation or alienation of families and the businesses they own. Individuals who have been stripped of any positive sense of themselves are forced to leave, if at all possible, or be completely destroyed; some family members have even killed themselves. Others have been utterly made powerless within their families and their family business, as just demonstrated in the Manweather family. Still others, under the reign of oppression, have escaped the character assassination by cutting themselves off entirely from their families of origin; however, they may still suffer terribly from this total alienation.

CHANGE IS POSSIBLE

When oppression rules in a family-owned business, every family member has a choice: "Do I have the courage and forethought to break the cycle, or shall I choose to remain silent and continue to betray myself and our family now and for generations to come?"

Change in dealing with oppression begins with recognizing the truth. We believe strongly in this statement attributed to Edmund Burke: "The only thing necessary for the triumph of evil is for good men to do nothing." We strongly accept that when family business members *do* something, change will occur.

In Part II, we take an extensive and detailed look at restoring justice and achieving reconciliation in business-owning families. But for now let us emphasize that the essential first step in combating oppression is for family members—particularly those with the most economic, historical, and psychological power—to acknowledge the existence, use, and harmful impact of an oppressive system in both their family and their business. Family members need to recognize that oppression exists and that it has set up the people in the family for unequal accesses to resources, life opportunities, and affirming family relationships. They need to recognize and accept that they themselves are part of the problem, and have contributed to and/or benefited from it.

So what are the best ways for business advisors and family members to move ahead when dealing with the presence of oppression in a family and its company?

Here are a few tools to use when approaching the three different roles family members play in a system of oppression.

Oppressors

In the beginning, oppressors usually need to be accommodated in order to enlist their participation in change efforts. When people have valuable skills to contribute to the company and are dedicated to its interests, it is most important to work toward changing the system and achieving justice in relationships. It never works to attempt to "out-escalate" the oppressor—this action, through changing roles, simply reinforces the oppressive system.

It is helpful to realize that people who play the oppressor role have incredible difficulty looking within themselves to admit any weaknesses and failings; they require a slow approach to changing. The oppressor, the perpetrator of wrongdoing, is basically coming either from a fear-based position or an angry, arrogant position. Regardless of origin, in the beginning oppressors need to feel that others (particularly anyone with power) are on their side, that they themselves are in the right, and that eventually they will prevail over whatever opposition or charges confront them.

Advisors should utilize family members with whom oppressors have good emotional connections, for they can support small behavioral changes in positive directions, such as beginning to show acceptance, tolerance, and gratitude for others in the family. Also, those wishing to facilitate change should consistently be supportive of the strength and wisdom of the oppressor by affirming his or her idealized self-image as the one who is putting so much effort into the company for the good of all. The person needs to be supported; the abusive behavior, however, is clearly not to be supported. Oppressors who are ultimately able to change will already possess the ability to be compassionate and have goodwill toward others; it is simply hidden behind their fear that others will discover their inadequacy.

Let us look at a recent case. Megan, who asked for our help, had never been part of the family business, an upscale wilderness resort which had long been a family dream that her deceased husband had started and that her four children now ran. Megan lived in a small home on the resort property and had ample opportunity to observe her children as they worked together. This was the source of her concern. She knew that Ryan, the oldest and currently in charge, "ran" his younger siblings with threats, put-downs, and an attitude of dismissal for their ineptitude. They were allowed little or no say in decisions of any kind because the "dumb kids," as Ryan called them, could never do anything right.

Megan, still the primary shareholder, asked us to try to remedy the situation before Ryan completely alienated his siblings. It was obvious when we met him that Ryan had always been both a "take-charge" and "I'll-do-it-myself" person. Barely five feet four inches tall, he puffed himself up with self-importance and portrayed himself as indispensable to the business. In a meeting with us, Megan, in a caring and concerned way, confronted Ryan with his abusive behaviors and his treatment of his brothers. After a long, slow, and careful discussion, Ryan was able to see how his judgmental, dictatorial, and demeaning behavior had affected others. Also, admitting to the work responsibilities that made his managerial position difficult for him, Ryan agreed to a plan for reallocating jobs and resources that kept him in his current position as company president but relieved him of many of the physically and emotionally taxing jobs that his siblings could do much more easily. With this reorganization Ryan felt happier, less frustrated, and more successful. His behavior changed and his siblings were allowed the freedom and responsibilities they deserved and were certainly able to handle.

Ryan was both willing and able to change. The change in the oppressive system, initiated when his mother moved out of the role of beneficiary and into the position of challenger, allowed Ryan to make the changes which also benefited him. We should point out, however—basing this comment on ample past experience—that many people in the oppressor role in family businesses prove simply unwilling to change. Or, if willing, are unable to develop the capacities of self-criticism and compassion for others. Many, in fact, will not hesitate to turn against others, even their closest family members, when things do not go the way they want them to.

For continuing family business success and the health and safety of the family, *do not* allow family members who are unwilling to look at themselves and reconcile differences to occupy positions of power and control over other family members or the resources of the company.

Oppressed

Another saying we believe in is from Eleanor Roosevelt: "No one can make you feel inferior without your consent."

The oppressed can position themselves to bring about basic change in their nonaffirming circumstances by breaking the silence and revealing oppressors' power games. However, oppressed people often initially need other people's help in first recognizing the abuse. Then they need encouragement to change their part in the drama by finding their own voice of protest against oppression—standing up to assert themselves. By accepting some responsibility for their position and taking on a new, positive self-definition, the oppressed can be empowered to take on different roles so as to effect changes in the oppressive system of the family business.

Some persons who find themselves in the role of the oppressed come from abusive backgrounds in which they were dependent and did not have any option other than to take whatever was dished out. However, as adults this situation of total dependence and inability is rarely the case. Others in the oppressed position are simply nice people who have never before directly experienced oppression and therefore have no idea or model for how to handle the abusive situation. This is typically the case with in-laws coming into a family business where oppressive systems have been imposed by both the family and its business. In-laws are frequently targeted by the oppressor.

The critical change in recovery is for victims to recognize their own *internal* oppressor, and after they have changed their conversations with themselves be willing to stand up to the identified perpetrators and change the external environment. The oppressed need to stop attacking and doubting themselves and replace their negative and demeaning internal conversations with a very different dialogue. To be successful, oppressors need people who will turn against themselves. To become challengers of oppression family members must refuse to cooperate by accommodating oppressors and putting themselves down. Drawing the self-boundary and knowing that, "this is not about me or my worth" is essential.

The second step is to devise a strategic way of responding to the oppressor so that blame for problems cannot be legitimately shifted, as has been allowed to happen in the past. For example, oppressors will insult people to trigger an angry response, for then the oppressor is able to say, "See, it really is the others. Just look at how they behave!"

Often the process of recovery from oppression is a long one. One must find the self that has been covered up and develop the resilience to bounce back when attacked—to "pick yourself up, dust yourself off, and start all over again."

Beneficiaries

Beneficiaries are frequently large in numbers—including family members, employees, outside board members, and even advisors. Beneficiaries go along with oppression to keep their jobs, protect their incomes, gain status in the community, and have the availability of perks and prestige. For beneficiaries, breaking the silence and confronting the system takes a commitment to honesty at any cost, and it requires both stamina and resilience. As we have learned, systems can be rigid and its adherents will quickly regroup when confronted by a foreign and unwanted reality. Oppressive family systems are especially rigid and changing one's role from beneficiary to challenger of oppression could mean leaving the company, the board, or the family.

As part of our initial evaluation of a new client company, we sat in on a board of directors meeting of a third-generation family business. The entire board membership was present and consisted of three siblings, two parents, the long-time accountant, an attorney, and an old family friend. One of the siblings, eventually to be a one-third shareholder and currently the CEO of this large manufacturing enterprise, had prepared the agenda. However, he had not given the agenda or the board information packet to anyone until that morning. This even included his sister, who served as president of the board and had shares equal to his.

When we finally were able to look at the packet we found that financial information was sketchy, and what was in the report was not annotated. Other reports were nonexistent and the agenda had been solely composed by the CEO.

We already knew from talking privately with various board members that serious concerns needed to be addressed. Yet there was little about these items on the agenda, some of which were extremely important. There was also no room for discussion. At one point during the meeting the sister/president asked a question that could have resulted in thoughtful consideration of a problem, but her brother, the CEO, summarily dismissed it. When she attempted to pursue the matter, the CEO threatened to walk out.

After that, little was said by anyone. The meeting was relatively brief, which we later learned was typical of previous meetings as well. The CEO totally controlled the meeting and met with little or no dissension. In addition, we noticed that it was the CEO rather than the board secretary who had written and submitted the minutes from the prior meeting and was again taking the minutes. When we asked about this later, some board members quietly told us that the minutes actually never bore any resemblance to the meetings they attended.

Following the meeting, we were concerned about the way people toed the line, their reluctance to challenge the leader, however constructively, and the paucity of ideas from some very bright people. So we asked each attendee about his or her experience. The board members had noticed the CEO's negative and dismissive comments and his attitude toward his sister; curiously, though, they had not noticed the ones aimed at themselves. They also tended to explain away the hostile remarks by saying, "He didn't mean that," "That's just the way John is," or, "He really is doing a good job." All were concerned about the lack of information and discussion, but considered that it would be pointless to inquire. So why bother?

Second, we asked the various people involved why they didn't speak up. Most said they wanted to retain their position on the board and in fact admitted that they liked not having to do much there, which in this case would involve asserting themselves and risking the CEO's ire.

Having been brought in by the parents and current owners of this very successful manufacturing company, we contracted to go ahead and work further with the family and also some of the outside board members. Our job in this effort was to help others become challengers of the oppressive system which bound them, this family and the company. People who watch and do nothing contribute to oppression. Each one must become actively involved in working toward the health and success of the business, regardless of what things or position they are frightened of losing.

CHALLENGING OPPRESSION

Several important steps can be taken when challenging oppression in family businesses. The first is to help some, if not all, family members recognize that oppression is a definite and central problem. The second step is to develop a willing group of family people ready to insist upon change. These steps go hand in hand, for in our experience it takes a cohesive, like-minded group to successfully challenge the roles and tactics used by family members who abuse their power. The third step is to find persons inside or outside the family who are not dependent on the other people, particularly the leader, for their self-esteem and income. It is important to utilize them as support in the change efforts.

Always remember that this is extraordinarily difficult work. Oppressive family systems are entrenched, and some have been so for generations. Many just cannot and will not change in the desired direction.

If people who have been oppressed in a family business finally come to accept the impossibility of the situation they are in and can find no way of impacting their families to make the essential changes needed for their survival, they must arrange for an exit that will protect their personal selves as well as any investments and assets in the family company. But that probably won't be the end of the story. They may still wish to remain as part of the family group, which almost inevitably will still include the oppressors and beneficiaries.

A bitter experience with oppression in a family business won't easily be forgotten or forgiven. What is the best way to deal with one's angry and hurt feelings at such times? How does one reconcile with the family when they have chosen for you to leave? This final case provides some suggestions.

The Parker family owned and managed a successful third-generation tool-and-die-making business. David, the remaining second-generation member and now seventy-four, had eliminated his brother from the business twenty-nine years earlier, and they had not spoken since. Ten years ago, having passed the company management onto his three children, Matt, Janet, and Marvin, he began his partial retirement. Then another generation of oppression began. Matt, the oldest son, president and CEO carried a big stick. He had no college degree and minimal business experience before joining his family company. Under his helm the company had been losing money for the past four years. His sister Janet, who had an MBA degree, was head of human resources, ran marathons in her personal time, and was well liked in the community. Marvin, the youngest, was employed and well paid by the company but had no real responsibilities and was generally left alone to do whatever he wished.

Over the past years, all three of the men in the Parker family, father and sons, had cooperated in underhanded ways to remove Janet from the company. She was devalued, demoted, and both privately and publicly shamed. For several years Janet had made numerous attempts to bring in someone who could work with the family to improve relationships, communication, and leadership skills. Matt was insulted by her insistent proposals, so nothing ever materialized.

The situation was at the point of no return when Janet contacted us. She wanted our help in exiting the company with some dignity, a fair return for selling her shares, and some hope of maintaining cordial family relationships following her departure. After the legal and financial arrangements were settled, however, Janet was unable to reconnect with her family of origin because her deep wounds had not yet healed. We encouraged her to speak up further about the mistreatment she had received in the family business, but she was concerned about what would happen when she saw family members again, even if it was just sitting around the Thanksgiving table.

We suggested that Janet begin expressing her feelings through a series of letters written to her father. Here are excerpts from a few of her letters:

On the night of the incident when the infamous blow-up doll named Janet was paraded in front of the whole company, I cried for hours in the garage before I walked into the house. I was incredibly hurt and shamed. Your comment to me later that "It was only a joke" was revealing. What kind of a father would further insult his daughter with a statement like that?

One of your reasons for getting me out of the business was because you thought I didn't work as hard as Matt. Does Marvin? You haven't kicked him out. The other reason you stated for getting me out was because Matt and I didn't get along. Whenever and wherever I attempted to contribute to the company (human resources, inventory, sales, marketing), I was put down—told my ideas were not important and that I was only interfering.

Eliminating me was easier than dealing with our dysfunctional family issues into which none of you men are willing to delve. You men in this family do whatever you want regardless of integrity or laws. You work through power, intimidation, and abuse.

That daughter whom you say you miss: do you even know who she is? Do you really even care? Are you afraid that our estrangement might look bad to your friends? That "good girl, damn fool" is no longer—she died with the job termination. I did my part for the family, and I allowed you and the boys to walk all over me. I will no longer subject myself to that.

As she expressed herself in this way, taking charge of herself in her relationships with her father and brothers, Janet grew in strength. She has now reconciled with her father and even manages to be in the same room with her brothers on holidays. Proud and happy with herself, she is still glad to be out of the family business and has moved on with her own family and her own career. Our work with Janet was successful.

After Janet was able to reconcile with her father our work with the Parker family began. Janet's father invited us in after he truly started listening to his daughter and her experience at his company. In addition, the business was stumbling even more. Currently, a movement is afoot to send Matt to business school and bring in an outside CEO while he's away, learning better how to run a business. He will thereby also improve his professional self-confidence, which as happens with oppressors, was shaky (though he wouldn't admit it), especially when he felt threatened by his sister's MBA credential.

Each of us, whatever the roles we play, must take responsibility for the very existence of oppression in our midst if we haven't worked to end it. The coercive tactics used to gain power over another person are learned in childhood but are maintained in adulthood in part because the targets of these tactics allow them to go on. When families refuse to confront maltreatment, make excuses for bad behavior, and reward business success, even at the expense of the dignity of their family members, the oppression continues. Families that lack an equitable structure and are unwilling to stop abusive behavior actually foster oppression.

Our next chapter is concerned with disengagement—the second major relationship problem encountered in family businesses. Many times fractures in relationships, which usually lead to disengagement, are the direct result of oppression.

Chapter 4

Disengaged Families

Since I left the business no one ever contacts me anymore. It's like I don't exist for them now. The business was a god; I defied it and now I'm not even in the family.

A client

We hold with the highest regard this idea: that people are more important than things. The people, the family members, in a family business are its greatest assets. We have emphasized this point before and will do so again. The network of committed family members who will guide the business and act as stewards of the business for future generations are the real wealth of the business—its human and intellectual capital. A business-owning family aiming to successfully preserve its wealth and well-being therefore must cherish and retain its people.

So what happens to a family and its business when family cohesion—the unity and solidarity that holds them together—is either destroyed or never existed? This chapter stresses the crucial importance of creating and maintaining cohesion in a business-owning family. It also considers the multiple causes, consequences, and techniques for repair when families disengage. By disengage we mean: unfasten, release, disconnect, liberate, divide, or cut loose—all of which are possibilities in the world of family business.

There are two distinct routes to disengagement in the business-owning family—families that disconnect or fracture, and families that have never connected. Both of these routes present serious and sometimes severe problems for the family business. Families in business often fracture or break apart as members choose to leave or are forced to leave because they have been stifled under oppressive systems or suffer from ruptured relationships and emotional wounds. Families also are unconnected because the current generation has never united and the promise of its accumulated human and intellectual capital is never realized. In the third and subsequent generations, families frequently never even get to know one another or learn to appreciate their relatives' personalities, skills, and capacities.

Thankfully, though, many families have managed to develop and protect their human capital while preserving their assets for four, five, and even more generations. For a hundred years or more each of them has built a collection of success stories about repairing relationships and about maintaining systems of governance that are based on honoring differences, shared values, and mutual positive regard.

THE IMPORTANCE OF COHESION IN FAMILIES

Cohesion and *cohesiveness,* the terms used to refer to the interpersonal bonds that exist in groups such as the family or a work group, the sense of belonging to the same unit, of "being on the same wavelength" as your partners, of sharing the same values and goals is universally recognized as the single most consistent factor that defines the healthy family. Accepting this conclusion leads us then to guess that the development of cohesiveness is probably the single most important goal of the business-owning family.

Cohesiveness, part of the experience of collaboration, is measurable (Olson, 1993; Moos and Moos, 1986) and has been shown time and again to result in more satisfaction with relationships and better outcomes in both the relationship and projects undertaken collaboratively. As we have stated many times, a successful family business involves mature individuals who work collaboratively and are committed to achieving a common goal: to successfully preserve the wealth of the family, which consists of its human, intellectual, and financial capital.

Cohesion exists at one end of a continuum—a continuum that describes the state of bonding in relationships. The terms *family solidarity* or *unity* are most frequently used to describe the cohesion end of the continuum. On the other end, many words are used to describe disengagement. We have chosen to use the words *fractured* or *sev-*

ered when referring to families who are disengaged because relationship bonds have been broken, sometimes slowly eroded away and sometimes violently trampled upon. We use the word *unconnected* to refer to families who are disengaged because the family members have never bonded.

FRACTURED OR SEVERED FAMILY CONNECTIONS

The separate causes of family disengagement are important to note because they require different processes for reunification. When families have been fractured, reconciliation is necessary. When families are disengaged because family members have never bonded, opportunities for bonding, understanding, and education about the family and business operations are the "treatments of choice."

Severed or fractured relationships leading to disengagement of the family can occur for any number of reasons, such as when parents get divorced, when children get married, when stepparents and stepchildren enter the scene, when people have battles and resentments over issues of position or inheritance, or when people have nasty fights or deep grievances. When families break apart because of any of these or other circumstances, loyalties are challenged, promises are broken, values are betrayed, and bitterness and disillusionment can become rampant. In contrast, some relationships rupture slowly, growing cool and creating emotional and social distancing when families and individuals cease to understand, respect, listen to, and care about one another, or when people are torn between preserving their own identity and dutifully conforming to externally imposed standards of "being a loyal family member."

Fractures can also occur as a direct result of oppressive family systems, which, as we learned in Chapter 3, are all too familiar in business-owning families. Oppression fractures relationships and forces disengagement, for if individuals are to survive they must emotionally and sometimes physically distance themselves from the central family and its business.

How do families, in spite of good intentions, end up with some or many of their members disengaged from one another—sometimes alienated, and sometimes at war? Many problems begin with the process of attachment, which sets the stage for the way human beings manage themselves and their relationships with others.

Studies in psychology and social anthropology indicate that a desire for a secure connection is basic to the nature of all human beings and drives people at any age to seek and strive for dependable attachments to others. Attachment behaviors among people let us know that a bond exists between individuals. Children internalize their early experiences of attachment, which ideally include quality connections with others and a desire to exist as a member of a particular family. Also, recent studies (Biringen et al., 1997) indicate that attachment behaviors, which lead to strong affective bonds with important others in the familial environment, contribute greatly to the development of the mature personality.

The implication is that attachment for individuals and high cohesion for families is part of normal development and that disengagement is what happens when the process goes awry. This is certainly true, but unfortunately, it is not all that simple, because even attachment has its dark side. Sometimes, the early experience of attachment has been so lacking in positive connections with others that isolation and alienation seem normal. At other times the nurturing and caregiving aspect of attachment and high cohesion can give way later to intrusiveness and the sticky experience of feeling nurtured and stuck at the same time (Werner et al., 2001).

Being able to establish and maintain individuality and a separate identity is a vital part of family cohesion. Cohesion is about separate individuals joining together with a common purpose and direction—individuals with the freedom to be themselves and the choice to be connected. When individuals have never benefited from stable early attachments or when they are constantly blocked from becoming and being themselves, relationships are unstable and rupture frequently, leading to fragmentation of the family.

Another circumstance leading to disengagement is some sort of trauma. Childhood trauma sensitizes children and makes them more vulnerable as adults (Nelson and Wampler, 2000). In addition, whenever any difficult situation occurs—when others become angry, for example—people's nervous systems, especially those traumatized as children, may overreact. They then protect themselves by avoiding, withdrawing, or otherwise disengaging from others (Johnson et al.,

2001). The experience of growing up in a household where serious physical or emotional abuse took place will have a very long-lasting effect, causing fractured relationships and sometimes estrangement from the entire family.

All of this does not mean that we are all marked for life from its very beginning. Far from it! Early experiences and early decisions, as was emphasized in Chapter 1, become part of the fabric of each person's personality—sometimes simply adjusted to, and sometimes redecided and changed with maturity.

But what does any of this have to do with business-owning families? In family business, where success depends on family members' ability to "work together," interpersonal bonds are constantly challenged. Repairing these bonds leads to a healthy maturation process for individual adults and to high family cohesion. However, when the inevitable disruptions of these bonds are not repaired, relationships fracture and families disengage. Some family members more easily than others are able to restore ruptured relationships, work collaboratively, and move toward mutual goals in the business.

Unfortunately, examples of fractured relationships and disengagement in business-owning families abound. The stories cited as follows of two different families' relationship ruptures and how these ruptures affected their businesses, are both notable not only because of the extensive media coverage they received, but also because they exemplify situations that are all too common.

In 1986 the Bingham family put its family media business, including the renowned *Louisville Courier Journal,* up for sale. The story was heavily reported in the nation's press for several reasons. First, the firm and the family had been an important part of Louisville's history and culture, plus the media was reporting on trouble in its own professional family. Second, the rift in the family apparently rang a responsive chord in the nation's psyche. In fact, four books were written about the Binghams, their empire, and their dispute.

The short version of the events leading to the sale of the business suggests that daughter Sallie's alienation from her brother, Barry Jr., the then-current manager, so upset Barry Sr. that he put the business on the auction block (Boylan, 1991).

The Bingham family story has been considered analogous to *King Lear,* and so too has another well-known situation: that of the Shoen family and their Phoenix, Arizona, U-Haul truck rental business. The long and short of their family business tale is truly a saga of disaffection. In 1986 after the father, Leonard Shoen, distributed stock to his children, they removed him from the business he had started with his wife in 1955. Numerous court battles ensued, including libel suits, allegations of murder, and other personal battles that played out in the public limelight. Ultimately the company went public, and the family feud went private. Leonard Shoen died at eighty-three in an auto accident that was ruled a suicide (Watkins, 1993).

Both of these family businesses were large companies with large amounts of money involved. But this is likely the only difference between them and hundreds upon hundreds of everyday examples of severed relationships in business-owning families. Stories of sundered relationships leading to fractures, disengagement, and even forced buyouts or sellouts are all too common. Repairing bonds in important family business relationships can save the life of companies, whether large firms or the small neighborhood restaurants or grocery stores—and perhaps the very lives of some of their people as well.

"Obsession, discomfort, and rage are the hallmarks of estrangement, and sorrow is its center" (Davis, 2002, p. 12). Unresolved relationship rifts trigger an interpersonal process that can easily get out of control, for negative affect quickly escalates and is contagious. When the interpersonal process is out of control, the strategy for self-protection that many if not most people use is withdrawal and avoidance, thus further escalating the relationship rupture. This information again alerts us to the importance of achieving reconciliation in ruptured relationships—hopefully before the pain and hurt has become too deep and the bonds are permanently broken.

The following case is an example of a family business that could have been destroyed. When couples are in business together and one of the partners breaks the marital bond through an extramarital affair, their joint enterprise is bound to be adversely affected.

Margaret and Gino Zoltan owned a successful advertising agency together. Married for twenty-eight years, they had two sons, ages twenty-five and twenty-three. Both children had graduated from college—one in business and the other in fine arts. While growing up, the boys had worked from time to time in the family business, and now that they were out of school both were considering a career in it. Margaret and Gino, thrilled with this idea, looked eagerly forward to mentoring their children and to reaching the point where they could just let go, semiretire, and enjoy themselves by doing other things.

Just when this transition was starting, though, Gino discovered that Margaret had been having an extramarital affair. Shocked and hurt, he felt a deep sense of betrayal. Immediately Margaret stopped the outside relationship, apologized to Gino, and wanted to make amends. She tried to explain, as best she could, how "I got myself into this mess." Gino, sensing the trouble to come, worked very hard to understand and let go of his extreme distress, but he could not. Fixating on Margaret's disregard of their marriage vows, he became more and more estranged, and finally moved out of their house.

But that was not enough to help quiet him, because seeing Margaret at the office on a daily basis continuously reawakened his hurt, feelings of betrayal, and rage to the point that he was simply unable to work and couldn't stop talking to his kids about his feelings. Gino tried psychotherapy, and though it was useful it still couldn't help him overcome the distress he felt whenever he saw Margaret. At this point Gino contacted us and asked for our help in dealing with the problems that the fractured marriage had brought into a once-successful and fulfilling business.

When we met the Zoltans it was quickly apparent that Gino and Margaret were so wounded and the relationship so ruptured that the only possible outcome was to help them, in as caring and respectful a way as possible, to dissolve the marriage and redirect the business. This process took several months and was successful in that the business stayed intact and in the family. Both parents agreed to exit at once, leaving everything in the hands of their offspring. Gino and Margaret also agreed to not talk to their sons about their personal difficulties. In addition, they hired someone from the outside who would temporarily act as the CEO and mentor their sons until one of the boys was ready to assume full responsibility for the business.

Marital problems, separation, and divorce are frequent causes of family fragmentation. However, fragmentation can be averted if business-owning parents, even when going their separate ways, work together to protect not only the relationship that each of them has with their children, but also the future of the family business, whether or not one or both of them remain involved in it.

Following is another example of fractured relationships, which led to a fragmented family and a major ownership change for the business. The following open letter tells a touching story of how the future of an individual, a family, and the family business could have been different if reconciliation had been sought.

Hello to everyone!

This letter marks a most important time in my life, and I hope that through my words I can communicate that importance to you, my friends and colleagues for many years.

This letter is a farewell; it is my good-bye to you all, since my life's journey at this company is now over. As many of you know, the third of January was my last day to work at and own a significant portion of the Redi Company. Since that day I still continue to wake up early in the morning, like I used to do, as my mind and body prepare themselves to go off to work. Each day for me has been an emotional and intellectual roller-coaster ride, filled with sadness and joy, disappointment and relief.

From a historical perspective, my journey with the company began in 1950, when I was growing in my mother's womb, and from that time on and throughout my childhood the company became part of me, and I became a part of the company. It was always the central focus at the family dinner table, not because of our discussions but because one or both of my parents were conspicuously absent. They would be at the office or at conventions, tending to the company's needs. While I was a kid, our annual family station-wagon vacations always included a stop or two at other packing companies. At first I resented it. However, I did grow to love the business.

As a very young kid, I tried the typical jobs available to kids my age. However, when I was eight years old I finally got a job that I really liked. Thanks to my parents, I was hired on at the company, on a part-time, round-the-year basis. I began by cleaning the tools, sweeping the floor, and picking the berries. I continued to work there and learn until I was sixteen. This was a great life—but not without some pretty steep hills to climb. It was actually tough, working at a company where my parents were both owners and chief executives. I didn't want to be treated like a little rich kid that needed to be baby-sat. To offset any preconceived notion that I might be a slouch, I decided early on to always work very hard and get things done. To never accept defeat, never be defeated.

I want to point out now that all during my childhood years of working here I was always treated wonderfully. Thank you for that, all of you who knew me then! You were always fair, kind, and supportive. You made me feel important and capable, just for being myself—and not the bosses' son.

After completing graduate school I returned to the company, fully prepared to offer and use whatever I'd learned. There I worked directly under my father and mother and the company's division managers. I found the same fair, kind, and supportive environment.

I worked with my parents until they both retired. It was then that my brother with my encouragement, joined me in sharing the company's helm.

Within a few years my experience at the company began to change. For several years my responsibilities in setting up and managing our large new facility took me away from the helm. When I returned I found that substantial changes had occurred during my absence. The company's original warm and friendly environment was gone, I didn't know most of the guys on the executive committee, and even the nature of the business itself was different than before. From that point forward it became more and more difficult for my brother and I to work together. Being two quite different people, except for our mutual ingrained love for the company, we had very different ideas about how and where the Redi Company ought to grow, and how it should be managed. We could not find common ground—so rather than rip the company and ourselves to shreds, I chose to leave my family's company. I left because of my love for my aging parents, but also because of my love for the company itself. I left it, too, because of my love for all of you, and my love for the communities in which the company does business.

My choice to end this long journey in life was the correct choice. But it leaves me with multiple scars. I chose to walk away from work that was very rewarding to me in many ways—intellectually, emotionally, and financially. At the same time I walked away from my pride, my pain, my frustration, and despair. I walked away from the absolute pleasure of all of our successes and the tremendous sense of competence.

Finally, I want to make clear that I'm still with all of you, all the way! I want the company, under my brother's leadership, to succeed in every one of its future endeavors. And I want all of you to achieve your greatest personal challenges.

Thank you for making the company an incredible journey for me . . . and good-bye.

The Redi Company's success continues, but the family itself is fractured. The siblings no longer speak to each other. As for their elderly parents, they grieve the loss of their family and their long-held dream of passing the ownership and management of their business onto both of their children, who would share it harmoniously.

UNCONNECTED BUSINESS-OWNING FAMILIES

In the initial generations of a family business, disengagement usually occurs because of ruptured relationships, a process frequently traumatic to those involved. In later generations disengagement is similarly caused by fractured relationships but can also simply be the result of distance—distancing caused either from the fragmentation of earlier generations or from the natural evolution or circumstances of the generations.

In many family business circumstances oppression is not a factor, no family members have been traumatized, and relationships have not been fractured. However, the needed connections among family members simply do not exist, either because they have simply faded away or never been established. These families too are disengaged and the relationship bonds must be established for cohesion to develop and collaboration to become a reality.

For instance, we recently completed a consultation with the Moon family, owners of a chain of travel agencies. Justin and Foster, who were half brothers, had inherited the business from their father. Never raised together, they were not particularly close though they worked well together, with each one managing different offices and sharing jointly in the overall management and ownership. Other than the business and their deceased father, they had little in common and lived very separate personal lives. Their children, seven in all, knew one another by looks, but that was all.

As the half cousins grew older, four of them became interested and active in the business. Yet there was little existing basis for trust—that requisite hallmark of successful family businesses—to build on. In this instance there was no relationship rift; family attachment bonds had simply never been formed. Recognizing that this lack of cohesiveness might cause serious problems in the future, the two owner brothers called us in.

After our initial contacts we recommended that the entire group of cousins and their current families spend a week away together while under our guidance. There they would all not only get to know one another socially, but they would also participate in noncompetitive trust- and team-building activities plus work together to establish a family mission statement. In addition, they would begin to learn about their different but connected family histories.

The week proved to be great fun and a productive experience for all. Of course, since the Moon agency was part of the travel industry, the entire family enjoyed the special perks of their family business. Today, the cousins continue both working and playing together. They have established their own governance structures, and little else has been needed from us. The opportunity to know and understand one another helped them to establish cohesion.

There are some parallels in the story of another family enterprise, Cross County Waste Management Resources, now in its fourth generation. In this family, as in many multiple-generation families, the bonds had been weakened over time and with distance as people moved elsewhere, resulting in a loss of connection to the core of the family and the family business. For the members of the fourth generation, many who lived far from corporate center, it was as if this was a public company in which they were just stockholders.

When several family members requested that their stock be bought back, management was surprised and concerned. They simply hadn't realized that a number of the family members were unattached and simply didn't have any sense of commitment to the family business and its values. After all, management was doing an admirable job keeping way ahead of current environmental concerns, and they had even been publicly recognized several times for their innovative work. The desire on some of the younger generation's part to sell shares came as an emotional shock and the managers realized that they did not have the cash for a buyout. To obtain it they would have to bring in outside investors, which they were loath to do.

Brought in during this predicament to advise the family business managers, we were again able to help a family business work through a disengagement condition that threatened the company's survival as a wholly family-owned firm. We did this by: educating the scattered family members about the company they owned and the income and career opportunities open to them if they held on to their shares; planning opportunities for the family to get to know one another and to visit the family company they all shared; and encouraging them to become active and contribute creative ideas. This newly vibrant family firm provided the possibility of future employment for interested and qualified members of the upcoming generation and initiated an owners' decision-making policy which included and valued input from all family.

RECOGNIZING DISENGAGEMENT

Every family business that wishes to retain as much of its "human capital" as possible needs to be constantly attentive to recognizing signs and causes of disengagement in individual members. The foremost way to learn about those who are in the process of disconnecting from the family business for whatever reason is for them to simply talk about the fact that they are getting ready to leave, and then to give the reasons why. If someone delivers that kind of message there still may be time to act decisively and work things out satisfactorily on both sides.

However, more often than not people don't speak up. Several important things can be learned from the previous two stories of family companies in which bonding had never taken place. First, the not-yet-engaged or disengaging family member appears very much like every other family member. Second, families who hold a dominant belief in the solidarity of their family may not even notice that some family members are disaffected. Third, many times the failure to detect detachment or estrangement is because the belief system or culture of the family modifies or restricts what people know and say.

So if people with little knowledge, reservations, or doubts can't or don't talk about them, it is impossible to see, hear, or think about differences or dissonance. When any individual or family creates an illusion, a strongly held false belief, the family culture makes it almost impossible to admit the "emperor has no clothes."

Let's consider now the case of the Woods family. Warren Woods was a successful upper-level manager in his father's company that leased mobile units as temporary classrooms to schools whose needs fluctuated on a year-to-year basis, and to businesses expanding too rapidly for a building program to keep pace. Warren, who had always dreamed of running the family business, finally got his opportunity when his father decided to retire, some twenty years ago. During the first ten years of his leadership, Warren successfully tripled the size of the business and developed several new and successful ventures but never once indicated any interest in or intention to ever have his own children involved in any way with him or the business.

We were called in by Warren, when he was exactly the same age as his father was upon retirement. At that time, his sixty-fifth year, Warren had changed his mind and expected us to help him persuade and then prepare his children to join with him in the business. Warren was shocked, however, when we declined to "persuade" anyone but instead offered to help him discover what each of his children, at this stage of their adult lives, wanted for themselves.

Soon after beginning with the Woods family, it became apparent that Warren had seriously miscalculated his ability to draw his children in at this point in their lives. It quickly became clear that none of his six children wanted the close association with him or the business he had recently decided to offer to them, in fact they didn't want anything to do with it, and they certainly did not want to give up their own already well-established careers.

Shortly after Warren had taken over the helm of his father's business, his eldest son had actually begged his father to come into the business and had tried to make a career at the company. However, he himself told us that he had quickly become disillusioned and felt unappreciated. He was particularly hard hit by his father's dismissive attitude toward him, and believed he had wasted several important years of his life trying to do the "right thing" as the dutiful son. He was, at the time of our interview, happily and successfully employed elsewhere.

Early in our dealings with the Woods family we recognized the disaffection in the parents marriage. When listening to Warren it became immediately clear to us that he had always been fixated on his own interests and goals, neglecting to take those of his wife into account. Although he and his wife had been together for over forty-five years, it was not a happy union. Warren liked to socialize; Mary did not. She preferred to focus on their children, whereas Warren had really wanted her to focus mainly on him. Mary also had a strong bond with her family of origin, which Warren resented. In fact, the more he pushed for her attention over the years, the more distant Mary became. They disagreed constantly, and although Mary avoided fighting whenever possible, Warren persisted in trying to coerce her into being the person and companion he wanted her to be.

In their young years Warren's children had tried hard to please their father, but they too had never achieved any closeness with him—and never measured up to his fantasies and expectations regarding them. Mary and the children, on the other hand, had always had a warm relationship but their family cohesion did not include Warren. The children's response to the tense domestic atmosphere surrounding them while they grew up, and still continuing now, was predictable: they were emotionally detached from their father and felt no gratitude for what he was, in his eyes, doing for them by inviting them into the business.

We recommended marital counseling for Warren and Mary and they began but never finished the process. Each acknowledgment of some breach between them caused new pain, so neither of them had the desire or resilience to go on. They simply retreated to their old patterns with each other, and the family balance of many years was reestablished.

Nowadays Warren is away from home eighty percent of the time, while Mary stays contentedly at home usually visiting with her grand-children. The business was recently purchased by outsiders and Warren's children remain detached from him. For years Warren had confused himself and his own dreams with the reality of his family situation, and for years he missed the clues telling him what was actually happening.

In the early years, Mary Woods and many of her six children had a continual line of excuses for not participating in Warren's traveling adventures or business interests. In turn, Warren always had excuses for not involving himself in his family's daily life, and he would demand their presence at things only he was interested in. As adults, Warren's children had ready reasons to refuse involvement in his business.

Sometimes disengagement is obvious when we track the amount of time people spend with one another, but all too often we need to look deeper into the communication patterns. Excuse making is one form of communication that signals disengagement. When individuals make excuses, it means they have disengaged. By not being accountable they have, at least momentarily, stepped outside of the relationship. When making excuses is a part of a pattern it can be problematic because credibility and trust are lost (Schlenker et al., 2001).

Triangulation, another common strategy people use to disengage, was discussed previously from a theoretical perspective. The Woods family is triangulation in action. When disagreement occurs between two (or more people) and one cannot internally manage the feelings the disagreement evokes, he or she talks about the problem to a third person rather than to the other party directly. In the Woods family, Warren, throughout his life, triangulated with the business and with his many other solitary interests as a way of disengaging from his wife and children. Mary triangulated with the children and successfully avoided bonding with her husband. The children disengaged by gossiping among themselves and jointly outlawing the business. Regardless of the form, any pattern of triangulation means that the bond between the parties is weakened and family cohesion is diminished.

In a more general sense, excuse making and triangulation are all part of the way people avoid one another. Although avoidance does not always lead to disengagement, the pattern of avoidance within the family is an important indicator of a disengagement.

THE PROSPECT OF RECONCILIATION

The glue that holds family members in relationship and allows family teams to work collaboratively is family cohesion or unity. Family cohesion is about people knowing, understanding, respecting, and caring about one another. When these bonds or attachments are absent in a family business, they must be consciously built. When the bonds are ruptured and not repaired, the rifts must be reconciled or families will fracture and disengage, causing people to be either seriously wounded and perhaps deprived of familial connections that would benefit them in many ways.

Such a scenario is nowhere better visible than in the case of the fractured Bingham family in Louisville, which we described earlier. Daughter Sallie was both disengaged and disaffected, and her position triggered the tragedy suffered by both the family and the family business. Sallie was not responsible for the problems in the family, but by the time her pain came to light, family events had taken on a life of their own—with an almost inevitable result.

The case of the Bingham family leaves us wondering whether or not something would have been different if the relationship ruptures and family disengagement had been noted earlier. Would reconciliation have been possible? If the family had been saved, wouldn't its business have been, too?

In Part II we present the tools for successfully reconciling relationship ruptures and collaboratively managing human differences. These tools, if used properly, can make the difference between family business success or failure, and between family estrangement or cohesion.

PART II:
THE RECONCILIATION MODEL IN PRACTICE

Without memory there is no healing.
Without forgiveness there is no future.

Archbishop Desmond Tutu

History, despite its wrenching pain,
Cannot be unlived, and if faced
With courage, need not be lived again.

Maya Angelou

Chapter 5

A Reconciliation Model Overview

I can't believe it; I just can't believe it. We actually accomplished what we came to do—my sons are talking again after seven long years of hell for all of us.

A client

Optimally, a family business is an alliance that combines love with a commitment to productive work. Its success depends on the sustained communication and cooperation of people with kinship connections who have widely differing viewpoints, skills, and personality styles. Unfortunately, many family businesses, of whatever size and kind, falter and eventually fail. Instead of providing strength, synergy, and resilience, the "ties that bind" constrict, chafe, and stifle both the people and the enterprise.

We have developed a model for resolving ruptured relationships in business-owning families. The Reconciliation Model was designed to assist advisors and family members in managing human differences, repairing relationship ruptures, mending individual wounds, and resolving long-standing or new family discords.

Our Reconciliation Model, outlined in this chapter and detailed in succeeding chapters, provides a guide for recognizing, reconsidering, and then rebuilding wounded family relationships that impede successful family business operations. The three-stage process begins by recognizing the truth about the difficult and discordant realities of the interpersonal situation (Chapter 6). It then addresses the hurts, wounds, and abuses that occurred in the past and now reverberate in the present as unresolved family conflicts and relationship rifts (Chapter 7). The process concludes with rebuilding relationships to improve the prospects for sustained success in the family business for the benefit not only of current family members, but also of future generations (Chapter 8).

WHY FAMILY BUSINESS RELATIONSHIPS NEED REPAIR

Breaks in relationships are inevitable, and they occur regularly, especially, it seems, when family members work together. Many small breaks, caused perhaps by irritable remarks and irritating behavior, repair automatically in the course of a regular day's work. People go on their way without having to discuss every hurt, affront, or insult. However, some breaks are not repaired automatically, perhaps because they are both reflections and repetitions of aspects of a traumatized past relationship, or else are so immense in offensive content that they cannot be mended easily. Family discord that fails to fade and go away over time requires special attention. When it occurs and endures in a way that seriously interferes with the well-being of a family's business enterprise, the need to resolve the matter can become acute. A diagram of the rupture-reconciliation process is shown in Figure 5.1.

A family business is a complex mass of intertwined relationships especially vulnerable to wounds, violations, and ruptures. This vulnerability comes at least in part from the interpersonal dilemma easily fostered in family business environments. It is expressed in the ambivalent complaint, "I can't live with you, and I can't live without you!"

Many family business relationships have the earmarks of this classic hostile-dependent relationship, which is characterized by power plays for money and position, and by resulting anger, competition, and escalated conflicts (Bader and Pearson, 1988). In hostile-dependent relationships people experience the urgency of their own personal needs, and allow their needs to take precedence over everything else, including the business.

Furthermore, the capacity for self-definition is restricted for people who have lived together (as parents and children, or spouses) and grown up together (as siblings and perhaps cousins) and then work together—especially persons who have never experienced other

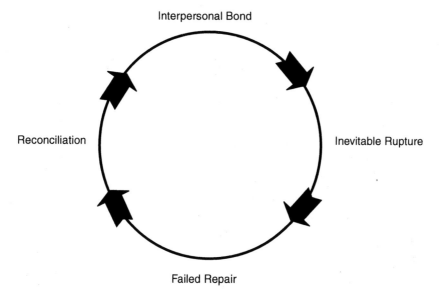

FIGURE 5.1. Relationship Cycle—Rupture, Reconciliation, and Repair (Based on Lewis, 2000)

work situations or pursued their own creative, intellectual, or entrepreneurial bents. People in such situations are apt to find it extremely difficult to identify and articulate their own thoughts and feelings, to express their own ideas, and to act in assertive ways.

In family businesses there is also a strong pull toward regressing into past feelings, responses, and behaviors. Negative feelings emerge quickly in the workplace and managing these emotions is hard to do especially when people already feel blamed, inadequate, and even bad about themselves. These conditions frequently create extremely volatile conflict situations because they are combined with an emotional and financial dependency on the family business along with the constant pressure from the demands of the business itself.

Conflict between people—characterized by tension, emotionality, disagreement, and polarization—occurs when bonding is either lacking or broken. Severed bonds cause people to quickly snap back into self-protective, established patterns of defense and responses from the past. Thus they experience the current problem not only with a reactive force to the precipitating event, but also with the impact of cumulative life experience.

The entrenched conflict and inevitable battles that accompany hostile-dependent relationships have the potential to destroy individuals, the family, and its business. This is because conflict quickly escalates and perpetuates itself; it is contagious and infects others, who inevitably get pulled into taking sides. Energy and time get deflected from the business, and morale shrinks. Therefore, it is crucial to skillfully intervene in defusing the resident animosity, for the longer it is allowed to go on unresolved, the worse it will become.

Nevertheless, conflict can sometimes actually serve a positive purpose. Because it creates distance between entwined persons, it permits the establishment of the self outside of the hostile-dependent relationship. Of course, this distancing also carries with it the future need—emotional, social, and probably economic—to reestablish the ruptured family connection. Thus a break in a family relationship can also be useful if it leads to relationship repair. It is possible, even probable, that a successful resolution of the conflict may help settle, and even prevent in the future, other relationship conflicts within the family and its business.

At various points in life people are called upon to review their relationships with others so as to find ways to mend important interpersonal connections that are broken or otherwise present difficulties. In a family business such times are apt to be far more numerous and frequent than in families whose members are not tied together by a common business. Sometimes this conflict-settling task is motivated from within, coming from a strong personal wish to reconcile. At other times the invitation to such an undertaking originates with other family members' desires for peacemaking. Many times settling serious, unrelenting discord among members who work in the family firm or are major shareholders can become an urgent matter.

Important research done in the field of marital and family relationships has focused on healthy relationships and the properties of relationships that have the best potential for repair after serious ruptures have occurred (Lewis et al., 1976, 1998, 2000). These linked relationship characteristics in which partners are more likely to listen attentively, ask for needed clarifications, respond empathetically, and where there is greater likelihood of repair rather than escalated conflict are as follows (Lewis, 2000):

- Relationship power is shared equally.
- A high level of mutual respect exists for one another's subjective reality, thus increasing the likelihood of greater self-disclosure.
- With greater self-disclosure comes increased opportunity to know and appreciate both similarities and differences in each other.
- Appreciation of similarities and differences leads to both increased understanding and augmented self-definition.

What significance does this research have for a family business? It provides the groundwork for reconciling relationships and for establishing mutual positive regard through the years, from one generation to the next, so that the business itself will benefit from growing healthy and successful relationships.

THE MODEL'S ORIGINS

Our Reconciliation Model offers an explicit method for bringing about new accord in family businesses. As seasoned mental health professionals, in designing this model we employed all of our knowledge and experience accumulated over many years of working with individuals, couples, and families.

The early format of the Reconciliation Model first appeared in the mid-1970s as a redecision relationship therapy—a three-stage model for therapeutic work with families and couples. We perfected this therapy model by integrating general systems theory, in the form of patterns of interaction, with personal history, in the form of early decisions, and noted how they operate in a reciprocal relationship. Over time, we refined our model to make it appropriate and effective when applied to our ongoing work as advisors to business-owning couples and families who live, love, and work together but who have begun to realize that relationship conflicts among them are decidedly interfering with the successful operation of their joint enterprise.

Simply stated, the main thrust of our relational work with family businesses is to help people learn to govern themselves differently in their business and family relationships. We work to expose family members' underlying conflicts, and then to aid them by: gaining new perspectives on the difficulties and the difficult people in their lives; enhancing their coping skills; persuading them to make changes in their immediate environments so as to reduce stress; and establishing supportive interpersonal relationships to assist in repair and recovery.

Reconciliation does not attempt to eliminate conflict, problems, or differences of opinion. Instead, the reconciliation effort concerns itself with reestablishing sundered relationship bonds, which will then allow family members to work together toward a common family goal. In addition, the new accord, bringing with it a structure for addressing future disagreements, can help to avoid future serious alienation, which almost certainly could again imperil the family business.

PROFILING THE MODEL

Our Reconciliation Model for family businesses is an integrative approach that does the following:

- Appreciates the mutual power and importance of individual and system dynamics
- Recognizes the confluence of past and present in the context of current relationship problems
- Honors the overlap of the present and the future
- Respects the roles and contributions of different professional viewpoints
- Fills the need for a practical approach to resolving relationship ruptures

The three stages are presented as a linear progression, but in actuality they do not follow one another neatly. Although we describe them as distinct entities for the purpose of clarity, they are rarely clearly demarcated. Movement back and forth among the three stages is continual. To resolve some family business problems, a concerted progression through the three stages can occur quickly. At other times, satisfactory movement through them all may require an extended time period. In some situations there is no need to even move into the second stage. In others, reconciling with the past may take years—even a change in generations, when the "old guard" eventually retires from the family's business activities, as it always must do, sooner or later.

In its actual application, then, the model is a shifting entity that flexibly accommodates the variable circumstances in family businesses and families as they actually are. When working with human beings and the relationships they form, the presenting situations and individual difficulties or even the pathologies must all be considered because they contribute to defining the application of the model. (A brief journey through the model is shown in Figure 5.2.)

Most important, remember that no quick solution exists for healing a business-owning family beset by serious relationship ruptures that have spilled over into or else began in the family enterprise. No magic formula can instantaneously remedy wounds that may have existed for a great many years, taking their toll in family discord which had, and still has, social, emotional, and financial consequences. When working toward reconciliation, patience, persistence, and options must be constant companions of family members and also of those serving as their advisors and consultants.

When seeking solutions to difficult problems among people, we always look for ways in which the strengths and resources of the individuals and families involved may be revealed and emphasized. Since a primary aim of every successful business-owning family is to develop the human and intellectual capital of its family resources, this too is an intention of the reconciliation effort.

Following are the three stages in the Reconciliation Model.

Stage I: Recognize

Before a problem can be resolved it must first be recognized and most families have understandable reservations regarding seeing, hearing, and speaking the truths of the family and its relations through the generations. This first stage of our model therefore seeks to both discover the ongoing and continuous patterns of family interactions that negatively impact the business and the business-owning

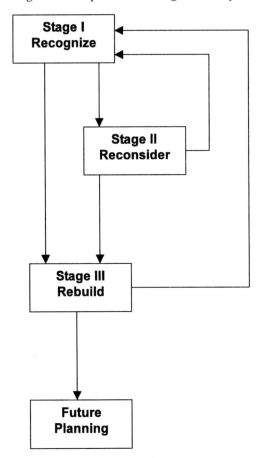

FIGURE 5.2. The Reconciliation Model

family, and to devise strategies for changing the relationship system. Our main tasks here are to: discover and identify the truths about current relationship problems; help the family members accept these truths, particularly the ones that have long been denied and buried; assist the family in reorienting their priorities; and form specific contracts for resolving the key relationship issues.

Stage I is the crucial preparation phase. Here we focus on learning as much as possible about the family and its problems and then design ways to interrupt long-established family patterns that bind individuals to the past and negatively affect problem-solving behaviors, coping skills, task mastery, self-esteem, social competence, and the ability to successfully collaborate as a member of the team at the top of a prosperous family business.

Stage I involves these tasks:

- Gathering information about the family and seeking relationship truths that lie beneath the behaviors, stories, myths, and false beliefs that have led to divisive and discordant interactions
- Making direct contact with family members and creating a common understanding of the problems
- Managing resistance and gaining acceptance of the proffered path to reconciliation
- Establishing contracts for relationship reconciliation and change
- Defining who participates in the reconciliation effort
- Preparing individuals and the family as a whole for reconciliation

Stage II: Reconsider

In this second stage family members reconsider their relationships by confronting both their present and their past, for the purpose of gaining confidence in mastering the present and participating differently with others in the future. The twin concepts—accept and reconsider—apply to looking honestly and empathetically at the perceptions of both self and others.

The main focus of Stage II is to facilitate a safe and structured process through which individual family members can reveal their personal histories and reconsider their relationship past with an eye toward achieving a collaborative future.

Stage II involves these tasks:

- Bringing the family together to focus on changing family interactions
- Establishing ground rules for individuals and family interaction
- Providing continuous support
- Helping people speak their truth by telling their personal stories
- Helping people manage themselves so they can listen, learn, and understand other family members

- Orchestrating responsive and respectful dialogue
- Supporting personal accountability and relationship mending
- Transition to the future of rebuilding relationships

Stage III: Rebuild

The third stage of our Reconciliation Model focuses on creating an affirming environment, building family cohesion, and developing excellent family teams. This stage extends over time, sometimes even years. In this stage needed changes are worked out in the everyday interactions of running and owning a successful family business. Stage III, then, is the time when family members learn, within the practical arena of being managers and owners of their family business, how to keep the wealth that belongs to their family—its human, intellectual, and financial capital—*in* the family for generations to come.

The target of Stage III is to set into permanent placement the four principles of an affirming environment, the cornerstones of quality relationships and a quality business. The four crucial goals of both advisors and family members are as follows:

- Build and preserve trust and mutual positive regard
- Foster collaboration
- Establish reconciliation policies and procedures
- Grow healthy, interacting families

APPLYING THE MODEL

Over many years and for thousands of hours we have listened to family business members and advisors talk about the challenges to family relationships within the workplace and the unhappy, counterproductive results of disagreements and discord. We have participated with hundreds of families as they struggled with reconciling their differences.

Certainly, each family is different, each business is different, and each problem has different roots and dimensions. However, despite the many relational variations to be found among them, family businesses have many features and factors in common. In each business-owning family the past, present, and future all have a common purpose: to provide both emotional and financial security for the family members. In each one, disparate persons—family members by virtue of biological, chosen, or imposed connections—interface and are mutually dependent. Each family business also has familiar struggles: between the forces of unity and freedom, between individuality and family loyalty, between nurturing and hostile dependency.

The greatest challenge in reconciling relationships in a family-owned business afflicted by serious interpersonal problems is to establish an environment conducive to healing the inevitable discords and relationship ruptures that intrude into the business operations. A sustained environment must be established for family members to: learn to accept themselves for whoever they are; learn to think for themselves; learn to soothe themselves; and learn to be compassionate toward others.

We have successfully applied our Reconciliation Model to all different family configurations and in many different formats. Most notably, we work with family-owned businesses either in intensive group meetings, at least of several days' duration, or in short-term ongoing consultations in which family members meet with us on a regular basis to resolve relationship wounds. In either of these formats the same basic tasks must be accomplished.

First, arrange the meeting situation so that everyone is able to participate. Second, establish a safe and accepting atmosphere where family members will actually reveal themselves. In such an environment people are able, perhaps at long last, to speak their own difficult truths in front of siblings, parents, and bosses. In front of the others people can also face, admit, and accept their own personal shortcomings, so as to move beyond the wall of shame that has surrounded them and defined their behaviors up to now.

Clearly, the crucial assignment of creating and sustaining an open, protected, and fully participatory meeting environment is a daunting one. Family business members customarily tend to restrict or distort their behaviors, thoughts, and feelings in the presence of other family members and outsiders. Also, some well-guarded information, such as family secrets, financial affairs, and estate plans, are sometimes withheld and, when given at all, frequently revealed reluctantly and only if asked for. Furthermore, problematic behavior patterns, often the cause of relationship ruptures to begin with, easily go underground and must be brought to the surface and challenged if they are to be changed and stopped from defining the future direction of the business.

Applying the Reconciliation Model also requires a great deal of flexibility. Unexpected situations may crop up, and the ability to manage surprises is a most important skill. Therefore, advisors need to be both willing and prepared to change direction at any time, as well as willing and able to do different things at different times, depending on the current climate of dialogue and interaction.

Family business members experiencing personal or business distress are frequently in conflict and people in conflict with others usually have communication patterns that are both confusing and destructive. It is common to hear noisy, angry, and aggressive conversations without any hint of empathy, negotiation, or give-and-take discussion. As the discord escalates, intense or out-of-control emotions and outbursts can erupt easily and family combatants tend to lose sight of the original cause of conflict and get sidetracked into seemingly irrelevant issues, which often actually carry the imprint of past struggles.

Clearly, advisors must be highly attentive to what is going on around them at all times, and be active in managing and containing participants' emotions to keep the direction of the interactions on course. Allowing personal attacks and other breaches of fairness or getting involved in frenetic irrelevancies usually encourages further violations.

The many human dilemmas and difficult choices faced in reconciling relationships are best met when each family member has an individual goal and purpose that transcends himself or herself. In other words, working not only for one's own well-being but also for a commonality of interests centered about what is best for the family as a whole will contribute significantly to the success of the family and its business—now, and for generations to come. Undeniably, the unique and durable power in a successful, well-run family enterprise comes from that family's ability to reconcile these many differences and create positive interpersonal dynamics and effective teamwork.

GUIDING PRINCIPLES FOR ADVISORS

The overall flow of the Reconciliation Model is based on a set of guidelines for professionals to apply as a means to facilitate reconciliation in a business-owning family.

- Be willing to do diligent background preparation and obtain abundant information about individual family members, details of the family dynamics, and the business itself.
- Maintain a positive focus and a constant eye to the future of the family and the business.
- Study current interactions to understand how they negatively impact relationships and will thereby impede the future success of the business.
- Help family members learn about themselves and how their behavior affects others.
- Motivate people to take responsibility for their own decisions and change.
- Move toward creating new and healthy relationship dynamics.

CONCLUSION

This chapter has presented an introduction to and overview of our Reconciliation Model, which can move family business relationships from a ruptured condition to one of close collaboration. It is based on our understanding of the complex interpersonal issues in business-owning families and experientially proven ways to address them. The reconciliation process outlined in this chapter is described in greater detail in the following three chapters; it is also exemplified in the four Interludes, which delineate our stage-by-stage work with the Sampson family.

The model will aid advisors of any professional background in their efforts to remedy the grievous predicament when a family business is disrupted because of relationship rifts. Knowledge of this process will help them to identify the areas of major difficulty and also to define and refine their skills for facilitating the necessary changes.

Sometimes a trusting relationship with any advisor is all that a family-owned business needs to help repair a current conflict that is interfering with its operations. At many other times, however, greater expertise in relationships is needed and should be called in.

Understanding the reconciliation process will also benefit family business participants, nonfamily members who occupy management positions in a closely held business, and family members who do not work in the business themselves yet have a stake in its success and who can possibly function as resources during and after the course of reconciliation.

In Chapters 6, 7, and 8 we take an in-depth look at the specific stages of the reconciliation process and the exact tools of reconciliation. In the four Interludes we present our reconciliation work with the Sampson family, owners and managers of the Sampson Seed Company.

Interlude 1: Meet the Sampsons, a Business-Owning Family

Our book was expressly written to provide relationship-mending guidance to advisors and consultants to business-owning families, and to concerned family members themselves. Of particular interest to readers will be our in-depth treatment, beginning with this first Interlude, of our work with the Sampson family, owners and managers of the Sampson Seed Company. By highlighting this family, we demonstrate our model for reconciling relationships, rebuilding trust, and creating a common vision for the future. We also show how we go about working directly with family members—as individuals, in small groups, and as a totality.

As relationship consultants to family businesses, our approach to working with client families always involves a major effort to repair troubled or ruptured relationships that are affecting the well-being of the business operation itself.

Each time we acquire a new consultation situation, we are faced with a unique set of people, and therefore, inevitably, a unique set of interpersonal problems. To give readers a sense of what this can be like for us as professionals, in four special sections we portray, stage by stage, our work over time with the Sampson family. We focus on the Sampsons because for us their conflicts typify, if perhaps in a magnified form, the kinds of relationship problems that unfortunately prevail in many family businesses.

This first Interlude tells how we initially became involved with the Sampsons and what we learned in the earliest stages of contact about the family's past and present, the individuals involved, and the business they owned together. Through considering this early phase of the consultation we demonstrate how we go about getting necessary information while becoming acquainted with the persons, problems, and possibilities in any family business that calls us in as relationship advisors.

As will be seen, this preliminary period launches our first exposure to a family and its presenting problems. From the very start we are consciously and actively preparing to make a relational, or systems, analysis of their interpersonal dynamics and salient issues. Our initial relational analyses are based on: family members' responses to questionnaires sent at the beginning of each new consultation; information provided in telephone conversations; experiences in in-person interviews; material coming from additional questionnaires if needed; and our impressions of character and behavior during initial interactions with individuals. When working as a team, as we usually do, we study the family history and its current situation, compare our various notes, and discuss any separate "takes" on the individuals involved to ultimately agree on what we initially consider and propose as the best route to resolving the family's critical, presenting problems.

Doing such an analysis, as portrayed in the second Sampson Interlude, tells us what is amiss within the family relationships and directs us to intervention strategies which will change relationships and give individual family members the best opportunities to heal. With the Sampsons, as will be revealed, the issues most evident from the start concerned the causes and consequences of family oppression and fragmentation.

The third Interlude, at the close of Chapter 7, concisely shows how the reconsidering stage of our Reconciliation Model actually worked in action with the Sampson family when they were brought together for an intensive family meeting. The fourth Interlude, following Chapter 8, reflects the rebuilding stage in which families work together to establish trust in the family and a prosperous future for the family business.

These four separate segments concerning the Sampsons demonstrate our particular approach to resolving tough, complex, and long-standing relationship issues. As such, this case study offers professional consultants, regardless of their areas of specialization, valuable tools for working with conflicted families. The Sampson case will also encourage family members to recognize the possible problems within their family and tackle relationship problems themselves, or at least to call in qualified professionals to help resolve the difficulties. This case study provides a good overview of how we have successfully aided many families in working through serious discords among its members. If not repaired, such relationship problems can certainly lead to the demise of the business and further social deterioration within the family itself.

FIRST CONTACTS

Early one morning our office voice mail recorded a message from a man identifying himself as Sam Sampson. He mentioned that he had recently spoken with a friend he had met some years ago in YPO (Young Presidents Organization). He wanted to find out if we might be able help him and his family business in the same way we had helped his friend. Returning Mr. Sampson's call soon afterward, we arranged for a more extensive phone conversation several days later, when all three of us could spend some time discussing his situation.

On the following Tuesday we had our first long talk with Sam Sampson. He told us he was president and CEO of the Sampson Seed Company, which had been in operation since 1944. Though he sounded anxious to talk, he was cautious at first. His friend, he said, had assured him that he could trust us—but what did that mean? He wondered whether we had ever worked with companies where the family members really didn't speak much to one another, or where one person was mostly responsible for everything.

Mr. Sampson also asked about how long all of this consultation would take, and when we could start. Also, would we be willing to travel to come to see him at the business's location in southern California, or should he come to our offices on the state's central coast? In addition, would we need to see any of the financial information for the company?

Throughout the long conversation we listened attentively and responded to Sam's questions with information about us and our extensive experience. We said that of course we'd be willing to travel to his location several hundred miles south of us; we actually needed to, to do our part of the work properly. We couldn't estimate right now how long a family reconciliation process might take among the Sampsons, not knowing much about the persons involved. But we could start with the initial information gathering as soon as two weeks from the time of this initial talk. Most important, we assured Sam of our stance on confidentiality. Following is the gist of what we told him:

> We uphold a strict confidentiality policy. We will never share information about you, your family, or the operation of your company with anyone outside the family unless we have requested and received written permission from all key family members to do so. We will keep personal confidentiality within the family unless critical information is determined to interfere with the health or welfare of other family members or the business. We support a policy that allows family members equal and open access to all information regarding the business and all information that affects interpersonal relationships within the family. We do not keep secrets and will work with you to be open and straightforward with one another.

After these initial clarifications we asked Sam if he would be willing to discuss his reason for contacting us and to briefly summarize his view of the main problems. As he began doing this, both the pressure behind his voice and the rapidity of his speech made it clear to us that talking about the problems was an unusual, somewhat frightening, but important move for him. Clearly and concisely, Sam then announced: "I am ready to leave the company and want to get on with doing different things in my own life as soon as possible."

We asked him, "Why do you want to do this now?" And he answered: "Since my father's death a year ago, the freedom I feel from my separation and hopefully soon-to-be divorce, and with my kids both grown up now, things just aren't the same for me anymore. I have nothing left to accomplish or even stay here for. I've decided that this is just a dead-end place to be. I've lived here all of my life so far and I really want to get out. Besides, everybody thinks of me and treats me like their workhorse; they really enjoy pushing me around. It seems to me that I've always just done what everyone else wanted me to. But now I want to do what *I* want to do! And I want to go away and see the world. Lord knows I've made *all* of us enough money . . . so why shouldn't I just take off now if I want to?"

Sam went on, revealing his feelings about his two siblings, who were equal, major shareholders in the business. His sister Joan, older than he, was a "silly woman, a worthless busybody"; she had become the laughingstock of the company . . . and, of the whole town! His older brother, David, long ago had gone off to another state, disavowing any responsibility for the business. But he was happy enough to get continuous earnings from it, and had received much more in the way of money and stock than was rightfully due him. David had always been the family troublemaker, and they had never gotten along, even as kids.

When we asked about the younger generation, Sam opined that a few of these family members seemed "okay" to him. Still, he said, "Basically I don't really care what happens to everything now. I only want to get out of this business . . . and this town." (The implication was that he wanted out of his extended family as well.) When we asked him why he didn't just pick up and go, he said emphatically, "I want every penny I can get. It really should be all mine, anyway. I *worked* for it!" Finally, we asked Sam if he had already announced to the others in the family his intention of leaving the company. His answer was "yes" and when we inquired what their reactions were he said he hadn't noticed—and didn't care.

By the close of our conversation Sam had agreed to several things. First, he would contact both of his siblings to inform them of his desire to engage professional help in resolving the current problems and developing an exit strategy for himself. He would recommend us to the family and tell them about his first contact with us. We were going to send him and each of his siblings an introductory packet of materials to peruse. We told Sam that the package would include the initial letter of engagement; our plans for gathering the information needed to construct an initial contract and formulate an initial plan for proceeding; our professional resumes; a statement of our fees and policies of operation; and a general release-of-information form for possible use with other professionals and consultants involved with the family business.

We explained that once the letter of engagement for this initial phase had been signed by him as CEO and returned to us, and we had received a fax from his siblings stating their agreement to speak with us, we would contact Joan and David by phone to introduce ourselves. Next, we would arrange for the next conversations, and get the names and addresses of the next generation so that we could send out initial questionnaires to each family member and his or her spouse, with the assurance that we would treat the questionnaires as strictly confidential.

When asked if there was anyone else we should speak with at this time, Sam suggested that we also talk directly to his nephew, Benton Bennington, the vice president in charge of operations at the Sampson Seed Company, and to Marsha Bennington, his niece and the vice president in charge of human resources and marketing.

The importance for Sam of getting on quickly with things became swiftly apparent to us. Within hours, Sam left a message saying that Joan and David would be sending their agreement letter and he was now just awaiting the packet from us.

Six days later we began calling the rest of the family members. Joan was willing to meet with us anywhere and would do anything else Sam wanted. She also said that she had actually been hoping for something like this to happen. When asked how she would briefly define the current business difficulties, she clearly stated, "The only problem is that Sam is wanting to leave, and I don't know what any of us will do without him. I think he has been depressed since his divorce, and now he's itching to do some wild new things in his life. I hope you will be able to stop him from doing anything rash."

David, on the other hand, was unwilling to commit to any in-person meetings. However, he was willing to take the first step and speak further with us on the phone. He also said he would fill out any questionnaires we sent him.

Marsha, like her mother, said she would be glad to talk with us and was extremely concerned about Sam who was like a father to her. She offered any help that we would need.

Finally, Benton—Joan's first born—acted rude and difficult when we called him. "I don't know what's going on here," he stated. "But then there isn't anything different in that. I keep this whole damn place going, and all I ever get for my efforts is a bunch of flack." He finally decided, though, that he would do what the others wanted him to because he knew he *had* to. But he warned us that his time was scarce, and we couldn't expect him to just jump through hoops each time we wanted something from him.

Questionnaires

After introductory phone contacts with the family members, our next step was to send out questionnaires. All thirteen of the second- and third-generation family members and their spouses returned their responses to us. Some were, as expected, more detailed and informative than others. David, his wife and children, answered, "I don't know" to many things; after all, they lived in another state, and it was apparent that David hadn't maintained much contact with his family of origin.

The form's questions, after eliciting factual information such as birth dates, marriage dates, and facts about any children, were pointed toward discovering each family member's view of one another and the relationship and business issues of the moment. They included the following items:

- Give three adjectives describing each person in the family.
- Define the current problems in the family and in the Sampson Seed Company.
- What was known about the origins of these problems?
- Who was directly involved in the problems?
- What would be the best resolutions for the current problems?
- What was considered to be the worst possible outcome if nothing in the family changes?

COMPILATION OF INITIAL FAMILY INFORMATION

Each person, including Benton, responded fairly quickly. By combining the material that the questionnaires provided with the information, opinions, and reactions gathered in further phone conversations, we formed our initial picture of the family members, Sampson Seed Company, and its history. We created a cast of characters as described by family members. This included the company's founder-partners, though both were deceased.

History

Bill and Marsha Sampson were only nineteen years old when they decided to begin their life's journey together. Both born and raised in the same southwestern city, each was brought up in poverty conditions during the Depression years. They had first met in junior high school. Several days after they graduated from high school, in June 1942, Bill and Marsha got married. The United States had entered World War II six months earlier, and their marriage was possible because Bill had been turned down from military service because of a bad leg. Together they talked of moving out of the city and giving the children they would have someday the advantages of fresh air and freedom that neither of them had ever experienced. Fulfilling this dream meant being out in the country and so in July they moved to California. There they quickly fell in love with and rented a cheap piece of land with a tumbledown house.

In their first years Bill and Marsha worked hard to make their "shack" livable. In addition, Bill went into the nearby town each day to work at the tannery there. Marsha stayed at home, tending to the garden and the chickens. In October 1943 she gave birth to their first child, Joan.

Marsha was creative and hardworking. She was also gentle, shy, and very accommodating to her husband, who was quite her opposite. Bill was loud, controlling, and always right. He had a wild streak, too. At the beginning of their marriage, so the story went, before Joan was born, sometimes he wouldn't come home for days at a time. When he finally did, Marsha was always understanding; she only hoped that he was okay.

The now-legendary view we got of them was this: Marsha and Bill Sampson had loved each other dearly, seldom fought, and always agreed that Bill knew best. They shared the values of family solidarity, hard work, honesty, freedom, and excellence in whatever they did.

Marsha's garden was gorgeous and soon grew to be the talk of their small town of 143 people. She started giving away seeds to her friends and neighbors; then she began selling her seeds in the town store. When the tannery closed in 1944, Marsha and Bill began working together full time, devoting all of their time and resources to the small seed production business. From that point forward, they depended on the seeds for their livelihood. After they launched the family enterprise, things just grew and grew. Eventually the company also grew seedlings for sale to wholesale and retail outlets, supplying customers both near and distant.

Within five short years, Marsha and Bill had produced three children, bought their house and some acreage, and started a budding flower and vegetable seed business. Over a half-century later, the Sampson Seed Company had become the community's major business and the main reason for its population expansion. The company occupies over 700 acres of land that contains seed-producing farmland as well as several dozen large greenhouses, a packing plant, an equipment warehouse, and several office and research buildings; it is tended to by more than one hundred employees.

The Sampson family business now bridges the second and third generations, with the members of a fourth generation growing up quickly. Following their original value system, Bill and Marsha in their joint will had distributed their assets and shares in the company in equal amounts to their children. Now, each sibling holds 26 percent, with the ten grandchildren holding the remaining 22 percent.

The future of this multimillion-dollar business no longer depends on the attachment of Bill and Marsha and their devotion to the basic down-home values of hard work and family. The future rests with their children, grandchildren, and even great-grandchildren.

The Current Players

From what we'd heard directly from and about them, it appeared that the second-generation members —Joan, David, and Sam—had fought incessantly and sometimes bitterly since the death of their mother six years ago. While alive, quiet and unassuming as she was, Marsha must have had an inner strength that bypassed her husband's domineering nature. Somehow she had held the family together socially and emotionally, albeit tenuously, in a way that Bill couldn't do once she was gone.

Joan and David had never shown any real interest in entering the business and just left its management up to Sam who seemed to have followed in his father's footsteps only by default. We were coming to the conclusion that the only goal the three siblings shared was getting as many dollars as possible from the business for their own personal spending requirements. Since Bill's death in the previous year, family cohesion had apparently proceeded from bad to worse; none of the three had a civil word for the others. We certainly had our work cut out for us.

Even before meeting many of them directly, we could now put together a composite vital-statistics directory of the Sampson Seed Company's current family shareholders. See the accompanying genogram (Figure 5.3) for a visual representation of this multigenerational family.

The Second Generation

> Joan Alice Sampson
> Age: Fifty-nine years
> Married: Jason Bennington, January 16, 1963
> Mother of four children: Benton, Marsha, May, and Jason Jr.
> Shareholder of 26 percent of Sampson Seed Company

Joan, Bill and Marsha's firstborn child, is a member of the family company's board of directors. Although as an adult she has never worked in the business, when young she was her mother's "right-hand girl." In the company's infancy, she would cut off the dry flower heads and strip them to carefully collect their seeds. She was a constant and definite asset to the young enterprise.

As a child, Joan had been cute, bright, and energetic—liked by both of her younger brothers. However, as both David and Sam pointed out, she had also been their father's obvious favorite. This always meant trouble for the whole family because whatever Joan wanted she always got. She had all sorts of ways of manipulating both her parents into compliance with her desires. The boys admitted their resentment.

Joan married Jason Bennington shortly after finishing high school. She had apparently married him for two reasons. First, she was pregnant with their first child. Second, her father liked Jason well enough and thought he could help manage the business—at least until Sam would be grown up, out of college, and ready to manage the company.

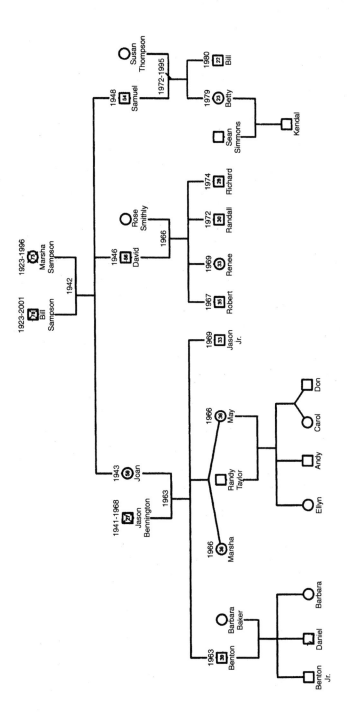

FIGURE 5.3. Sampson Family Genogram

Jason, a local boy and from a humble background, just like Joan's parents, hadn't finished high school, but he had practical sense and his ambitions focused on the land, not office matters. Unfortunately, Jason died early in his life when his tractor turned over on him, leaving Joan to raise their four children alone, with financial help from her parents.

As an adult Joan is described by everyone as innocent and unknowing. Yet she also has "temper tantrums" whenever she doesn't get what she wants. Her still-girlish demeanor has made her the focus of both jokes and anger from the third generation, including her own children.

> David William Sampson
> Age: Fifty-six years
> Married: Rose Smithly, August 2, 1967
> Father of four children: Robert, Renee, Randall, and Richard
> Shareholder of 26 percent of Sampson Seed Company

David was described by both his siblings as a kid who was always in trouble at home and at school, with Sam adding that, "It was well deserved." Although both small and slight in stature like his mother, David was rambunctious and at times a scrapper. His father often made fun of him and treated him harshly; as a result, he spent most of his time away from home. Once he completed high school at the age of seventeen, David moved to another state. There he quickly found a job with a small real estate developer. Several years later he married the boss's daughter, Rose. Together they had four children, Robert, Renee, Randall, and Richard.

When David wanted to join his father-in-law's development company and open up his own division, he persuaded his mother to lend him the capital to do so, which she managed to do despite the objections of her husband. David sees himself as a successful husband, parent, and businessman, respected in his community and contributing regularly to the welfare of others. He has not encouraged his wife and children to have contact with his family of origin, since he continues to feel both rejected and betrayed by his siblings. In fact, his feelings seemed confirmed because neither of his siblings knew anything about his current family or life.

Samuel Morgan Sampson
Age: Fifty-four years
Married: Susan Thompson, June 1, 1972
Father of two children: Betty and William
Shareholder of 26 percent of Sampson Seed Company

In boyhood, Sam, Bill and Marsha's last-born child, had been successful in school, popular with his peers, and openly cooperative and enthusiastic at home. Although known as "the sunshine kid," he had always seemed angry with his sister and brother. Almost from the start Sam was identified as the family star, both at home and in the community. Reportedly from day one he was considered to be the next leader of Sampson Seed Company. Sam went to a four-year university and then on to graduate school, graduating with honors in agricultural business. After completing an internship with an agricultural packaging company, he returned home.

During his university years Sam met Susan Thompson whom he married shortly after graduate school. They had two children. Seven years ago, Susan left Sam and they began divorce proceedings. Their daughter Betty moved away with her mother, while Bill II remained with his father. The divorce is still not settled and the family is divided, with Sam accusing "the women" of trying to take all the assets he'd acquired over the years from his dedicated work at the family company.

Since his father retired in 1992, Sam has been CEO of the company. Almost everyone reports that he has done an exemplary job and the only problems have been when his health has taken him out of the office for long periods of time.

The Third Generation: Joan's Children

Benton Bennington
Age: Thirty-nine years
Married and father of Benton Jr., Daniel, and Barbara
Shareholder of 4 percent of Sampson Seed Company

According to everyone, Benton, the first grandchild, was always his grandfather's and his father's favorite. As a one-year-old he had already joined his father and grandfather in the fields on the "tractor team," and as a youngster he was not only bright and accomplished, but also ruthless in his play with the other farm kids. He was further described as always being extremely angry with his mother and blaming her for his father's death.

Anointed "the next Sampson seed man" by his grandfather Bill, from the age of five Benton was groomed to ultimately take over the company management from Uncle Sam. To make sure that this would happen, Grandpa Bill issued Benton more shares of stock than any of the other grandchildren. Benton now had the not-so-secret goal of becoming CEO and running the family business before he turned forty. The current vice president of operations, he is described as good at his job, and much relied upon by Sam. However, few people ever dare to challenge Benton's opinions and actions, for he is unwilling to listen and acts offended and angry when confronted.

> Marsha Bennington
> Age: Thirty-six years
> Single, no children
> Shareholder of 2 percent of Sampson Seed Company

Marsha, named after her beloved grandmother, is described as smart, reliable, caring, and always keeping to herself. Her best friend is still her twin sister May. She says she has always hated her older brother and that she always will. A valued employee of the company, Marsha is vice president of human resources (HR). She is Uncle Sam's personal confidant, especially since his divorce.

> May Bennington Taylor
> Age: Thirty-six years
> Married and mother of Ellyn, Andy, Carol, and Don
> Shareholder of 2 percent of Sampson Seed Company

May is Marsha's twin sister and they remain best friends even as adults, talking to each other sometimes twice a day. Although May does not work at the company, her husband, Randy Taylor, is a longtime trusted employee. Randy's father had been Bill Sampson's best friend. Since they were youngsters, when all the little girls would get together with their grandmother Marsha at the ranch, May has kept contact with her Uncle David and his family. She actually refers to David's daughter, Renee, as her "third twin."

Jason Bennington Jr.
Age: Thirty-three years
Single, no children
Shareholder of 2 percent of Sampson Seed Company

Jason still lives with his mother. He is a talented artist who has actually sold some of his works. Whenever he is needed in the marketing department for contributing graphic design work, he willingly volunteers for a short period of time. He will do anything his mother asks him to; according to his siblings, Joan has promised him anything he ever wants.

The Third Generation: David's Children

Robert, Renee, Randall, and Richard
Each own 2 percent of Sampson Seed Company

David reported that all of his children are accomplished adults in their own right. They know little or nothing from direct experience with their father's family. Their cousin May keeps contact with Renee, who then passes information along to all the others, including himself. Otherwise, they know that it is only because of their grandmother Marsha that their father or they were remembered at all in the distribution of stock for Sampson Seeds.

The Third Generation: Sam's Children

Betty Sampson Simmons
Age: Twenty-three years
Married and mother of Kendal
Shareholder of 2 percent of Sampson Seed Company

Betty is described as bright, beautiful, capable, and very outspoken. Living half a state away from her father and brother, she currently works in the marketing department of a client company in the California food industry. Sam says he has not spoken to her since the time of the separation, when she sided with her mother. He said he is waiting for an apology, and for her to come to him. Betty and her brother rarely see each other now and have little in common.

> Bill Sampson, II
> Age: Twenty-one years
> Single, no children
> Shareholder of 2 percent of Sampson Seed Company

Not only is Bill the namesake of his grandfather, but it's said that he's also his spitting image, both physically and in personality. He is young, wild, and not yet fully educated. He has little to do with his mother and sister. In his own written words: "I could care less about that company . . . except it gives me money, and that's cool."

GETTING AN AGREEMENT TO PROCEED

After putting together the initial family profiles based on our phone interviews and the responses to the questionnaires, we prepared a preliminary or working plan and sent it for "buy-in" to Sam, Joan, and David.

The three principals agreed to the family participating in a critical four-day meeting to be scheduled sometime within the next three months. The second-generation family members had all accepted the necessity of doing some quick and intensive work in preparation for Sam's inevitable departure. Each of them knew that neither the family nor the company were prepared for a successful transition.

Joan was sure that Benton, May, Marsha, and Jason would go along with "whatever." David was fiercely clear that he would not be very willing to invite all of his family to attend the meeting, but that he would consider bringing Rose and that he'd even ask Renee what she thought. Sam didn't know if Bill would come, and he certainly wouldn't permit Betty to participate, saying, "This is none of her damn business!"

It was decided to hold the meeting in Carmel during a long weekend in October. Our fees were agreed upon and would be paid by the company. We took responsibility for arranging a meeting place and the accommodations.

We were now ready to proceed to the next steps. Between the time of agreement and the meeting we would be sending out more questionnaires; completing face-to-face interviews with each of the principals and everyone else who was willing to see us; and also freely talking with employees, the company accountants, and perhaps its lawyers. If any family member wanted to talk with us, they were free to call us at any time. Our contact person for all of the practical arrangements would be Marsha.

Chapter 6

Stage I: Recognize

We were told to tell the truth but when I asked questions, it was always "none of my business." Now, I see how much was hidden and I cry for their pain.

A client

Building a successful family and a successful family business requires facing the truth and seeing reality. But what is truth and how do you find it? Finding the truth of the family and helping family members see and accept the realities is a most crucial first step when working with troubled business-owning families.

All advisors to family-owned businesses, whether financial, legal, management, or relationship consultants, need to know how to observe and gather information related to the entire family business system and its various participants. We must really *look* at the family and become fully aware of the reality of their unique patterns of interaction, the way individual family members contribute to the patterns, and the special circumstances of the family and the business that influence the family at this moment in time. We cannot overemphasize the importance of taking the time and making the effort to closely examine a family and its business—and then keep on doing so until the details of its reality are slowly revealed. Only then can the best plans for assistance or intervention be designed.

This chapter is about gathering information and helping family members recognize hidden truths and prepare for changing relationships, thus better enabling the family to lead their enterprise in the desired direction. In this presentation of Stage I of the Reconciliation Model, we present a number of important tasks which we believe are useful to consultants in getting to know and far better understand the "real" family they will be guiding into the future.

ABOUT THE TRUTH

What is *real,* and who knows the truth? The answer is that no one person knows the "real truth," because what family members believe to be true depends on what information they have and then choose to pay attention to. That information is determined by culture, values, past experiences, and beliefs about self, others, and the world. In other words, how the present is perceived is based on the availability of information from the past, the current circumstances, the environment, and what family members have been allowed to see and say, if only to themselves.

Seeing the world consistently through a highly personalized pair of lenses, particularly when the lenses are colored by memories of the past, results in distortions of reality, from which we create beliefs and even illusions. Quite naturally, then, many families in business have skewed perceptions, whether positive or negative, of their family and family members, particularly when such illusions have existed for a long time. In addition, so much activity is apt to be going on within a business-owning family that its members tend to close their eyes and minds to present truths, especially if they contain seemingly irreconcilable conflicts with the family's long-held view of itself.

We don't mean to infer that family members intentionally lie; the point is that oftentimes family members do not see the facts before them because personal and family histories bind them to believe commonly accepted truths rather than present realities. Our objective is to help the family accept the present and plan appropriately for the future, while freeing themselves from the ties that bind them to the past.

During the early phase of consultation we approach gathering accurate and in-depth information from the position of knowing that different kinds of truth need to be sought and honored. We have found it quite helpful to acknowledge and work with the four categories of truth that were identified by the South African Truth and Reconciliation Commission (TRC, 1998; Bouraine, 2000) in its final report.

These are: (1) objective or factual truth; (2) personal or narrative truth; (3) social truth; and (4) healing and restorative truth.

This report on the Republic of South Africa's progress in working through truth telling to affect reconciliation of its nation, has supplied useful guidance to us—particularly because a family divided is similar to a nation divided. The dissociated and even warring groups within both nations and families have a common history, a common present, and a common future. As with a nation formed into factions, a family business hoping to secure its future needs to reunite. It can do this by seeking the truths and realities of the past and the present; reconciling disagreements over differently perceived truths, especially when they collide; and using its members' collective wisdom to establish a plan for a shared future.

The advisor's goal in a family business parallels the goal of the Commission's in South Africa: the promotion of future family business success through creating unity and reconciliation in relationships that have been split asunder or estranged. In this endeavor advisors seek to gather information and evidence that will make it possible to repair relationships, restore family justice, and prevent past violations from happening again.

Let's now consider how the four different kinds of truth are applied to the realities in family businesses.

Objective Truth

Objective truth is arrived at through collecting, in an impartial and caring way, information and evidence that relates to individuals and relationships in both the past and the present. At a glance this work may seem easy. In reality, though, family secrets—especially when bound up in the generations—are hard for family members to reveal. The popular but grimly apt metaphor of "skeletons in the closet" attests to that difficulty. It's sometimes very difficult to tell the truth, and it's especially difficult when other people don't want to listen. It's even more difficult to tell the truth when family members fear that they will be judged or even punished for what they say they believe or feel. In seeking objective truths, family members and advisors need to have patience and compassion and listen carefully without judgments.

As family business consultants we customarily seek to secure facts concerning the business, such as its history, finances, and markets. As relationship advisors, we work with the families and the family business accountants in order to make sure that we understand the reality of their financial situation. Some family members measure the success of the business from the perspective of the dividends they receive, others from the growth in sales volume, while others may look at the various perks available. Each of these gives a partial but incomplete view of the financial circumstances. Only through verifying factual information can we help the family evaluate their business from a common perspective.

In addition, of course, it is necessary to obtain a great deal of personal information. We search for contexts, causes, and patterns within the family that have created, support, or sustain serious interpersonal and behavioral problems. We also ask "circular questions" (Penn, 1982) such as what happened to whom, where, when, and how, and, very important, who was involved. This is because we have the responsibility to discover and challenge the individual and relationship illusions under which the family functions.

In today's world of family business some relationship truths are easier than others to unearth and challenge. For example, all one needs to do in some family companies is to examine the performances of different family members to observe that the males are not necessarily always smarter and more worthy than the females. Other patterns are more difficult to discover, such as the subtle abuse of one sibling by another, or the disenfranchisement of certain family members, which may have gone on one generation after another.

For the advisor, getting at the objective or factual truth about relationships means accepting that there may well be as many different versions of the truth as there are people involved in a family business—all of which will need to be investigated and considered.

Personal or Narrative Truth

Narrative truths are the stories people create to account for the facts and to fill in the gaps in the facts as they know them. This second truth, which is experience-based, is established through people's willingness to tell their own stories without interruptions and challenges, and their eventual opportunity to listen to others' stories, told under the same circumstances. Individual stories contain the facts, at least as each person believes them, of events that he or she has experienced or witnessed, and also his or her feelings about these events.

Opportunities for family members to present their personal stories are important steps for attaining both identity and worthiness within the family system. Everyone's personal truth needs to be acknowledged and validated, by advisors as well as by other family members, which involves recognition of the storyteller as a unique and valuable family member. Sharing personal truths helps restore memory and a sense of a worthwhile self. Family members experiencing a separate, unique, and worthwhile sense of themselves, who also know, respect, and care for others in the family, are the people most prepared to commit to the long-term life of the family business. Sharing personal truths in a family group setting, where an individual voice can help to break the silence of the family, contributes enormously to healing wounds and changing family relationship patterns.

Collective or Social Truth

Collective truth is the experience-based reality of the family that is established through interaction, discussion, and debate. When the different individual stories about similar events are gathered together the collective or social truth of the family is compiled. Collective truth emerges as family members become aware of various personal stories and of what other family members know, see, and feel. Part of helping a family create a bonding force, family cohesion, is to know and understand others and to develop a shared history which honors both individuality and family unity.

One of the great virtues of the Reconciliation Model is its mechanism for enabling individual and collective storytelling to take place in a communal setting, probably in ways never experienced before by most or even all of the family members.

Healing and Restorative Truth

The fourth and final truth is the healing and restorative truth obtained through acknowledgment and accountability for interpersonal wounds—the truth that makes reconciling relationships possible. Much more will be learned about the special value of this truth as we continue with the model.

Now let's consider the tasks, that when completed, aid family members and advisors in finding the relationship truth, understanding the family, and achieving reconciliation in ruptured relationships.

TASK #1: MAKE CONTACT

This initial period of fact gathering and making inquiries into the nature and configuration of the family relationships is when advisors first establish their direct connections with family members. Gathering information actually provides a wonderful opportunity to make contact, contact, and more contact. For a family business advisor, it is very important to make these first contacts with *everyone* in the family, whenever it is possible.

Making good personal contact is one of the best practices of effective consultation. The goal is to help each family member view the advisors as people who want to understand the situation from their own personal point of view. If we fail to do this, there will be little chance of learning the family truths so necessary to facilitating needed change. To help families effect relationship change, it is essential for the advisor to be regarded as a useful and trusted person by every family member, a tall order and a very important one.

For relationship consultation to progress productively, every family member needs to be regarded as important, and helped to feel important within the family system, regardless of their position, or no position at all, in the business. For us, this translates, simply, to making sure that we make contact with everyone—mothers, fathers, children, siblings, cousins, and in-laws—and ask for their honest input. Of course, some may say that they have nothing to share, but the long-term benefit is in the asking and making a connection, however brief.

Contact is an important issue within the family and the business as well. As we pointed out in Chapter 4, a major problem for many business-owning families, especially long-established ones with many members, is the very lack of contact within the family itself. Problems arise when family members are not counted, not heard, and not understood by one another. As part of a successful consultation, family members start to learn how to make satisfying contacts with one another. They begin to recognize and value one another's uniqueness as individuals, to recognize and value the differences between people, and to recognize, value, and respect what each and every person has to offer to the family and its business, the essence of good contact.

Thus the advisor who is successful at the early stage of the consultation in acknowledging the uniqueness and value of all family members and in gathering the truths about the family is both making contact and teaching others the process of successfully making contact. This is an essential part of reconciling relationships so that beneficial changes can begin to take place. As has been aptly said, "Contact is the lifeblood for growth, the means for changing oneself and one's experience of the world. . . . Through contact . . . one does not have to try to change; change simply occurs" (Polster and Polster, 1974, p. 101).

TASK #2: SEEK RELATIONSHIP TRUTH

For a family business to succeed over time, dealing with the truth is difficult but imperative. Remember Hans Christian Andersen's tale, "The Emperor's New Clothes"? It is applicable to many business-owning families. Sometimes family members simply say and even believe what they think the others want to hear, rather than speaking their own truth. Sometimes, as in the tale, one person will cry out, "But the Emperor has no clothes!" Sometimes, but not always, others too will show the courage of their own convictions. At such times the "emperor" of the family business (and often there is one) even suspects that these other members are right; still, he or she continues to walk more proudly than ever, as courtiers hold high the train of a garment that really isn't there at all.

"Telling it like it is"—revealing how some unresolved relationship situations have ugly and even perilous problems that nobody has wanted to talk about, let alone *do anything about*—can be a large challenge. It usually requires real bravery. Also, even hearing and accepting an unpleasant truth takes an act of courage. Furthermore, holding oneself accountable for playing a part in supporting an oppressor or some false ideal or shopworn illusion is a risk-taking act. Each deed, heroic in itself, can also have other positive human consequences, since it frequently causes others to take similar actions.

One way of gathering information about relationship truth in the family business is to witness the family system in action and another is to ask each family member to answer a series of relationship-focused questions. These questions differ with each family and each circumstance, and, of course, are also general in nature. Our intent is twofold. First, we are interested in the objective truth: the facts and details of the events and circumstances of the business-owning family. Second, since we are also interested in establishing a relational focus, we proceed to gather relational information through the personal or narrative truth supplied by family members and the specific questions which when answered tell us about the system.

To gather relational truth we listen to discover the interpersonal patterns of the family by soliciting feedback about form, differences, and changes in relationships. Examples of such questions are: Who notices first when . . . ; Who intervenes when . . . ; Who does nothing when . . . ; How would the business get along without . . . ; or, What is your explanation for . . . ? We then use the feedback provided by family members to lead us to the succeeding questions.

Relational truth or a relational "diagnosis" (Kaslow, 1996) can also be made from observations of the ongoing processes and inferences about the interaction process developed from collateral data, such as family life cycles, the family genogram, and other indirect reports. How one decides which approach to use, and when, is really part of the "art," rather than the science, of a professional consultation.

When systems or relational truth—as compared to individual truth—is achieved, two very different things are said: (1) something is amiss within the entire pattern of relationships in the family; and (2) when the relationship patterns are changed, individuals will have the opportunity to change and manage themselves in a more consistent, productive, and healthy manner. In addition, this shift paves the way to establishing healthy decision-making and problem-solving processes for the future.

We often ask questions similar to the following as a way of both obtaining initial relational information and helping individuals to define themselves. We frame our request for information by asking people to give us their answers in the first person present tense and without blaming references to others.

- What is your description of the current problem and what is your proposed solution?
- Who in your family would agree most with your definition and solution and why?
- Who in your family would disagree most and why?
- How do you want to manage yourself during the most difficult parts of this consultation?
- Who will be most pleased if you succeed and who will be most displeased and why do you believe they will feel this way?
- What are the two most significant historical events that you believe reflect the roots of the current family problems? These descriptions should include who was involved and how each person reacted along with the resolution at the time.
- What are the things you would most like to see happen during the reconciliation process and the things you would absolutely *not* want to happen?
- What else do you think we should be aware of to ensure maximum success?

The search for relationship information, as stated, is best conducted by focusing on the interaction process among family members, and also between family members and "outsiders" such as nonfamily employees. Such a relational perspective helps shift the dialogue from a particular problem with individuals to a wider, more dynamic one of the process itself, which is a paradigm shift crucial to successful change.

TASK #3: CREATE COMMON UNDERSTANDING

Developing a common understanding of the problem and a shared vision of the path to resolution is essential. The varied techniques used by advisors to develop this common understanding all share the same idea: since we frame our own reality, it is the clash of different ways of seeing things that causes dissonance in relationships. Therefore, the goal in creating common understanding is to arrive at an interpretation of the problems that is close enough to, and yet significantly different from, any individual's perception. This allows everyone to "buy into" and accept the common understanding as a new and different explanation for the problems.

In business-owning families the many different perceptions and understandings that must be taken into consideration are often surprisingly similar at their core. Therefore, the accuracy and precision of the advisor's interpretation or understanding is not usually as important as how he or she articulates the interpretation to each of the family members. Tools for developing common understanding are: to frame the problem in general relationship terms that are nonthreatening to individuals and to the family unit, and to create a positive connotation so that each family member can see himself or herself as valuable and participating in the best interests of the family.

As an example, the accepted common family understanding of the Sampson family was that a need existed to immediately create a viable and accepted plan for transition of the business to new leadership and that plan would be worked out best in a way that would allow shareholders to have the opportunity to state their interests and be considered.

TASK #4: DETERMINE WHO PARTICIPATES

As professionals, we need to determine how each family member participates in the problem. We also need to determine who participates in the reconciliation process, and why. To do this we consider our own analysis of the problem. We also ask each family member how they believe they themselves and others are involved. We inquire about who has issues with other family members and who each family member thinks needs to make changes for the good of the family and the business.

We consider that there are both insiders and outsiders to relationship problems in a family business. Insiders are directly involved in the problems and outsiders are impacted but do not participate. In small families who own businesses everyone is an insider; since all insiders participate in some form or another in the problems, they should also participate in the reconciliation efforts. In some larger families, though, there are many and distant family members barely connected with the business at all, and these people are considered to be outsiders to the dynamics of the problems, although certainly impacted by the problems and also the solutions.

Insiders to the problem are generally easy to discover, since they are active participants in the ongoing interplay of relationship wounding. They occupy different roles in specific relationship problems: those of victim, persecutor, and rescuer. However, insiders are not always family members. Outside professionals and advisors as well as trusted managers can all be insiders if they participate in supporting the conflict in ways such as keeping secrets, carrying out plans unknown to others, or forming alliances that undermine either family unity or, frequently, a particular family member.

Insider-victims usually identify themselves, for they consider themselves as the injured party. Some people in the role of victim have difficulty talking about the conflict that afflicts them, especially if fear, concern about retaliation, and personal shame contribute to keeping them stuck. Others, however, become highly vocal in their protest against what they see as unforgivable and unjust. Victim-insiders rarely refuse to participate in a reconciliation process. In fact, they are usually quite supportive of the effort as they see themselves as having nothing further to lose . . . and much to gain. Victims generally need support in accepting responsibility for their circumstances and finding ways to get out of their hole.

Insider-persecutors perpetrate family ruptures yet rarely see themselves doing so; in fact, they usually tend to both see and portray themselves as victims of other people's incompetence, laziness, or wiles. Persecutors often present as righteous, sacrificing, and burdened—after all, it is much easier and more acceptable to act as a put-upon victim.

Some people in persecutor roles will openly admit that they would like to get rid of all the other family members who are simply incompetent and undeserving relatives who occupy positions in the business or receive what they consider unearned benefits. Persecutors generally and notably resist getting involved in a reconciliation effort. Avoiding exposure of their real motivations and often denying any hostility, they claim they are "too busy keeping it all together for the benefit of the business" to take time to meet with relationship advisors or attend family conferences.

Insider-rescuers come in many sizes and shapes. The rescuer role has two possibilities: active supporter of the victim or passive supporter of the persecutor. Rescuers often stand to benefit, either materially or emotionally, from the sustained relationship conflict. Rescuers can also be professionals who are involved with the family business, such as lawyers, accountants, and consultants who get caught because they do not take a systems focus in looking at the problems and solutions.

Active rescuers are people who are engaged somehow in the family interplay; they believe they are helping the victims by becoming involved in the controversy. They step in with good intentions but further aggravate the difficulties by simply smoothing feathers, lending an ear, trying to negotiate, making promises, and keeping secrets—anything that enables the problems to continue. Their actions unfortunately simply stir the boiling pot and delay resolution. Through their participation active rescuers get included and gain self-esteem because the continuing conflict gives them a place and a reason to be there.

Passive rescuers are the silent people who, knowingly or unknowingly, support the persecutor, because they know what is going on but won't say or do anything to expose the problems, confront the participants, or resolve the conflict. Passive rescuers gain the personal benefit of being left alone and not having to get involved. Frequently, this benefit is monetary, as is the case with in-law spouses or outside consultants who are passive in their advisory role, even though they are aware of serious problems.

All insiders to the conflict should be included in the reconciliation process, regardless of the roles they are currently playing. Nonfamily members are not involved in the actual reconciliation process; however, it is essential to address their roles and confront their parts in maintaining relationship problems.

Remember that the insider roles of victim, persecutor, and rescuer are constantly shifting in a family. Every rescuer will eventually become a victim and every victim will eventually become a persecutor. The circumstances of the problems will be different and the roles will be different. These roles, although similar in some ways to the roles described for oppressive systems, are different in that they represent temporary stances that people take whenever there are interpersonal difficulties. This is in contrast to the roles in oppressive systems, which are integral parts of an ongoing and overwhelming system dynamic, sometimes continuing for generations.

Finally, in many families, particularly large ones, some of the people are actually outsiders to the problem. These people, who have a stake in supporting a successful resolution, are separate from the emotional entanglements. These outsiders can be called upon to support changes but they are generally not included as part of an actual reconciliation process. When working toward reconciliation people are vulnerable and expose their inner selves, and it is much safer for them when the confidential circle is closely contained.

TASK #5: UNDERSTAND CHANGE. AND OVERCOME RESISTANCE

Crucial to a professional's practice-oriented wisdom when guiding a family business is an understanding of and appreciation for the process of change that must take place for the business-owning family to be successful in the years ahead. Also crucial is an understanding of resistance to change and how to overcome it.

So how do we proceed with reconciliation when people are, for one reason or another, not available to change? Examining change across many different health-related behaviors, researchers (Prochaska and DiClemente, 1992) have developed a model for evaluating individual readiness to change. Business leaders have also looked at the principles for "taking charge of change" (Smith, 1997). The results of these investigations suggest that readiness for change is one of the most important determinants of positive outcome.

In preparing family business members for change, we aim first to help each person acquire an awareness and understanding of the family relationship problem. This is done by gathering factual truth, defining problems as systems issues, and encouraging each person to take partial ownership of the relationship problem through helping him or her understand that when any family business member has a problem, everyone has a problem.

Next, we aim to create interest and desire to participate in the change process—recognizing that change is needed and must happen. We alert family members not just to the identified problems, but also educate them about what will be different after relationships are reconciled. Many people need reassurance, because they feel fearful of the unknown and about how things will be different when change occurs. They may be particularly frightened about losing face, status, position, resources, and family relationships. As people weigh the pros and cons of change, they usually need gentle nudging, support, information, and alternative ways to look at things. Family members must become convinced that the negative aspects of the problem far outweigh their concerns about changing.

When relationships are at the center of the problem, the difference in readiness among family members also becomes a critical issue. When some people in a family group are ready sooner than others to commit to this process of change, it is important to work diligently with the system and get all involved in the reconciliation efforts. For example, siblings working hard in a family business in which parents continually "buy off" a brother who blackmails their parents are ready to do whatever it takes to resolve the problems. On the other hand, the third sibling is resistant and the parents are not yet ready to take the firm actions needed—getting everyone involved is essential.

People's willingness and ability to change attitudes and behaviors is critical to the success of the reconciliation process. Both a willingness to change their behaviors and the ability to learn new ways to relate to others is crucial in making change happen. In our many years of experience we have found that there is always a place in the family business for any family member who is willing to change and learn. Unfortunately, we have also found that when family members are unwilling to participate in change, no matter what their capacities or role, new troubles loom ahead. So, in the reconciliation process we welcome people even if they participate grudgingly or under duress, and we always hope to enlist them in the change efforts.

There are many reasons why family members may be resistant to the reconciliation process. Concern over personal and family exposure is one of the foremost: e.g., "We have always been a private family and we don't wash our dirty linen in public." Family secrets, financial information and practices, and various personal problems with family members—such as substance abuse, depression, and other disorders—are generally held very close to the vest in family businesses, and reluctance to reveal and openly discuss these issues may lie underneath.

Participation in a change effort may also be seen as an enormous threat to those who anticipate that change will bring with it a loss of personal or positional power. Or it can simply seem unsafe because people are deeply distrustful of one another, sometimes for sensible reasons based on past experience. Fear, self-doubt, personal weakness, and a questionable ability to manage oneself in the reconciliation environment are all real issues that support resistance.

Family members are also usually concerned about the professional facilitator's ability to skillfully manage the delicate process of reconciliation. The most frequently expressed scare is that the conflict will get out of hand and the meeting will become hostile and emotional. This is why the first stage of the model in which advisors make contact with the individual family members as they gather information is critical in establishing confidence and trust in the advisor's ability to maintain diplomatic impartiality as well as enforce the ground rules for conduct that were agreed upon.

Whatever the reasons underlying resistance, it should always be remembered that nonparticipation is a most powerful position. It must be confronted and never allowed to interrupt the reconciliation efforts of others. One option for dealing with this resistance is to make it clear that the family intends to proceed despite the absence of the withholding person, regardless of the ultimate outcome to him or her. Sending this message that the family will not be controlled by one person is sometimes enough to get participation.

Another option, if all else fails, is that family members must sometimes be willing to take high-level risks. These risks may include redefining positions, and being willing to withhold funds and personal support in last-ditch attempts to gain compliance in resolving relationship problems. This is especially vital when the high cost of maintaining the conflict, in social, emotional, and even economic terms, is too risky for both the family and the business to bear.

TASK #6: FORM CONTRACTS

The foundation of a successful relationship consultation, as well as success in the reconciliation effort itself, is the contract. This explicit agreement, written or verbal, is made between the professional and the business-owning family. A contract centers the consultation and reminds participants of their obligations and objectives. A contract brings two disparate units, the family and the professional, together under the same umbrella and provides them with a common purpose.

Contracts also focus attention, problem-solving abilities, and energy, while outlining and supporting individual and family strengths. Furthermore, a contract establishes a boundary that defines the working environment, lays out the work to be done, sets limits on expectations, and both prescribes and proscribes behaviors. With a contract as a point of reference, distractions or interpersonal maneuvering become obvious, so that they can then either be explored or handled directly, according to the immediate need.

A contract focusing on reconciling family relationships is a mutually constructed blueprint for both protection and change. Usually it encompasses the common understanding of the engagement and attends to individual needs and obligations while keeping the well-being of the family and its business uppermost in mind.

As will be seen in Interlude 2 each member of the Sampson family agreed to the following basic terms of their consultation contract: "I agree to fully participate in the family meeting arranged for October 24 to 28 in Carmel, California. I support the purpose of the meeting which I understand to be: promoting family unity and establishing new leadership teams for Sampson Seed Company. I agree to participate in accomplishing these goals by being available to openly explore family relationship patterns of both the past and the present and participating with others in a manner that will best support the successful future of the company."

In working toward a mutually agreed-upon relational contract, we state the process in behaviorally specific terms based on observable information, and emphasize the significance of the problem's effect on the entire family and business. Who owns what part of the problem must be sorted out and stated and at no time should an individual or a specific group of people such as "the cousins" be defined as *The Problem*.

If the family focuses on a single person or several people as the purported source of their main problem, at least two distinct things are being said: (1) something is quite amiss with that individual or individuals, and (2) changing whatever is amiss will completely correct the problem. Buying into this linear viewpoint is wrong because it neglects the family system's view that everyone has some responsibility in either creating the problem or permitting it to amplify, or both. Such an individual focus results in sidetracking the underlying issues involved in a relationship rupture, or in some other relationship violation or injustice and can lead to an unsuccessful consultation and business future.

A crucial task in forming the overall relationship contract is linking up the different levels of the family system and getting everyone to work simultaneously toward a common goal or shared vision. To enlist each person's support, honor individuality, take skeptics seriously, and provide tactical positive plans for each person in support of the overall plan.

Many individual contracts for change will support this overall contract and are continuously being defined. When reading Interlude 3 of the Sampson family case, it is easy to see the multiple individual contracts that interface to support the overall effort. These contracts are stated in ways such as: Will you . . . ; Are you able to . . . ; or, later, You will need to . . . are you willing to do this?

A different example of a contract made to support an overall reconciliation contract is seen in this new case: Rosine initially refused to participate in a scheduled family meeting to discuss her desire to leave the family company and sell her shares. We had previously been informed that she had already consulted lawyers and engaged someone to represent her. In a private meeting Rosine told us of the pain and frustration she felt when her siblings refused to include her in decision making; when her brothers degraded and devalued her; and when there was conversation about removing her from the vice presidency of the family's real estate holdings.

After validating for Rosine that these things were actually happening, something we were able to do because we had actually witnessed some of the behaviors, we were able to get Rosine to meet with her siblings. At the meeting we were then able to contract with everyone for concrete changes which would offer more protection to Rosine— changes such as reorganizing space and responsibilities in a way that would lessen her daily contact with her siblings. Rosine then felt safe enough to participate in the family reconciliation process, where eventually the entire family contracted to "keep the family and the company holdings intact."

TASK #7: PREPARE FAMILY MEMBERS
FOR PARTICIPATION IN RECONCILIATION EFFORTS

How well family members are prepared for taking part in the reconciliation work itself can make or break the process. Good preparation reduces personal risk, gets influential family members to support the effort, and establishes a framework for the future when reconciliation practices are integrated as part of the family culture.

Preparation has two distinct parts: education about the process, or getting everyone to be "on the same page"; and creating safety for the participants.

We set the stage for reconciliation through educating participants during our individual meetings with them. This work is done with insiders after we have completed most of our information gathering, formed our initial hypotheses about what changes will have the most impact on the family, and outlined a plan for proceeding. We present the concept and process of reconciliation: that of building trust and collaboration through reaching a common truth about the ruptures that have occurred. We go into some detail about the importance of family members telling their stories in order to reveal their own truths. In giving this information we aim to lay the groundwork for all participants to explore the various ways in which their own behavior and attitudes may have contributed to the problems.

Part of educating involves clarifying our own role in facilitating the reconciliation meetings, which is to do whatever is necessary to provide a safe atmosphere for each family member to:

- Develop the ongoing ability to identify and express their thoughts, feelings, values, memories, and capabilities when in the presence of family members
- Build the capacity to be interested in, responsive to, and supportive of others while maintaining themselves and managing their own reactions
- Participate in ways that support the desired changes and the future prosperity of both the family and the business

The second element of preparation is assuring, as much as possible, that people will be safe. The most crucial part of safety is protecting family members against a shaming experience. Advisors who are planning to conduct family reconciliation processes would do well to understand shame and its potency. Shame and the defenses against shame are self-protective mechanisms that help people avoid vulnerability and loss of contact in relationships. Tomkins (1963) wrote that shame is the affect present when a person has experienced such personal calamities as a loss of dignity, defeat, transgression, or alienation. To feel shame, then, is to feel "seen," and to see oneself in a painfully diminished sense. Therefore, as professionals who guide relationship change, it is our utmost responsibility to build in every possible protection against a shame-producing environment.

People create their own stories about themselves, others, and their circumstances. In this way they protect themselves and mitigate the shame that would come from being "found out" to be someone different than who they appear to be and say they are, or even different from whomever they may actually think they are. In reconciling relationships family members are asked to come out from behind their self-protective stories and reveal themselves. In doing this, they invariably expose themselves to potential shame. So, very crucially, the advisor must provide protection against shaming.

Providing the most effective protection from shame is done by continually emphasizing the strengths and resources of individuals and the family, and by controlling the boundaries and limits of interactions. This is best accomplished through: the use of contracts, which define the problem and the work to be done; ground rules that help to contain the conflicts and protect against negative consequences for what has been revealed; and, a firm commitment to making any violation of safety the first order of business, as soon as it is apparent.

The assurance of a safe environment for self-disclosure is essential in getting people to initially agree to enter into the reconciliation process. It is not surprising that many family members are frightened of meeting all together in the effort to achieve reconciliation. Some anticipate the process of "truth and consequences"—a dangerous game in which they have everything to lose. Others, usually the disenfranchised, anticipate noisy, psyche-crushing conflicts, having to challenge entrenched family authority all on their own, and even facing ostracism from the family. No matter what the form of the fear, the advisor's job is to stay involved and act as an agent of education and safety up to the very moment of actually getting together.

Maintaining a continuously positive focus will encourage full participation. It allows individuals to reveal themselves, safely and honestly, even though this can be a most difficult thing to do in the context of the family and the family business. A positive focus supports relationship loyalty and thereby assists greatly with problem solving and behavioral change.

In the next Sampson Interlude we show the process of gathering information and setting the stage for reconciliation. In Chapter 7, Stage II of the model, we delineate the tools used during the actual meetings for achieving reconciliation in ruptured or estranged relationships—relationships with a long history behind them, a tormented present, and a promising, interdependent future. Restoring justice in ruptured relationships comes through the incredibly potent process of safely unmasking individuals and the family and guiding all toward understanding, acceptance, and sometimes even forgiveness of one another.

Interlude 2: Setting the Stage for Reconciliation

The second phase of our consultation process with a conflicted family business requires an assessment of the primary problem or problems, as is often the case. Therefore, it initially involves having in-depth interviews or conversations with individual family members, meeting them in person whenever possible. This is often a daunting task because of most people's understandable reluctance to reveal to strangers what they really think, feel, and know. Moreover, they are expected to do this with consultants usually chosen by someone else and whom they certainly don't yet trust. In addition, for us there are often geography challenges to overcome: many of the businesses with whom we consult are distant from our home base.

We must always stay neutral, yet remain interested and caring, in our connections with each family member in turn as we learn about his or her circumstances and hear individual stories. As we ask questions and listen to the various responses we are constantly storing our impressions of each person and his or her place in the relationship network, which gradually begins to take shape through the interviews. We then start putting together our "best guesses" about the main family relationship problems, their roots in the past, and the possibilities for reconciling interpersonal differences. In this phase we typically work as a team to facilitate contact, contrast how we each heard the same story, and compare our impressions of and reactions to the different individuals and relationships.

For reconciliation work to progress productively, each family member (including the in-law spouses) must be regarded by us as important—sometimes even to be helped to feel important within the family system. In families where oppression reigns or some pieces of the family unit have been fragmented, in-person contact and even basic communication have been routinely negated and avoided. Therefore, it is easy for professionals also to get caught up in these dynamics, and miss hearing about and understanding the entire picture.

To make progress in the reconciliation process, family business members often need to learn how to make satisfying and productive contact. They need to learn to recognize and value one another's uniqueness and contribution to the organization and family, and value the differences among them, especially in the persons most unlike themselves.

Getting started on the work ahead is critical for the relationship advisor. Establishing a satisfactory initial direct contact with everyone is essential as a model and a goal. (Occasionally, of course, it will be necessary to omit certain individuals when the logistics of their situations make a meeting almost impossible.) Three practical suggestions for this preliminary contact and interview are:

- Let everyone know that they are important and possess valuable information for helping resolve the family business problems.
- Look for each person's strengths and explore how to utilize them.
- Help each family member to get what they need in the present, and to view themselves as an integral part of the family's future.

ARRANGING INTERVIEWS
WITH SAMPSON FAMILY MEMBERS

Bill and Marsha Sampson were the founders and architects of both the family and the family business. Since their deaths, the Sampson Seed Company now belongs to all the second- and third-generation family members, who are collectively charged with caring for and growing their inherited shares. The future of the business therefore depends on Marsha and Bill's children and grandchildren, who carry both the blessings and burdens of the past. These are people who, as we already have glimpsed, desperately need to learn new ways to relate to one another and to manage themselves in the present. Since the time when the elder Sampsons first started it all, both the family and the family business have undergone profound changes.

The early information we acquired in Phase I of our contact with the Sampson family had been gathered from family members' written and telephone responses about themselves and their descriptions of others. A critical difference in Phase II of the reconciliation work is that the needed additional information about the Sampsons, individually and collectively, will come from our in-person contacts with family members, which we will then process using our professional experience and expertise to reach a concerted plan for healing the various disaffected relationships.

Our plan for launching the second phase of our consultation arrangement with the Sampson family is simple: to meet with each family member whenever possible. Through both direct observation and self-report approaches we will gain information about individual members and the family system. We will secure personal willingness to participate and support others' participation in an effort to reconcile the discords among the Sampson family shareholders and within the family business management. We aim to develop an understanding of how the family system operates by delineating the early decision/script position of all family members who occupy integral positions in the current problems.

To arrange for appointments in advance, we telephone each person we hope to meet and either talk with them directly or leave messages requesting a returned call. Within a short time we set up the necessary appointments. We also schedule time to visit corporate headquarters and consequently see the town where Sampson Seed Company is located—the town that owes much of its growth and prosperity to the family company. Moreover, we hoped to be able to arrange for a flight to visit David and his family on another day soon afterward.

The rest of this Interlude reports on our journey to conduct interviews with Sampson family members. When we arrived at Sampson Seed Company we were initially given a tour of the office premises and introduced briefly to some of the key employees. This was followed by our first four family interviews.

MEETING WITH LOCAL FAMILY MEMBERS

Samuel Morgan Sampson

Our first interview is with Sam. He is eager to say many things, just as he had been earlier on the phone in our first talk. (We can't help noting later, as we go about our round of interviews and plant tours, that whenever we passed him in a corridor he also always asks, "How's it going?" He even phoned us several times at the hotel with the same question. Clearly, Sam felt anxious and wanted reassurance from us about our progress.) Our task was to keep him informed without revealing confidentiality, and also without being perceived by the others as "Sam's people." Thus, we soon make the decision to meet with him again only after finishing all the other interviews.

We meet Sam Sampson in his large, spacious office. Easy to talk with, he readily gives us his view of things along with information about the company and himself. He offers us all of the important documents, such as financial reports, as well as pleasant amenities such as food and drink. We notice that it is always his niece Marsha, not his administrative assistant, who brings whatever is needed. When we eventually inquire about this, Sam becomes misty-eyed and says, "Marsha is the only family person I can really trust. I have no parents anymore, my wife left me years ago, and my son is still just a kid. . . . And, damn her soul, my daughter just won't speak to me at all."

Next, we ask him to tell us more about what most troubles him personally, leading to his decision to leave the company at this time. "I hate this place!" he replies. "I'm up all night worrying about things. Nothing here is any fun. Maybe I've just outgrown this narrow little valley. I want to see the world before I die, and now just seems like the right time for me to get out."

We ask Sam to tell us what he believes are the roots of the present problems. We also ask him to give us his version of these problems and how they could interfere with his attaining his goal of exiting the business without causing it irreparable harm.

SAM: There is only one current problem. When I leave this place, I think everyone will want to do the same thing—take their money out. But we simply can't do that and have anything left of the business. Someone will just have to come in from the outside to take over for me because neither of my siblings could do it. As you'll see, Benton is quite qualified but he is also a pompous ass who could destroy everything. And Marsha, the only other family member around, isn't up to speed yet. So you see, you'll have to find some way to get me out—but only me! That's your job as far as I'm concerned. And good luck to you . . . because the three of us siblings, holding equal shares, have always been at war.

This last statement provides us with the invitation to explore some of the family history.

RUTH: What was it like, Sam, to grow up with your parents and siblings?

SAM: My mother was great to grow up with because she was gentle and never ragged on me for anything. But she never helped me out with much, either. David was always her favorite; she was sure dumb about that. My dad was extremely harsh with all of us and, I have to admit, especially with David. He—my dad, I mean—had control over everything in my parents' life, and he tried to do that with all of us, too. Home was a loud place all the time because he was constantly yelling and throwing out put-downs, particularly to my mother and David. I think Dad really had good intentions, but it sure was hell to be around him! On the other hand, look what he left us.

LES: Sam, how did you manage with all that commotion going on around you?

SAM: I just got good grades and never let them see when I wanted to do something that Dad wouldn't approve of. David, of course, was always in trouble, so it was easy to get the attention away from me. Besides, David as an older brother was awful to me. I think he was out to do me in from the very start of my life. So why should I care if he took the hits all the time from our dad?

RUTH: And what about your sister?

SAM: Well, Joan could always smile, or cry, and that would persuade Dad to either leave her alone or let her have something or do something she wanted. She was clearly his favorite . . . and she knew it and used it.

RUTH: So, Sam, you figured out how to survive by being the model and accomplished son. Is that right?

SAM: You are so right! But that's only part of it. Eventually I got stuck with taking care of everything, including my brother and sister, when I got hooked into this company. Everyone in this stupid family takes advantage of me. Dad never even said thank you for all I did around here, especially after he got me to take over the real day-to-day management from him. So now I've had it, with everybody and everything . . . and I want out.

With these statements Sam has revealed himself. When young, he had learned to take advantage of David's plight with their father, manipulating the situation at home so that he was never wrong or in trouble. He views himself now as the perennial victim of the rest of his "stupid" family, despite being successfully secretive about his own dalliances away from the straight and narrow path set down for him as the "good" son. Seen from the beginning as the family star both at home and in the larger community that depended on the company as the main resource for local employment and prosperity, he had always been the heir apparent, the next leader of Sampson Seeds.

Today, Sam is still angry with his "useless" siblings who, in his mind, continue to be the underlying cause of many of his problems. He denigrates David and his personal and business successes, just as his father did, while Joan is still insignificant to him except that he views her as a great manipulator and someone whose "needy" behavior is blocking his getaway from the company.

Sam had decided early that he would show his father and mother that he was worthy and would do anything to get the recognition and approval that was never forthcoming from them—his dad in particular. As soon as Sam's parents had both died there was no more reason for him to continue with anything that had to do with the company they started. He doesn't have to keep proving himself to them any longer.

Joan Alice Sampson Bennington

From the moment we spoke with Joan by phone we experienced what was confirmed by others' statements. When she wanted to, she could get everybody irritated and angry with one another, yet at the same time get everybody on her side. For instance, her easy familiarity with Les over the phone could have made Ruth feel left out and upset with Les.

Now, meeting her in person, we are reminded of that earlier feeling. We immediately notice tension coming up between ourselves about her, while at the same time both of us were defending different things about her in our later disagreements. We quickly think how difficult it's going to be to get anything clear, decisive, and permanent from her. We also appreciate the difficulties her brothers—"the boys" of her childhood—and her own children would have had with her. But most important, we begin sensing what Joan has had to give up in order to survive in both her childhood and her adult life.

Joan, at sixty, is a striking-looking woman who is pleasant in her manner and caring in her behaviors. It's easy to be with her except for the irritation between us. She describes the current big problem besetting the family business as "the devastation which would befall everyone if Sam were to actually leave us now." We ask her to say more about what she means by this.

JOAN: Sam has been a good chief and I feel I can trust him where everything is concerned, both in the business and with family stuff. You know, he has always been very good to us ever since Jason died, and he runs the company now without a hitch—especially since Dad died and got out of his way, because they have such different managing styles. If Sam leaves, there's just no one else who can take his place. My older son, Benton, of course thinks he is capable of being the CEO. But he pushes everybody around except Sam. If he were in charge, it would become again just like it was when Dad was screaming at everyone all the time. Sam's different. Oh, I know he doesn't like me—never has, really—but he would never hurt me or my kids.

LES: Joan, you have just given us a lot of information. Let's see if we can go further. First, tell us more about Sam. You sounded scared when you spoke a moment ago. What was that related to, him or to Benton?

JOAN: Well, both, really. Can I speak confidentially to you now? I have never said this to anyone before, but it's time now.

LES: Yes, of course you may, for the time being. However, we might encourage you to talk with others, sometime later on.

JOAN: Okay. This story is probably long overdue. I want to begin with my husband, Jason, and his death. Jason was just like Dad in many ways except that he never finished high school. I loved him a lot, but he was an insecure and edgy person, He often turned to alcohol as a way to calm himself after work. Then things got pretty horrible in our house. I was unable to recognize the depth of his difficulties, because the way he treated us at home was the way I had grown up. When I began to see the kids on the receiving end of his abusiveness, I still couldn't do anything but blame myself—all the while making excuses for him and his behavior. I can talk about these things to you now because I got a lot of help when I went to therapy and Al-Anon after his death.

When Jason turned the tractor over on himself, he was stone drunk, but no one ever knew that except my father and me, not even my mother. No one even knows about this today, especially our kids. I've always made their father out to be a wonderful guy. Certainly I was devastated by his death. But, I have to admit, I was also relieved not to have to keep going through such hell at home. Well, Benton has always blamed me for his father's death and that's a big problem between us.

But wait . . . that isn't all. Sam is a drinker too, a quiet one, but he drinks a lot, especially since Susan left. She just couldn't take it any longer. But nobody in the family talks about Sam's drinking, and I'm not sure most of them even notice it, because he does it after work hours. But I think Marsha knows, and that's why Marsha is always taking care of him, protecting him. . . . Please don't let anyone know about this, okay?

RUTH: But dealing with this problem of Sam's sounds really essential for the health of the business, the family, and Sam himself. We will have to find a way to deal with these issues . . . so what do you suggest?

JOAN: I can tell people, especially Benton, about Jason. Maybe having that information about him would help clear up some things about the past.

RUTH: That will give us a good start. Thanks.

Next, we inquire about how Joan survived her family when she was growing up. She quickly volunteers: "It was easy to get my father on my side, to have him like me, by just being agreeable and always telling him good things about himself. My mother was never any problem; I could talk her into most anything as long as I did it behind Dad's back. Sam was a good guy, so he had no problems with either of our parents. But David took the brunt of everything."

When we ask Joan what outcome she would like to have for herself from the family meeting, she says, "I want the meeting to end with family members liking and respecting me. No one does now, I know that. You have probably already heard a lot of complaints about me. I don't want that to be the case anymore. My life ahead of me is too short! Also, I want Sam to get better and not do things anymore to hurt himself, like the drinking. And I want David and his family to visit us sometimes. That's all . . . except, of course, I want Sam to stay around and keep running the company."

Only on the surface does Joan come across as a flake or a lightweight. It's evident to us that underneath her exterior she is extremely thoughtful and caring about all her family, and she's hurt by her son Benton's contemptuous treatment of her. In other words, she is definitely not as most of the others had described her. Joan has a surprising depth of understanding and experience with looking at herself; these qualities will be very helpful to us in getting at the core of the family's relationship problems.

Marsha Bennington

Marsha, too, seems eager to meet with us. She says she's especially concerned about her Uncle Sam. When we ask her what these concerns are and what she thinks would be the best resolution to them, Marsha replies: "To help my uncle stay alive and continue to run this company."

Startled by her statement, we wonder aloud if she literally means "stay alive" and find out that Sam frequently tells her that his life has been just too hard, that he's feeling sad and miserable, and he just doesn't want "to be here anymore." But does that mean here in the business, or here on Earth? She says she cares deeply about Sam, and her interpretation is that he could easily get rid of himself, especially when he's drinking too much. Sam has been much like a father to her ever since her own father died in that tragic accident. She was only three years old at the time and had never really known her dad very well.

When we ask about her childhood, Marsha reports: "Nothing ever seemed safe or happy, except that I had my sister May, and Sam was around a lot, too. Mom was an emotional mess; she has always clung to Jason, her 'baby boy.' Benton just terrorized all of us, and I still hate him for it. So, May and I made our own private world and just hung out together. We got through fine, and we're still best friends."

Marsha has quickly made the picture clear from her perspective. To this point she has been easy to talk with and cooperative in whatever we've asked. However, when we shift the focus to exploring her current situation and connections with others in the family, she becomes visibly stiff. Noticing how the atmosphere has suddenly turned cold, we silently recall the information from the earlier phase of our explorations—people seemed to know little about Marsha personally. She was seen as integral in the business and helpful to others; yet no one except May had even visited her current home, probably because she'd never invited them to do so.

Our interview ends with our not understanding the abrupt, visible change in Marsha's demeanor. We're baffled at being unable now to penetrate what seems like a personal wall erected between us. We're unsure about what, if anything, this would mean to our work in the future.

May and Randy Taylor

Our next couple of hours are spent with May and Randy at their home. Since they are the parents of four young children, including three-year-old twins, it is easier for them to meet us at their home than to have May escape to the company's office, where Randy himself works. They both come across at once as caring and cooperative parents—a delight for us. May and Randy had requested to be together at the meeting with us because, as May now says, "There is nothing we don't know about each other or wouldn't say with the other one present. After all, we almost grew up together . . . and Randy is practically blood kin."

Randy and May had met when they were just kids, and both worked summers at the company. They have been together ever since. Randy tells us he is in charge of factory and facility operations; he works directly under Benton, who also oversees the field operations. May is a full-time mother and wife. Furthermore, according to Randy, "May holds all of the Sampson family together."

When we inquire what this function involves, May answers: "Well, having good family relationships means a lot to me. First of all, I'm never going to work in that damn company; that's a place Randy can have all to himself—without me! I've seen it wear my parents down, make my brother Benton into a real monster, and it's the only life my sister has. None of that's for me! But I do love all of them in spite of everything, so I try to have all the birthdays and holidays here . . . things like that. Mom just never did any of those things."

When Les wonders if that's all, May easily continues on. "No, that's not all, if you want to know about any of the problems. You see, my brother Benton is a big problem for us, and it's really bad. He insults my husband constantly and he even tried to get him fired. I don't know what to do except tell Marsha sometimes. But that's a problem too, because she seems jealous or something. Since the day Randy and I met, Marsha and Randy have both always sort of wanted me to be just alone with each of them. I try to make it okay, but Marsha is usually hurt. When we were growing up, we were practically inseparable. Now Randy wants her to live her own life, and not hang so much around me. But he understands more about twins now that we have our own twins and he sees how involved they always are with each other."

Then we ask what current problems they're aware of at Sampson Seeds. May and Randy know only that Marsha sometimes has said that Sam seems unhappy with his CEO responsibilities and even with his life, so he's talking about retiring. The biggest thing for them personally, then, is whether Randy could continue to work under Benton and how any management change would affect their own lives.

We also inquire about May's connection with her cousins, and learn that she really likes both Renee, David's daughter, and Sam's daughter, Betty. She remembers all the good times they had as kids together with their grandmother.

In visiting this young couple we get our first real sense of the third-generation Sampson family outside of the workplace. Caring, responsible, and principled people, they express a willingness to do whatever they can if called upon to help. They will attend the scheduled meeting in Carmel so long as, if the children come, they can bring a child care person for them. The company, of course, would need to pay for the expenses of the trip, since finances are a difficult issue at this time in their family-rearing lives.

This interview with the Taylors ended our first full day at the Sampson Seed Company. On the next day we were going to have a breakfast meeting with Jason Jr., to be followed by an interview with Benton and an informational tour of both field and packaging operations. If time allowed, we would also meet with the chief financial officer (CFO), a nonfamily employee and recent hire. We were informed that Benton's wife, Barbara, would be unable to meet with us at this time because she had to attend to other pressing matters.

Jason Bennington Jr.

Our breakfast meeting with Jason goes well. A tall and lean young man, he sees himself as separate and uninvolved with the family business, and most of its interpersonal commotion, and wants it to stay that way. Yes, he and his partner do live with his mother, but that has nothing to do with the company. She has a big house and they have separated it into his art studio, their living quarters, and her living quarters.

We ask about problems he's aware of at the Sampson Seed Company. He doesn't know of any or even care to know; in fact, if anybody wants his stock, they can have it! Sure, he offers his artistic consultation on marketing materials when his mother asks him to do this, but that's the extent of his involvement. He says he'd do just about anything for his mother: after all, she is the only parent he has ever known, because his father died just before he was born.

We want to know about his relationship with his siblings. "The twins are fine persons and were great to grow up with," he replies. "They always had each other, while Mom and I had each other. And as for Benton . . . well, he didn't deserve to have anybody." When asked for more information about his older brother, Jason says: "Benton has always been mean and aggressive with all of us, which includes my mother, and that really makes me angry."

We then ask whether he'll attend the family meeting to take place in Carmel; Jason states that if his mother needs him there and wants him to go, he will, otherwise, no. Finally, we'd like to find out if there's anything else he thinks we should know. "Well," he volunteers, "you probably already heard from others that I am gay. Some of the family would rather see me dead than that way. Benton and Barbara won't even bring the kids over to the house to see Mom because Ryan and I live there with her. I think Marsha may be gay, too; but if so she would never let anybody know it—even me. She keeps saying she is still looking for the 'right man,' but she and Sophie have lived together for the last four years, and I can usually tell these things."

Benton Bennington

We are scheduled to meet Benton in the conference room at 9:30 a.m. When he finally rushes in shortly after 10:00 a.m., we learn that some sort of emergency has occurred; therefore he'll be able to spend only a few short minutes with us. He is only there, he says, because Sam was now down in the plant and had sent him up to talk with us. "So . . . what do you want of me?" he asks sharply. With this one quick interchange, we felt put on the defensive.

RUTH: It sounds like things are hard right now, Benton, so thanks at least for this brief time. What we would like to know is your view of the current problems in the family and the company, plus your view of the solutions. Everyone we have spoken with remarks about your importance here at the company, and of course we would very much value your input.

BENTON: The short of it is that I actually run this place, while Uncle Sam keeps the top stuff together. All of the other family members could be easily replaced, and we'd be better off for it. Sam wants to leave and I'm all for his getting out. He deserves to retire now, and I know I can handle everything once he's gone.

LES: To handle it all sounds like a tall order.

BENTON: No problem, really—at least for me. After all, all my life I've been looking forward to taking over when my turn comes up. I was the very first grandson. I remember how sometimes Grandpa Bill and my dad and I would be out together at sunset, looking at the buildings and the fields beyond them, and Grandpa would always tell me, "Someday this whole spread will be all yours to command, Benton." The way I see it, that time has now arrived.

LES: You mentioned your father. How old were you when he had the accident?

BENTON (in a soft voice now): I was almost seven. I saw it all, you know. Grandpa and I were there just after it happened. It was awful.

RUTH: I'm sure it was terrible for you and that you probably still flash back to that scene. Do you know how it happened? Because your dad must have been a good tractor driver . . .

BENTON: Sure I know! My parents had had a big fight in the afternoon, and my mom—excuse me, I mean Joan—had been really upset at him about something. She was always upset at Dad and I hated her for that. She's not much different now, either.

By now Benton, obviously agitated, is pacing around the room. His voice has been getting louder and louder. He heads toward the door, saying he needs to go now. But he turns back and asks if there is anything else we need to know from him. So we ask what more he wants *us* to know at this point.

BENTON: I want you to know that this company is mine and I intend to keep it that way. I want you to know that my mother interferes with everything and is a total bitch. It was because of her that my dad died and it is because of her that we didn't acquire the farming operation down the road last year . . . and I really needed to get that land! I don't know how she convinced Sam not to buy it, but she sure messed us up.

RUTH: Just before you leave, how about telling us something about your siblings and your cousins? We really appreciate getting your perspective.

BENTON: That won't take long. None of them, including my sister May's husband, count for anything, as you'll see for yourselves. And by the way, my wife Barbara doesn't want my mother to see the kids, since all she does is interfere there, too.

With that final comment, Benton is gone. Of course he has actually told us a lot, stayed longer than he had said he would, and stirred up many feelings within us. His aggressiveness, contempt for others, and anger at his mother have at times been overwhelming. It's clear enough why others in the family dislike and avoid him. But we had also detected a sadness when he spoke about losing his father in his boyhood. It gives us hope that we'll be able ultimately to work with him and to make inroads into his relationships with the other family members.

We won't see Benton again until the meeting in Carmel. Our subsequent tour of the seed company's various facilities, including greenhouse nurseries and fields, is conducted by one of Benton's people—not Randy, whom we had hoped would escort us around. Finally, we check back in with Sam to tell him that things have gone well overall and that we're now setting off for home. When we turn down his attempts to get details and ask more questions, he handles this with understanding. What he really wants to know is that the process is moving ahead, and we've just assured him of that.

MEETING WITH DAVID SAMPSON AND HIS FAMILY

On the following Monday we flew to Phoenix. David had finally consented to our coming to interview him and his family. This change came when May, after our meeting with her and Randy, called her cousin Renee and reported on our conversation and the hopes we had expressed for bringing about a family reconciliation. Renee then had encouraged her father not only to see us, but to introduce us to the whole family.

Arriving late in the day, we are immediately taken to our hotel, where we are given the presidential suite. It turns out that David Sampson owns this small luxury establishment. Dinner is scheduled for 7:00 p.m. at Renee's house, with all of David's family members present. We plan to meet alone with David the next morning.

The evening is great for us, and it also seems very important to everyone there. The whole family is curious to hear anything we could tell them about the others in the larger Sampson clan. We also learn many things about David and his family, which we hadn't been told about before. All four of David and Rose's children are married; there are six grandchildren so far. Rose has never even met some of her nephews and nieces on David's side, while Robert, Randall, and Richard have never seen any of their cousins. David and Renee are the only ones who know the rest of the Sampson clan. Renee knows her female cousins because of her grandmother's efforts during their girlhood to bring them together, and she regularly corresponds with May and Betty. She had even been in both of their weddings.

This is obviously a close family whose members get along well with one another. All the second-generation offspring work together in the family business here in Phoenix. Years earlier, David had joined Rose's father's company, which is now Smithly, Sampson & Sons, or SS&S Development Resources.

Finally, we learn that this entire family has been meeting regularly for several years now with a local family business consultant, who has helped them a lot. Above all, David's four offspring are all very much in favor of our helping to get their father's relationship with his siblings straightened out. The boys say that they've long been aware that their father often seems sad and lonely, especially during holidays, probably because he's cut off entirely from his family of origin.

David William Sampson

At the beginning of the individual meeting with us, David seems hesitant and even fearful. He voices his reluctance to talk with us but says, "I know I have to do this because things sound like they're going to change now. And besides, Rose and Renee both want me to."

DAVID: I'd like to ask first if you two already think the worst of me. I'm sure that when you talked to the others, especially to my brother and sister, they told you I was a pretty bad character!

RUTH: Yes, we have talked with them. But what makes you think that they would give us a negative picture of you?

DAVID: Well, ever since we were little I felt that both Joan and Sam hated me. Now that I think of it, maybe that's because my dad didn't like me at all. For years he really wanted me out of the house, away from the family. And he'd even go after me with this pipe thing he had. (He was sweating a lot now, remembering back.) This is hard to talk about and I have no idea why I am telling you this.

LES: If it's possible, David, could you tell us more about growing up in your family? If that brings up too much pain for you, it is certainly okay to stop at any time.

DAVID: Oh, I can go on. Everyone in my family here has been telling me that I have to do it, to take this opportunity to talk about my childhood, the past. So . . . it seems that I was a problem kid from the start, even though I've always been small and slight in stature just like my mother. As a youngster my father and my siblings made fun of me all the time, and I was always expected to step aside for them. For a long while I tried to do just what Dad wanted, but I never seemed to be able to do it right. At times I'd give up and take the beatings when they came. But more and more I would hide out in the woods, or just anyplace that was away from home. But this would actually make my dad even angrier because he thought I was defying him. So then when I finally did come home he would hit me a lot, and harder. My dad and I got worse and worse with each other, and Joan and Sam seemed to enjoy watching me being punished. But not my mom. When Dad wasn't around, she'd give me lots of love and special treats, as if to make up for not defending me. Dad made it clear that he had just given up on me, as a total embarrassment and a complete failure. So when I finished high school, I just picked up and left it all behind me.

RUTH: How did your mom deal with all of this?

DAVID: She always let me know that she loved me, no matter what, and was sorry about what went on, but that she couldn't do anything about Dad. After I took off, she would write me letters and send me money and gifts, but I was never allowed to contact her at home. I would actually write or call her at her friend's house. When Renee was little, Mom would ask to have her come there and be with the other little-girl cousins. But it always had to be when Dad was away—on a business trip, or hunting or fishing or something.

LES: All of this is really important, David, and I am sorry for all of the pain you have experienced. I have two questions now. First, with all this bad history, how did you end up with one-third of the family company? And second, what can we do to help end the family rifts for you now?

DAVID: The first answer is easy. Mom always promised me that even if she had to divorce my dad, she would see that I got my equal share in the family inheritance. After all, that had been my parents' plan even before I was born, when they started the company. Also, I don't know if you know this, but she sent me some money to get started when Rose and I were married. I don't know whether Dad ever found out about that side money. But Sam knows and has always been angry about it. I think he had always really wanted Mom to look out for his welfare, too . . . even though in our childhood he did a lot better than me on his own. As for your second question, I have no answer for it. This family reconciliation issue is too new for me . . .

Our interview with David ends with his commitment to participate in the family meeting. He's even willing to bring his wife and daughter along if we want them there—which of course we do. He doubts if any of his sons will be able to come. As we walk out of David's office to head for home, David comments: "Wow, you guys don't mess around, do you?"

Rose and Renee, who drive us to the airport, have enthusiastically agreed to come to the Carmel meeting. Our visit to this branch of the family has left us both saddened and heartened. David still suffers enormous pain from the past treatment by his family of origin. Feeling misunderstood, betrayed, and rejected by both his father and his siblings, he desperately needs validation for his experience. For us, though, the situation seems hopeful. With the support of his current family and a lot of courage, David is willing to take emotional risks and participate further. We also know from our talks with Joan and Sam that for the first time in many years they seemed willing to include David in their lives.

At this time, two important contacts remain for us: Sam's children, Betty Simmons and her brother, Bill Sampson II. We have already scheduled a phone conversation with Betty at midday tomorrow, but we are still trying to locate Bill. According to his father, young Bill is traveling around the West Coast with his surfboard in tow—"He's twenty-two years old and a real adventurer, that one!" He didn't have a clue as to where we might catch him.

Betty Simmons

Over the phone Sam's daughter comes across to us as bright, articulate, and fiercely protective of her mother. She makes it clear that she is determined to never again cross paths with her father, whom she describes as, "a wimpy, mean drunk who always makes his plight everyone else's fault—especially Mom and me." As we explore this experience-based attitude with her, we never hear even a crack in her rigid perception of her growing-up years. Actually, she sounds a lot *like* her father in his pronouncements, and we can't help wondering if we'll ever be successful in helping either one of them to move out of their tightly held corners.

Basically, Betty is unaware of, or uninformed about, anything currently going on in the company and any problems in management. However, she definitely wants to remain a shareholder so as to have something "to pass along" to her children. "It's a really dependable moneymaker, right?" she says. But she says rather firmly she'd never consider attending any meeting that her father is involved in. When asked why, she answers: "I wouldn't be able to hang on to myself and keep all the anger from coming out. Then everyone will blame me for being such a bitch. I know, because this has happened many times in the past. That whole family loves my dad. No one knows how he really treated us. To the outside world, though, he seems like such a good guy."

At this point, we accept this impasse, having decided that no immediate reason exists to push anything with reconciling father and daughter. We have plenty of other interpersonal issues to handle already. Betty is doing fine in her own married life and, pregnant with her second child, she has many plans for the future. However, we do mark this fractured relationship as a possible future target for reconciliation, when and if Betty and Sam are more ready for it.

William Sampson II

We never succeed in contacting young Bill so that we might meet with him in person before the family meeting. He continues on with his travels, which are fully financed by his father, apparently only checking in when he wants more funds. Sam obviously has no difficulty with indulging his son. In fact, he seems to vicariously enjoy Bill's footloose, adventuresome activities. It's as if he himself is gearing up to a similar opportunity to roam without any responsibilities in the world or any obligation toward anyone else—a state of being that he has never yet achieved, dutiful son that he has always been.

But we are expecting Bill to be at the upcoming family meeting because Sam has promised him that at Carmel he would have ample time for surfing.

Returning home at last, we are now prepared to move ahead with specific planning for the four-day Sampson family meeting. We have completed our in-person contacts with the available and willing family members and must now begin planning for what is to happen when we finally bring everyone together as a large family unit. As is usual for us, the long, intensive get-together will include a combination of group, subgroup, and individual sessions. These are set up according to the goals of the reconciliation but also will be flexible enough to accommodate the emerging and possibly urgent needs at any time.

An incredible amount of planning and evaluating work lies ahead of us in the coming month, and we are experiencing much pressure to get it done quickly. Time seems to be running out for Sam. He's anxious to get the matter of his successor decided, and nobody in the family appears to favor the idea of Benton taking over—except, of course, for Benton himself. It is imperative for us to respond to this problematic situation to the best of our abilities. Addressing it has brought the Sampsons' various relationship conflicts and ruptures, past and present, to the foreground of our own attention.

Even the Sampsons themselves are beginning to understand that Sam's desire to leave the family-owned company is not *The Problem:* it has only served as the trigger to get professional help. The real problem is far more complex and lies much deeper in various people's current discordant relationships with one another. So the solution to the business predicament must necessarily come from reconciliation of as many of these family rifts as possible.

In the next week we will begin spending many hours processing, individually and together as a team, everything we learned, experienced, and hypothesized about the Sampsons, their interpersonal connections, and the family business itself in which they all have shares and some of them have jobs or positions on the board of directors.

To prepare the Sampsons for participating in the meeting we will send all the future attendees some reading materials and additional questions to think about. We will also ask them to take the self-scoring Myers-Briggs Type Indicator inventory (MBTI). The MBTI provides a useful and gentle way of understanding family members, their similarities and their differences, by looking at personality preferences, and considering the strengths and weaknesses of each personality style within the organizational setting and the family. Family members will complete these on their own and bring them to the first session of the Carmel meeting.

When putting together the relationship puzzle of the Sampson family, we have noted that distinct differences exist between the family members' impressions of themselves and others and our direct observations of them. Significantly, what is *missing or not said* by family members is just as important as, if not more than, what *is* covered in conversations. We won't ignore these discrepancies.

One of the great challenges in planning for a family group meeting that will go on for several days is anticipating different scenarios that may occur, based on acquired knowledge of the individual family members as well as our considerable experience of moderating previous family-reconciling meetings.

We have learned a lot about the Sampson family in a short time and as we think ahead we are aware of the following: in spite of warnings to the contrary, most of the people we met were open and willing to talk about themselves; there were important secrets that really weren't secrets, such as Sam's drinking and secrets that really were secrets, such as the stories surrounding Jason's life and death; the family had its beginnings in an oppressive system and currently is both disengaged and fragmented.

It becomes clear that at least some of our task will be to create opportunities for the secrets to come out in a safe atmosphere and to help family members learn to manage their feelings and stay present in the face of Benton's anticipated outbursts. All of this is a challenge but not uncommon when working from a reconciliation framework.

Chapter 7

Stage II: Reconsider

Afterward, we never spoke again until years later when we finally talked and she apologized. Now, I've stopped hurting and I've even stopped hating her.

A client

Reconciliation in family business relationships occurs when, after a period of alienation, people make a commitment to work out their differences and create a shared future. Relationships can be reconciled when family members reconsider the past through collectively restoring memory for the purposes of validating experiences, rebuilding an individual's sense of sanity, worth, and dignity, and repairing interpersonal bonds.

Healing begins when people who feel misunderstood, undervalued, or wronged by others can reconsider the past by talking to relatives about the events and interactions that created personal wounds and discord. As family members listen and validate experiences, they begin to recover a sense of self, self-worth, and personal power. Acknowledgment of the past is critical in conflict-ridden business-owning families if they are to build unity and commitment for the future.

Reflecting again on the relevance of the monumental reconciliation efforts in South Africa, we quote Archbishop Desmond Tutu:

> To pursue the path of healing, we need to remember what we have endured. . . . We recognize that the past can't be remade through punishment. Instead—since we know memories will persist for a long time—we aim to acknowledge those memories. This is critical if we are to build a democracy of self-respecting citizens. (Tutu, cited in Greer, 1998, p. 6)

165

Reconciling differences and repairing relationships can sometimes be a laborious process. To busy people it may appear, annoyingly, to interfere with "the business of the business." Yet it is often crucial to the viability of the family business in both the near and far futures.

Advisors who work with reconciling relationships have tremendous power to affect the business-owning family and the business they share. We are called upon to explain the behaviors of family members and to define what is happening and why. We are allowed to ask questions about the details of the most important and treasured parts of people's lives. Our questions open up dark areas, suggest causes of problems, and point toward solutions. We have the power to lead the family toward healing and the power to create enormous harm. How we use that power is up to each one of us and our professional ethics and expertise.

This chapter presents the most important tools for use in reconsidering and repairing the past to achieve reconciliation in damaged relationships. These tools can help validate individual experiences and foster the acquisition of knowledge and understanding of others, resulting in empathy toward them. If used carelessly or without knowledge the tools for reconsidering the past can do harm. However, if applied with care and trained excellence they can lead people toward repairing vital relationships. This will allow family members to move ahead with one another in newly cooperative attitudes and actions that support both the family as a unit and the business it conducts.

TOOL #1: PROVIDE A SAFE PLACE

Reconsidering the past is a difficult and emotionally stressful process and is best accomplished when people are sheltered from their usual work and family environments. When distractions are eliminated and family members can totally focus on the tasks of telling their own stories and listening to the others, the work of reconciling ruptured relationships and repairing family-connected wounds has the greatest opportunity of being completed. Reconsidering and repairing the past asks people to face themselves and their family members—a task which requires incredible internal resources and constant attention to the process and people involved.

To be successful it is necessary to work with families away from the office and in an environment that is neutral for all participants. Many times we have been invited to families' homes, summer cabins, and even resorts owned by the family. Although this clearly reduces financial expenses, the emotional expenses and the challenges to our leadership can be far too great. We need to be in charge of the working environment and in control of any outside interference.

In taking charge and defining the working environment we also require limited and set times when family members, even executives, can have phone or e-mail contact with their business or other situations. More times than not, some critical relationship change has been sacrificed when a business issue or crisis, news of a court case, or a call from an accountant has been allowed to intrude. In addition, when working to achieve reconciliation, we even ask that younger children be either left at home or else with a trusted baby-sitter who is brought along to care for them while their parents are engaged in reconciliation work.

It is also important to provide the environment for informal socializing as well as undisturbed time outside the group. This free time needs to be planned for and protected, since this is when family members have an opportunity to rest and restore themselves, become newly acquainted with one another, and get ready for the next important steps in the reconciliation effort.

The reasons for taking the family away from their accustomed places apply regardless of the amount of time allowed for the family meeting. Whether working together for four hours, four days, or several weeks, we require that the family get away from the inevitable clamor and demands of their everyday lives. We also take care of family members by making sure that food and other creature comforts are supplied to ease this most difficult journey they are taking with themselves and other family members.

TOOL #2: ESTABLISH GROUND RULES

Ground rules empower family members, making them more able to go ahead with difficult tasks. Ground rules for participating in the reconciliation process are set prior to getting the family together.

Since we are most interested in an informed and conscious commitment to the reconciliation process, everyone in the family is asked to carefully consider the rules well in advance of their attendance at the family meeting.

We establish ground rules to give power to participants and to protect them from breaches of confidentiality, shame, personal attacks, interruptions, and other harmful acts. We ask that family members respect one another through prompt and total attendance at the meetings, unless a prior arrangement was made for them to do something else. All family members are expected to abide by the rules during every aspect of the process. Whenever a violation of these rules occurs, it becomes the most immediate issue to be confronted and worked with.

Since each family situation is unique, different ground rules may need to be established to accommodate different family circumstances. However, in general, here is a set of commonly applied operating principles for the reconciliation process.

- The entire reconciliation process is confidential, and all information, whether acquired inside or outside of the planned meetings, will be held in highest regard and in strictest confidence.
- Each person will treat every other person with respect and be available to help other family members do likewise.
- Each person will ask for what he or she needs.
- Each person will take responsibility for his or her own behavior.
- Each person will be held accountable to others for his or her own behavior.
- Each person will accept every other family member as equal in family relationships.
- All family members will make themselves available for the entire meeting and participate fully to the end of the process.
- Everyone agrees that the facilitators are in charge and will accept their direction when it is needed to ensure safety.
- Each person will take all opportunities to extend himself or herself in supportive and positive ways to other family members.

Knowing that all the other participants have agreed in principle to the ground rules provides an initial sense of safety in taking part in the meetings, which usually are regarded in advance with apprehension by everyone. Ground rules, along with controlling the meeting environment, are a way to help establish the facilitators as leaders of the reconciliation sessions. This again is an important element in reassuring family members that they will be protected during the difficult process of revealing themselves.

Moreover, ground rules actually serve as a test of sorts for the participants. How a family member reacts to the rules and whether or not they are followed or ignored are predictors of the future. Family members who show themselves as repeatedly uninterested or unwilling to cooperate with problem-solving efforts are unlikely to be able to change in desired directions. Since present behavior is known to be one of the best indicators of future behavior, how family members, regardless of their current position in the family or the business, handle the rules is certainly an important indicator of suitability for future positions.

TOOL #3: PROVIDE CONTINUOUS SUPPORT

As facilitators enabling a family reconciliation, we constantly provide strong support by helping family members face not only their own fears but also the uncertainties brought about by the presence of persons they feel and believe have hurt them. Advisors need to understand the full meaning of support and what is involved in supporting family members throughout the process of healing relationship wounds.

Providing support requires: a willingness to take an active approach in guiding the reconciliation efforts; a solid professional base, which includes a sense of timing the interventions; skills in bringing up difficult issues; an ability to confront harmful interactions, contain conflict, and manage angry escalation; confident ease with the work of constantly reassuring and affirming family members; and a plentiful supply of time, energy, and patience.

Active support keeps the family participating in relationship problem solving; it is the vehicle for maintaining safety in a process that requires effort from all. Support encourages learning and openness. It allows family members to express what they know and who they are. Inactivity in any of the dimensions of support usually magnifies relationship problems and can quickly lead to discouragement and even harm.

Support has many different faces. Frequently we support individuals, sometimes even before they have agreed to participate in reconciliation efforts, by rehearsing with them ahead of time. Before facing other family members we help them collect their inner resources and prepare ahead for scenarios with both the worst and the best possible outcomes. We are also supportive during the meeting period itself when we offer alternative working environments that allow people to ready themselves for making striking disclosures and major changes in front of the entire family. Thus we suggest variants such as meeting one-on-one or in family dyads or other small-group configurations where participants will feel more at ease. These smaller meetings also serve as a safety measure for mitigating shame. In the Sampson family reconciliation, we changed group configurations on a regular basis, according to what the issues were at the moment and what configuration would best allow us to achieve success.

Finally, we are supportive when we take on issues and individuals that the family itself has not yet been able to manage. Only through a willingness to confront the real problems, head-on if necessary, can advisors keep themselves out of the objectionable roles of "rescuer" or "beneficiary" of the family and its difficulties. Creating an atmosphere in which family members can speak the truth and hear the truth as other family members know it requires paying deliberate attention to the deceptions and avoidance that set the stage for continued distrust. It takes an aware, committed, and supportive facilitator to continually confront uncomfortable subject matter and interpersonal violations.

TOOL #4: ACKNOWLEDGE MEMORIES

When everything about safety, support, and preparation comes together, we are ready to help people tell their stories and speak their truth. This process, which allows those involved in conflict situations to safely present themselves, their feelings, and their memories, is the central step in reconciliation and healing relationships in business-owning families.

Ample psychological research has produced evidence that people begin to recover emotionally when they are allowed to express their own stories and receive validation for their experiences. Recent research has demonstrated that the process of repairing ruptured relationships promotes individual personality maturation; through reconciliation people take steps toward creating new internal models of themselves (Lewis, 2000). Therefore, since one of the greatest assets of the family business is its individual family members, achieving reconciliation surely will add to the human capital of the family.

When people speak about the circumstances and the injuries they believe they have sustained, personal healing begins. Telling one's personal story is especially productive when it is done in the presence of family members who are believed by the storyteller to have wronged or misjudged them. Yet talking candidly and articulately when deep emotions are involved is an incredibly difficult thing to do. Advisors facilitating reconciliation can aid family members in this complex and trying endeavor by: controlling the storytelling environment; respectfully requesting additional information when needed; and constantly expressing genuine support, encouragement, and appreciation for all those involved in the efforts.

Since birth we have all told ourselves stories about ourselves, about our history, and about the environment around us. Our personal stories serve to orient, guide, and sustain us because they help us explain to ourselves the events that have happened to us in our own particular world. Telling ourselves stories also assists us in making sense of the unexpected and in establishing some predictability in circumstances that otherwise might seem random or even chaotic. The content of our personal stories is based in and around our early decisions and is congruent with the way we see ourselves and behave with others.

In this reconsidering stage we focus on understanding current conflicts by drawing parallels with the past and acknowledging the memories of related events. Since past experiences are reenacted in present discords, our goal is to shift the focus to also include earlier difficulties that have inflicted the present wounds. Through acknowledging past memories we allow for a resolution of the problem at its roots and a broader range of solutions to the current issue. Further benefits occur when family members involved in the original problem situation are present. It allows dialoguing and a new story, a collective truth, to be built. Then everyone is still together in the whole story, but in a much different way.

Amazing power and release are experienced when people speak their own truth, thereby freeing themselves from early decisions and the surrounding stories of the past. When old stories are updated and new stories are constructed, individuals make redecisions about themselves, others, and the world they live in.

We have found the following procedures to be particularly useful in helping family members speak their truth:

- Obtain a detailed account of the problem from participants on all sides of the story. Since it is important to us to minimize surprises at the family meeting, this account may be obtained in individual meetings prior to getting everyone together. It should include such information as: why or how this relationship is a problem; how often and in what form the conflict occurs; an account of the history of the relationship rupture and its consequences; and the storyteller's historical and current reactions.
- Begin by outlining areas of relationship strength and then lead the storyteller slowly into the major areas of difficulty. This makes it easier for both the teller and the listeners to manage their own feelings.
- Always focus on the relationship itself as the problem rather than any person or group of people.
- Keep constant control of the overall process by deciding who will begin, who will follow, and when dialoguing will occur.
- Manage the storytelling by: keeping people in the first person; staying on point and halting any sidetracking; stopping any personal attacks or blaming; and leading people to related historical events which contribute to the present distress.
- Frequently point out individual strengths and use them on behalf of the future.
- Always, always be sure there is enough time to complete the process.

TOOL #5: TEACH PEOPLE TO LISTEN—
TO LEARN AND UNDERSTAND

Reconciling relationships requires change on behalf of all participants, and change begins with new learning and understanding about oneself and others. Listening to learn and understand is first of all about being cognizant of what you are thinking and feeling while someone else is talking. It is about managing yourself when you perceive that you are being attacked and maybe feeling in need of defending yourself. It is about hearing important information even when you are feeling uncomfortable.

Listening to learn and understand is also about hearing others in a considerate, caring, and respectful way. Through listening with interest and sensitivity, however, anyone who wishes can develop awareness of and appreciation for others in the family who are different from themselves.

Listening carefully and intently requires intention, willingness, and keeping oneself emotionally separate from the problems being expressed. It is aided by keeping in mind these tenets:

• People are not the problem; the relationship is the problem.
• People are more important than things.

These points frequently need to be emphasized over and over again. When people manage to stay separate and distinct from feeling accused and accusing themselves, they are better able to understand others and to discover what part they have played in the hurt and pain experienced by others.

Family business members who participate in the reconciliation process often have a large personal and even financial stake in its outcome. Therefore, many are extremely challenged to manage their own emotional responses while also acquiring new learning and understanding of others. Managing feelings during a highly charged encounter is a skill that few people seem to come by naturally. However, it can be learned, and therefore taught.

Many easy stress-reduction techniques can be used while listening to others. Therefore, before going ahead with the actual reconsidering of the relationship, we teach listeners how to listen by reviewing techniques that will help them hear uncomfortable things about themselves. One technique is to help people define nurturing statements that they can use to soothe themselves under stress. Most important, though, we emphasize that while hearing others out, each family member needs to hold onto his or her own personal values, truths, and particular vision of the family business.

It is easier for people to listen and understand others when they start with smaller issues and work up to the more emotionally charged problems. It is always less stressful to listen to and manage one's own feelings on the small things. People are usually afraid to both tell their truth and also to hear the truth from others. They are afraid of many things such as being exposed and looking weak or foolish, losing face, and being proven wrong.

As professionals we learn to listen with the "third ear" by focusing on what happens first, what happens next, and then what leads to the next interaction. This is a most important function. Along with noting what is said, to whom, and in what tone of voice, we need to be aware of what wasn't said and, therefore, what is missing that should be there. This knowledge directs us in the next steps and in rebuilding relationships. Finally, we also need to recognize and point out what doesn't match between what is seen and heard. We pay close attention to the nonverbal messages and responses, such as facial expressions, gestures, and movements—the "body language" of both the speakers and listeners.

Monitoring while listening is an immensely important job because facilitators need to respond rapidly and assertively to any insensitive remarks and intrusions. Interruptions in storytelling need to be stopped immediately and listeners helped to continue containing themselves. Defensive statements, counterattacks, and discounts such as "I cannot believe he said that" have no place in problem-solving efforts. Finally, in managing the environment, advisors must always make sure that people are allowed to follow through to the completion of their story. Astute management of the situation helps to provide safety and protection against additional wounding from others' remarks and behavior, as well as exposure and shame in the family. It is a way of taking care of each and every one involved.

TOOL #6: ORCHESTRATE RESPONSIVE
AND RESPECTFUL DIALOGUE

Dialoguing is a joint process in which relationships begin to develop new meaning. Up until this point, the reconsidering process has focused on hearing and understanding the storyteller's monologue—the individuals' ready-made interpretation of interpersonal events that have negatively impacted them. It is now time to shift the focus to developing a shared form of communication aimed at building different understanding and new alliances.

Dialogue directed toward increased knowledge and understanding of one another and the relationship happens after family members have had sufficient opportunity to define and express themselves through telling their stories. In dialoguing, attention is first paid to clarifying points and understanding the person who has just been the storyteller. This is done when responders reflect what they have heard and understood and then ask for clarification of things from the initiator of the story. Second, attention is paid to the impact of the story on others—listeners' perceptions at the time of the storytellers' distress and what they think, feel, and plan to do now with this new knowledge. Dialoguing is frequently a long, intensive, and extensive exchange leading to a new common understanding and collective truth.

The dialogue at this stage of the reconsideration is carefully structured and strictly focused. Following are some guidelines for facilitating effective family dialogue directed toward achieving reconciliation:

- Develop a common understanding of the problem and build an agreement on how the troubled relationship might be repaired.
- Utilize reflective listening and conversation by frequently summarizing what has been said and checking out whether or not things have been heard correctly.
- Identify needs, wants, and questions of the participants.
- Teach people how to respond differently than they customarily would to someone's given point of view, and how to ask for more information so as to better understand and support others.
- Reframe issues in positive ways, which no longer allow any family member to see things in the negative way of the past.

- Create options and proposals for rebuilding trust, such as what each participant could do to begin building the relationship in a new and collaborative direction.

People, often unconsciously, effectively block successful dialoguing by using passivity, discounting, blaming, overemotional responses, overrational discourse, needless detailing, generalizing, and trying to incite arguments. Whatever the block, it must be recognized, identified, and removed by the facilitator, who then can replace it with an alternative way to move the dialogue along toward reconciliation.

Many people need help in participating suitably in family dialogues. In addition to dealing with blocking behaviors, we help family members identify and talk about their "normal" responses to others, such as starting to argue and defend themselves, or automatically trying to fix things to alleviate the tension in and around them. This is a way of aiding them in adopting new ways of responding. We also emphasize, over and over again, that expressing feelings, especially anger, is constructive since it is about having a voice, making differences known, and defining oneself. The focus of the advisor is not on stifling feelings but on helping people manage the ways they express themselves. Learning new and different ways of expression usually leads to better understanding, acceptance, and positive self-esteem.

Advisors should help participants stay in touch with their strengths as individuals, family members, and business members, plus their own personal values about how they want to be during these difficult discussions. Nurturing and protecting the sense of positive self-esteem for everyone involved in the dialogue leads to a mending of the relationship wounds and a productive resolution of the interpersonal conflict. As a final point, we emphasize the vulnerability of people involved in the reconciliation effort and focus on helping people make caring responses.

Simply stated, the job of facilitating the dialogue in reconciliation processes involves helping all family members take responsibility for their own change while understanding, helping, and crediting others in their family.

TOOL #7: HELP PARTICIPANTS APOLOGIZE
AND MOVE TOWARD FORGIVENESS

When ruptured relationships exist within a business-owning family, individuals, as well as the family and the business, are at risk. Failure to reconcile unresolved feelings of anger, blame, and hurt can cause not just significant business problems, but also both physical and deep-seated emotional problems for individual family members. Current literature (Gordon and Baucom, 1998) reveals an increasing interest in apologies and the nature of forgiveness and their importance for physical health, emotional well-being, and relationship repair.

Apologizing and forgiving are behaviors of choice—transitional acts that aid family members in reestablishing necessary goodwill, rebuilding relationships, and refocusing on the future. They are opposite sides of the same coin. Who needs to do what, and when, are really questions of who is willing and able to move first to resolve issues for the common good.

Making an apology is a decision to take responsibility for one's behavior and be accountable to others for what you have done, intentionally or unintentionally. Forgiving, first an internal and then an interpersonal act, is a decision to release oneself from anger and grief and then to reenter the relationship. Sincere apologies and forgiveness cannot be structured or demanded in the reconciliation process; ultimately both must arise naturally from the participants.

It is critical for all involved in the reconciliation process to understand what these verbal testimonies mean so that they can be supported and brought forth as genuine offerings. Family members need to know that they are not going to "lose face" if they apologize to or forgive their adversary . . . or do both.

Apologies

An apology is a form of restitution for injuries inflicted, whether unintentional or intended, that symbolizes a willingness to return the relationship to a shared power status. Apologies open the door and invite injured family members to reenter the relationship and regain self-esteem and relationship power.

Making an apology is a choice, which hopefully is given freely and made with sincerity. Apologies are neither excuses nor perfunctory "I'm sorry, now let's move on" statements. Real apologies are expressions of regret for having said or done something that created problems for another person. Apologies say, "I recognize my own behavior and take responsibility for my actions and I know that the impact my behavior had on others was injurious to them."

Apologies are necessary for individual healing and reconciliation of differences. The balance of power in the relationship system was disrupted and apologies help return that relationship balance to an equally shared state. Apologies open the channels to forgiveness and rebuilding trust. In fact, in restoring justice it is the combination of acknowledgment, validation, and apology that make forgiveness even possible. Apologies also make it easier for collaboration to be renewed in a family business relationship, because persons have regained a sense of influence and control within the relationship and feel safer to move on and rebuild the working relationship.

Unfortunately, for some who abuse their power and are seeking even more power, apologizing is not an option. Nor are these same persons interested in receiving anyone's forgiveness, since they are unlikely ever to admit to having done anything seriously hurtful or wrong. When this is the circumstance advisors sometimes need to step in to indicate the grim scenario that will probably ensue if a family member, especially one in a controlling position in the business, refuses to accept responsibility for hurting others in the family.

Forgiveness

The ability to forgive evolves over time and is an internal and, if chosen, an interpersonal act. Internally, forgiveness involves strengthening the inner self by taking less personal offense, reducing anger and blaming, and acquiring increased understanding of situations that formerly led to feelings of shame, hurt, and anger. Interpersonal forgiveness involves pardoning but never condoning another person's violations.

To forgive means to release one's judgments and feelings about the motives and character of others who are perceived to have caused harm. Forgiveness allows individuals to stop dwelling on the negative; it does not mean that the past is forgotten. In fact, many relationship violations are never forgotten, but with forgiveness the violations begin to occupy a different internal space that shields people from being so vulnerable to new wounding.

Moreover, forgiving does not mean that future hurtful acts done by persons who caused earlier afflictions will be excused, avoided, or ignored. Nor does it mean that permission is given for relationships to go back to the way they were before, or that past offenders are now freed from accountability for their actions. Instead, forgiving is a conscious choice to release oneself from the burden of anger and resentment, as well as from an overwhelming preoccupation with hurts, which for some people can be an obsession. Forgiveness can also help others release themselves from the anger they hold toward themselves for having participated in the problem, if only as bystanders.

The value of forgiveness stands on a solid clinical and ethical foundation. Clinically, it is based on information on recovery from stress and trauma. For many people with religious beliefs, forgiveness is well embedded in their conscience or ethics. When given freely, forgiveness reduces interpersonal hurts and creates an environment of positive intention and interaction. Forgiveness is also a tool, which in family business situations, facilitates the rebuilding of trust and the development of collaborative teams at the top.

Genuine forgiveness empowers individuals and releases the family from the stranglehold of the constant replay of hurts and resentments. Forgiveness moves the family forward because it diminishes the negative effects of those inevitable relationship ruptures and therefore helps family members focus on the present and the future.

Every business-owning family will struggle, many times over, to recover from interpersonal traumas. When the goal is reconciliation it is important to keep in mind that *forgiveness is a desirable but not an essential ingredient.* As facilitators we know that after reconsidering the relationship people can, and often do, choose to collaborate effectively, yet never forgive. On the other hand, some family members choose to forgive but never again join the family business team; in this way they remain in their family but are lost as resources to the business.

TOOL #8: CONSIDER THE FUTURE

The last step in Stage II is to help create an open dialogue based on the shared reality of the reconsidered relationship. This step attends to the form of the communication that occurs within the family and aims to guide the conversation between people as they consider their future together as competent and capable partners.

Family business members usually need help and support in adjusting to both the system and the individual changes that hopefully result from reconsidering relationships. By helping people talk about and plan their shared future and noting where major problems will arise, we transition to the next stage of reconciliation: rebuilding relationships. We prepare the family members to learn to carry themselves successfully into the future through educating them about techniques for enhancing their communication processes and predicting some of the pitfalls in the long journey ahead.

In summary, what governs the future success of the family business is the business-owning family's ability to reconsider and repair relationships, and move ahead to nurture and protect the sense of positive self-esteem for each and every family member. "True self-esteem is a genuine sense of one's self as worthy of nurturance and protection, capable of growth and development" (Basch, 1988, p. 24).

Interlude 3: The Heart of the Work

We are just one week away from the scheduled meeting in Carmel with the assembled Sampson family. Over the past month we have worked to carefully prepare ourselves and the family for getting together, reconciling the relationship rifts, and resolving the important problem of Sam's intended departure from the family company. Tensions are high as evidenced by the enormous number of phone calls we have been fielding. With the exception of the funerals of their parents, the principal Sampsons have not met together for over thirty years. Everyone in their own way has needed reassurance and support, for it takes both courage and conviction to confront the converging past and present, to face estranged family members, and oneself in the process.

The two of us are about as ready as we can possibly be. First, we have checked and rechecked the facilities where we'll be meeting and the family will be staying. We've done as much as possible to make sure that everyone will be comfortable and have their personal needs met. Private meeting rooms have been secured, and there will be plenty of space for getting together in both the large and smaller groups, and also time and a place for being alone when someone chooses to be.

As for ourselves, for four days we will be spending most of our waking time with the Sampson family, observing, connecting, working, but occasionally resting from the sure-to-be-intense conversations and some probable collisions.

As a result of our initial contacts and information gathering, we have defined the overall focus of the meeting. Everyone has agreed and contracted to work on these goals:

1. To work toward reconciling relationships within the Sampson family's three second-generation members
2. To work toward reconciliation of the relationships within the Bennington family

3. To encourage connection and communication among the third generation, both siblings and cousins

4. To begin establishing mutually agreed-upon plans and structures for the future operation and governance of the Sampson Seed Company

Our task will be large, and we already know that it will not be completed when we finish on the coming Sunday afternoon. However, we are hopeful of successfully planting the seeds of change. By the time the four-day session ends, individuals and relationships are bound to be different.

Our plan had been for all of the shareholders in the third generation and their spouses to be in attendance. However, not entirely to our surprise, Barbara had refused to participate, and Benton expressed her position when he told us that "there is no way my wife will be subject to my other family members and their problems." Randall and Richard would both be out of the country on their own family's business. Both Betty and Sam had, as we expected, continued to refuse to be together in any way.

These twelve family members would be present:

Joan Sampson Bennington	David Sampson
Benton Bennington	Rose Sampson
Marsha Bennington	Renee Sampson
May Bennington Taylor	Robert Sampson
Randy Taylor	Sam Sampson
Jason Bennington	William (Bill) Sampson II

To prepare for their arrival and participation, each person completed the self-scoring Myers-Briggs Type Indicator inventory, or MBTI. We had also asked each of them to focus on themselves and the kind of person that they would like to be during these four intense days. In numerous ways we have reminded and rereminded everyone that reconciliation is about "Being the kind of person you want to be, in your own eyes, and repairing interpersonal bonds with your family members."

We have summarized what we know and don't know so far about the Sampsons, individually, relationally, and collectively. We have outlined the issues that need to be covered to help this family reach their stated goals, and we have made our initial guesses about how to structure the meeting in order to meet both family and individual needs and goals.

Our contacts thus far have enabled us to summarize what we now know:

- The second-generation members, even though they grew up in the same household, have never really bonded. Because their family-of-origin system worked to pit them against one another, Joan, David, and Sam learned to survive "each on their own." One focus will be to create common ground through mutual understanding and validation within the sibling system. Right now their only point of relationship is through their mutual ownership of Sampson Seed Company.
- The male members of the third generation are essentially strangers to everyone, except within the individual sibling systems, and the female members know only a little about one another.
- Sam is devaluing his life and has made a loud cry for help for himself and the company he has successfully nurtured for years, both before and after his father's death several years ago. We will need to focus on helping Sam find a meaningful future for himself and encourage supportive family connections.
- The financial information and the company forecast, which we have seen, show that they are presently doing well and are well positioned for the future.
- Joan is much different than she appears; we will need to help her show her real self.
- David suffers deep emotional pain and is ready to reunite with his family of origin. Fortunately, he has a very caring and supportive nuclear family and has numerous major business successes of his own.
- Everyone sees Benton as a serious problem and a threat to any family accord and company morale, even though he is apparently competent in his job. We will need to deal directly with this threat and help him gain others' trust through changing his attitude and behavior. At some point, Barbara, Benton's wife, will need to be integrated into the greater family.

- Marsha, a person with total access to all company information and the inside ear of the CEO, is very guarded, sketchy, and protective of her private life.
- May, well regarded by everyone, is a very important cohesive force in the cousins' generation. We will want to use her as a resource.
- Bill is immature and indulged, and no one, including his father, considers him important for the future of Sampson Seed Company. However, we also know that Bill could someday be a major shareholder in the third generation, depending on his father's decisions regarding selling his shares in the family business.

ARRIVAL

The convergence period of the four-day family meeting is difficult and stressful. Everyone except Benton has arrived on the evening before we are scheduled to start. Still, no one except May, Marsha, and Renee, who knew each other as girls and have stayed in contact, choose to connect before our officially scheduled morning meeting. Family members are obviously avoiding one another, and the nonverbal tensions are high.

We have made brief contacts with everyone except Bill, whom we still haven't even met. He is nowhere to be found, but according to Sam he's down at the ocean with his surfboard. Our purpose this evening is to make sure that everyone is comfortable and to observe, when possible, any unstructured interactions. Therefore, we view with relief and delight "the girls" giggling as they remember their times together years ago with their grandmother, Marsha. We are saddened that Betty isn't here to share in the connection among the cousins. We saw her as clearly interested in being included in her cousins' fun, but this reunion will just have to wait.

DAY ONE: MORNING

We planned to begin the family meeting at 9:00 a.m. with everyone in attendance together. However, Benton still hadn't arrived, and Sam said he told Bill he didn't have to be there. Our aim was to begin the session by establishing some common positive purposes. We wrote each person's responses to our written questionnaire on a flip chart where everybody could see "the three most important resolutions that you want to occur in these four days." Everybody was curious about what the others wanted, making it possible for us to begin to point out the similarities and points of agreement.

In addition, we planned to do some initial communications work: talking about similarities and differences and surprises by focusing on results from the MBTI personality inventory.

Benton arrives shortly before we are due to take the morning break. Luckily, we haven't yet begun the communications work. During the break we send Sam to find Bill. Privately, we've made it clear to Sam that it's his responsibility to require Bill's attendance at each session unless we announce ahead of time that Bill's presence is not needed. Before resuming we also take the opportunity to speak privately with Benton and remind him about his commitment to participate fully. Benton does not yet grasp how much he has to gain by being cooperative.

In the information packet sent to all participants several weeks before the meeting, we had included the ground rules for getting together and creating a successful outcome. Benton, Bill, and Sam appeared defiant and openly challenged our leadership through their disregard for our request that everyone be present at the start. It was imperative for us to respond immediately as we did at the break.

When we enter the meeting room to resume the first session, many family members are just standing or sitting quietly staring at the floor. Renee and Rose surround David, Jason hangs close to Joan, and Sam sits alone, while Benton and Bill chat loudly as they pace together in the back of the room. We ask everyone to sit down and proceed with verbally preparing the group for what is to come in the days ahead. We then recap the ground rules and ask for public acceptance of these rules, done person by person—only securing it reluctantly from Benton and Bill.

With this initial procedural business over, we ask people to relate a positive experience they had in the past when summoning up their courage to participate in a difficult process. Robert is particularly helpful when he relates his experience of having to work for another company before he could join his father and grandfather at SS&S. He admits that he had been enraged about it to begin with, but now sees it as a truly valuable and absolutely necessary experience. Upon hearing this, Benton does a complete double take and shortly thereafter actually sits down next to Robert, his cousin, who up until now, has been a complete stranger.

The morning ends with the focus on personality types using the MBTI results. This allows for introducing each person through a discussion of his or her relating, learning, and leading style and seeing where and how each person fits into the family unit. There is excitement in the room when each person sees himself or herself in relation to the others on the summary graph of the MBTI on the flip chart in the front of the room.

In the connecting process, David and Sam actually speak with each other for the first time in years, Benton and Randy have a civil conversation, and Rose talks with some family members for the very first time. The morning ends on a more lively, open, and energetic note—a sign to us that we've been successful in establishing some sense of safety and cooperation. We had already announced that we would be meeting with only Sam, Joan, and David in the afternoon, and that we would see everyone else together again the next morning. The second generation siblings had all known ahead of time that we would want to have at least one full session solely with them, and each had cautiously agreed to this.

Each day lunch will be catered for the group as a whole. We do this because it gives us flexibility in our scheduling and forces the family to interface outside of the meeting room. Time will be available later for being alone, we assure them, if anyone wants that. As it is, we've observed that Sam is isolating himself, except that Marsha always seems to be by his side, attempting to bring him in. Joan has been acting quite subdued, and we hear others inquire if she feels sick, for this pensiveness is not at all like her.

DAY ONE: AFTERNOON

The meeting with the three disengaged Sampson siblings is taking place in the smaller, more private room, where the windows are large and the view of the gardens and distant ocean is beautiful. We can see Rose in the distance; she has positioned herself in a chair with a book, clearly making herself available to David if she's needed.

We begin by giving each of them a lovely picture book about siblings and their life journey together (Kelsh and Quindlen, 1998). We also verbalize our purpose for this particular session: to begin to repair the personal damage in their relationships. Next, we simply ask each person to express what he or she is feeling now and to state what he or she most wants to have happen by the end of the afternoon. This shows how the advance work with individuals is so important. With our prior guidance, all three have each diligently prepared themselves for these intensely difficult conversations and contacts.

SAM: I'm willing to begin. . . . I want my brother and sister to admit how hard I have worked, and to buy me out of this hellhole I have been sitting in for the past years, just to take care of them. I've earned good money but now I can see it wasn't worth it.

DAVID (firing back): Well, here we go again! Nothing has changed, has it? You have always played the victim, and I'm always the bad guy to you.

RUTH: Okay, so each of you begins with feelings about not having been valued and respected by the other one. We'll get back to that, but first let's finish with what each of you wants to have happen today.

JOAN: I want to help Sam get what's important to him, but I also want him to stay at the company for now. I don't think we can do without him yet. And yes, I too want my brothers to respect and value me. . . . It feels funny being the oldest one now, with our folks gone.

LES: And you, David? We haven't heard yet what you want.

DAVID: Thanks. I think I want to be part of this team. Really, I mean it! I know I've always sort of copped out on the entire package deal … but no one knows what it's been like for me.

LES: David, I appreciate your admitting that you have had a part in the problems. That recognition will be important for each of you to do eventually. And learning what it has been like for all of you over these many years is what we are about this afternoon.

RUTH: David, what do you mean by wanting "to be part of this team"?

DAVID: Well, many things. I've worked very hard to get my kids to co-operate and be close, both in the family and in our business, and I know that's because we never did that when we were young. I've wanted them to trust one another and to find their own places . . . for them all to be proud of owning the business, even if they never actually work there. (Turning to Sam.) I get mad when one of them isn't there to do his or her part, and I understand how you can feel that way about me, only much more so. And another reason is that I really want to help you now, Sam, if I can. It never seemed like I was a good older brother to you, because it was always me who was in the most trouble with Dad. So maybe it's time to do that.

SAM (clearly moved but holding back his feelings): I just don't know what to say, David. I never even imagined you would ever be this way.

LES: You know, often we tend to see ourselves and one another as we know our parents saw us. Maybe this is one of those times. What I remember is that your dad labeled David as defiant and uncooperative and not caring. Perhaps you, David, would act that way to meet his expectations; and you, Sam, have seen David through your father's eyes instead of your own. This meeting is actually about learning to see yourselves and one another through your own updated eyes.

During this time Ruth has been helping Joan keep herself quiet and emotionally contained while being attentive to what her brothers are saying.

RUTH: And Joan, you have done a good job just listening. What do you think?

JOAN: I think I have a lot to learn and a lot to say.

We are off to a good beginning. With good preparation, firm structuring, and consistently framing things in the positive, we have been able to subdue and avert the deep underlying conflicts and keep the problem defined as the damaged relationships rather than any one person. After a brief stretch we return. We're going to ask each person to talk in turn about what it was like to grow up in the family.

To Joan we say: "Tell all of us what it was like for you growing up as the only daughter, the oldest child, and in difficult economic times for the family because the business was just beginning."

To David we say: "Tell us about being the middle child, the first boy, and someone who was physically and emotionally abused by your father."

To Sam we say: "Tell us about being the youngest and the one who was always expected to follow in your father's footsteps."

Our statements clearly frame the stories so as to target what we already know are the core individual and relationship issues for these three siblings.

DAVID: Well, I've had to look at this childhood stuff a lot because my life has been a mess at some times. But now it is much better, thanks to my wife and kids. I've been reminded here that all of us (looking around at his siblings) grew up in an abusive, oppressive family. Not that Dad was a bad guy or anything like that, but he sure made life hell for all the rest of us. Maybe just because it was me and I was the first boy, I don't know, or maybe it was the way he was with all of us . . . but he always had to be right about everything, and no one else had any right to a different way or opinion. (Both Sam and Joan nod in agreement with this.) And no matter what I did, it was never good enough for him. But I really tried . . . or at least I did when I was a little kid, before I had to give it all up as hopeless.

I know you guys don't think I ever even cared what anyone thought of me, but I really did. (His voice is cracking now.) Whenever I tried to find out what Dad wanted from me, he would say I was talking back or attacking him. Then he'd go after me with that pipe thing, so I'd run away. And Mom would never do anything to stop him. He would always tell her what to do and what to think, and she would just go along with him and his way . . . at least when he was around her.

The thing that maybe hurt the most, though, was you guys, because you seemed to always agree with him and you even tried to make everything be my fault. Don't you realize that I didn't have anybody on my side? For the longest time I thought the fighting in the house was because there was something really wrong with me, and that if only I was gone it would be okay for everyone else, even Dad. So that's why I always stayed away as much as I could, and then finally took off. I only wish I had had the courage to go a lot sooner than seventeen. (David hangs his head.) Well, that's all for now from me.

LES (with a gentle hand on David's shoulder): Thanks for speaking freely about who you are and what things were like for you.

JOAN (crying softly): Can I say something now?

RUTH: Sure, as long as it is about you and what it was like for you.

JOAN: I know exactly what David means. Only there was another part too. Dad was drinking most of the time, even in those years, so that was a big problem also. I know because he and Jason were just alike in so many ways, and they became real buddies. Well, anyway, as a little kid I was always afraid of Dad and I didn't want him to yell at me like he did at Mom and you, David.

SAM (interrupting and sarcastic): Well, he never did . . . because you would always just cry or smile at him, and then he would give you anything!

LES: Sam, Joan needs to tell her own story without interruption. Joan, will you go ahead?

JOAN: You are right, though, Sam. I did do it that way. It seemed like that was all I knew how to do, to keep Dad from punishing me, too. I couldn't even think right when he was screaming and running after David with that pipe. I was just frozen like a little girl statue.

SAM (pushing in again): And you still act like a little girl who can always get her way!

RUTH: Sam, it's not okay to attack and blame others. There will be plenty of time for you to talk here this afternoon.

JOAN: It's okay. I'm used to it.

RUTH: No, it is not okay. And your part in the problems is that you let that kind of thing go on. You don't stop him, but you should . . . just like your mother should have stopped your father from abusing her and you kids.

JOAN (in a loud and frantic voice): Oh, my God . . . and like I should have stopped Jason!

RUTH: Yes, you should have stopped Jason. But there's still time for you to help your kids with this—we will look at that later. If you want to be taken seriously and valued as an adult, you have to follow through with doing the hard things, and from there you will grow in your own self-respect.

JOAN: I think I understand this. And I'm feeling more ready now to talk with my kids about their father.

LES: Sam, what are you thinking now?

SAM: I never thought about any of these things. I just always figured that if I did it all right, Dad would stay away from me. I was glad David was always such a jerk because I could always blame him for whatever went on, and Dad would believe me. (David takes a very big breath at this point.) Dad always liked Joan best and she never had to do anything. He demanded that I go to the company with him, and he told me when I was about three that I would be the next head guy—it had to be someone with the Sampson name. I guess he'd already decided that David was hopeless. So I was stupid and did just as he wanted.

I hate my life and I hate myself for being his puppet. And now that he is finally gone, what is there for me? . . . Absolutely nothing! I am fifty-four years old and can't even decide what I want to eat sometimes, much less what is fun or where I want to go. Worst of all, I'm now (pointing his finger at Joan and David) your puppet. But this time I'll get out of it all, no matter what I have to do!

RUTH: Let's explore what you mean by that. A lot of people have expressed concern about your drinking and maybe your hurting yourself.

SAM: I'm surprised that anyone notices or cares.

DAVID: Sam, I care . . . and I thank you for staying around to be there to run the company after Dad was ready for that. I just never realized that taking on Dad's job one day could be a problem for you. In fact, I was always jealous that he thought you were better than me.

SAM: And I was jealous that Mom looked out for you and your interests in spite of everything. She gave you money to start your own business. And she'd always say, "Oh, Sam, David is okay; he can handle anything." I was enraged too when she insisted that they divide the business evenly among us, because you really didn't deserve anything. The only time she stood up for anything was for you. But maybe, I'm wondering just now, if that was the same old thing, and I am still letting Dad do my thinking for me.

JOAN: Sam, I have always cared about you, but you always seem to be so angry with me and act as if I'm a dumb bother all the time. Yet when Jason died, it was you who looked out for us all and gave my children a caring and gentle ear. I am forever grateful to you for that, and much more. I will try to do whatever you need—and you are *not* a puppet!

LES: This seems like a good place to take a brief stretch.

Our brief stretch turned into a long break, something everybody clearly needed. Before going outside to meet Rose, David approached Sam and put his arms around him. Joan also touched him gently and said, "I am so thankful for you being who you are." With this Sam turned away, clearly having a hard time holding it together. He spent the rest of the time staring out the window, his eyes watering and his jaw quivering. Joan sat with her head in her hands and asked Ruth when she could talk with her own family about their father.

When we resumed, Les began.

LES: We will be finishing soon for the day. A lot of very important things have happened already. You have all journeyed miles from where you were when Sam first called us. This afternoon is an example of how your relationships can actually be when each one of you listens to the others, understands yourself and your siblings in new ways, and responds in caring ways. Now, what else is important for you to say to one another before we finish for today?

DAVID: I want you both to understand that I was never against you; I was only trying to save myself when we were growing up. You can't even imagine how important it is to me to hear what each of you has been saying about yourselves and to me.

JOAN (quickly jumping in): I do understand now, David, and I'm really sorry for never supporting you or trying to stop Dad from hurting you. Of course, I couldn't really have done anything. But I'm sorry he did all that to you. It wasn't you—it was him, please believe that! Ruth just helped me think about how to talk to my kids about their father, and it is the same situation. Just like it wasn't about you, it wasn't about me either, or my kids.

RUTH: Sam, do you have a response to David?

SAM (slowly): It's a little hard for me because I have always wished that I had chosen your way, David, instead of mine. Look at how it is right now: you have it all! But I have nothing like that. So obviously mine was the wrong way. You still have a wife, you have your own business rather than the one our parents started, and you have four kids who care about you. I have nothing much to show for all these years of effort. But maybe it is time for me to do something different. . . . Being a victim was Mom's role. (Turning and looking straight at David.) Okay, I honor you for choosing your own way, and I'm sorry you had to take all of that hate from our dad. I'm embarrassed and mad at myself that I was never man enough to stand up to him like you did.

RUTH: Sam, before we finish for the day, what do you want for yourself?

SAM: I don't think I can handle any more. I'm full for right now.

LES: And how about you, Joan?

JOAN: I need to know that it is okay with both of you that I talk to my children about the past and our family. I realize now that I've made a lot of mistakes by hiding truths and just pretending that everything in our lives is just fun and roses. It has hurt the kids, especially Benton, and I need to make it right with them.

SAM: Sure, there's no reason to keep anything secret anymore. Our folks, and Jason too, are all gone, so it's only us now, anyway. I think it's about time we started doing it our way.

DAVID: No problem here. And Joan, tell Benton, if you want to, that I know what it is like to be thought of as the bad guy . . . and it stinks.

This ends our first day. David goes off to find Rose and bring her to join him and his sister and brother, which must have been a first in their lifetime together. While Sam heads to the bar to order champagne, Joan walks slowly by herself to where they are to meet.

For us, the first day has been quite successful. But we are both tired and a lot of work still lies ahead for everyone. We are especially concerned about Sam. He seems depressed, and admittedly has an issue with alcohol. He needs much more attention than we will be able to give him in the following three days, and we want to be both sensitive and successful in getting him to accept appropriate help. Both his sister and brother, we now know, will be helpful resources in Sam's behalf.

On our way to the beach for our own walk, we notice the second-generation Sampsons sitting together. They are looking at the book we gave them earlier and bringing up, "Do you remember when we . . ." That's exactly what we'd hoped for.

DAY TWO: MORNING

We've requested that every family member be present each morning. This is our way of checking in with individuals, the separate families, and the entire family group. As we enter the meeting room, Bill is acting highly upset over having to be there again. Moreover, we notice that he's being very belligerent and abusive with his father, who is meekly trying to get him to quiet down and stay.

As Ruth walks by the two of them, she simply says: "It is time to sit down now. Sam, would you sit across the room from Bill? Please join your brother and sister over there." If Bill's looks could kill, Ruth would soon be six feet under. Bill chooses to sit next to Benton, who again has set himself apart from the others, especially his mother, whom he glances at in a hostile manner.

We begin with the general check-in. Then, after a brief on-the-spot agreement with each other, we divide the group into three smaller units that will meet together for the rest of the morning. David and his family are sent off to discuss an important issue among themselves: Since they had been estranged from the rest of the family for so long, would any of them want to be part of the Sampson Seed Company business in a more active way? If so, how do they envision their involvement in it? We notice Benton immediately tensing up when he hears this announcement, but he says nothing.

Meanwhile, Joan and her family, including Randy, are to meet with Ruth, and Sam and Bill are to meet with Les.

Meeting with Sam and Bill

We have decided that this meeting between father and son is essential and must take place quickly. As his grandfather's namesake, young Bill Sampson has somehow managed to assume the role of his father's oppressor. Sam is obviously continuing on in the same early-decision position he had taken with his father, and he's doing whatever he can to please and quiet his son. Not only does the pair's relational interaction keep Sam entrapped in his early decision, made in childhood, but it's extremely harmful to Bill as well. If we are going to be successful with the family as a whole we have to change the pattern in this father-son dyad—and sooner rather than later.

LES: Sam, you allow your son to abuse you, just like your father did. Are you willing to do everything possible to change that?

SAM: What do you mean? I never thought about that . . .

BILL (in a very loud and aggressive voice): Yeah. Don't let him lie to you, Dad. He doesn't know what he's talking about!

LES: Oh, but I do, Bill. And your dad knows it. He just needs to summon up his courage and deal directly with you. He lets you use him and push him around. And you are disrespectful not just to him, but to everyone else. You act arrogant and as if you are entitled to do whatever you want, at any time. That's not okay. You'll discover that this behavior and attitude will get you into some big trouble when outside of the family.

BILL (standing and shouting): Shut up, you stupid old man!

SAM (getting up to face his son and then speaking with a commanding voice): That's enough, Son. Les is correct. I have let everything go to pieces ever since your mother left, and I've especially let you do whatever you feel like doing. But now I see that what I've really done is encourage you to be someone that I hope you aren't. If I can reverse that, I am going to do it . . .

BILL: Dad, don't do this!

SAM (turning to Les): What do you think I should do?

LES: First of all, Sam, I think you know very well what you should do because you know what you wanted your mother to do differently.

I trust and support you in following your own lead now with your son.

BILL: Dad, I'm not putting up with this shit anymore. I'm out of here!

SAM: That's okay for the moment, Bill. But I expect you to be with us all at lunch and to treat me and everyone else with consideration. And if you don't do that and follow through for the rest of this meeting, don't expect to receive your stipend for next month. Or in the months afterward, either. You'll have to learn to be accountable, or else.

BILL (moving toward the door): You're a damn fool, Dad! (He slams the door behind him.)

LES: He's a tough kid, Sam, and you did a really good job just now. I hope it helps you both. There is one other thing I really would like you to consider.

SAM: What is that?

LES: Connections with your daughter, Betty. The first move will be up to you.

SAM: Man . . . you just don't stop, do you?

LES: No, not for awhile yet. Well, how about if you just think about it, at least? (Sam nods in agreement.)

Les now heads over to join Ruth after Sam says he's going to look for David and see if he wants to go for a walk.

Meeting with Joan, Benton, Marsha, May, Randy, and Jason

As this small group convenes, Benton is anxiously pacing in front of the windows, Jason is sitting in a protective position by his mother's side, May and Randy are sitting close together, hanging onto each other, and Marsha, who has placed herself separately, looks somber and pensive.

RUTH: These four days are going to bring many changes to your lives. We've seen a few changes already taking place. Some of these changes will come in the form of family information—which may at first be hard to hear, and even harder to understand. It will require patience and courage on each of your parts to listen and understand, and then to make your own personal changes.

Benton, Marsha, May, and Jason: your mother has some things to say to you all. I hope that you will hear her out with compassion before you form your own opinions and share your feelings.

JOAN: This is going to be very difficult for me . . . but the time has come for me to tell you all the real truth about many things that have affected your lives up to now. Maybe I'm wrong; maybe you already know what I am about to say . . . but I don't think so.

I will start with telling you a bit about what it was like for me when your uncles and I grew up. Your grandfather was a good, hardworking man who provided well for all of us. If not for him and your grandmother, none of us would have the company and the good life that we have now. However, my father could often be terrible, too. He was physically and emotionally abusive to all of us . . . especially, I might say, to your uncle David. He also had a serious drinking problem. I don't want to go into much more of this except to say that maybe the most horrible part was that none of us did anything to stop any of his abuse, not even when we were adults and should have been able to speak up and do something.

Next, and most important for all of you to know, is that your own father was this same way; he had a serious drinking problem and was an abusive man. I have never said anything about this because I wanted you to think well of him and remember him in a good way. I realize now that my silence was wrong. But I did what I did and now I have to change it. I still want you to remember your father in a good way, but you also have to know the truth. The night he died he was stone drunk. He had gone out on the tractor against everyone's advice, but that's the way he was when he was angry and drinking. . . . He didn't listen to anyone about anything.

Also, he always threatened to do something reckless and even kill himself when I wouldn't do whatever he wanted. Just before he left on the afternoon of his accident we had argued. He wanted me to give him the money I'd just gotten from the company dividend so he could go out and buy a new sports car. After I refused, he stormed out, saying that I was stingy and selfish and he would never be back. Then when I learned of the accident that killed him, I fell apart. For many years I blamed myself for his death.

Jason, you were born into all of this just four months after he died. Since your birth I have never depended emotionally on anyone except you . . . and now I am sensing what a bad thing I must have done to you in that way.

Marsha, your father was very mean to you, even though you were just a little girl. I don't know why he was this way with you—because he wasn't with your twin sister. But I could never do anything about it. I don't know how much you remember about any of this, but I do know you don't trust me . . . and I don't blame you. I hope you can forgive me someday.

May, you were your dad's favorite child, and you could really charm him, even at two years old.

And Benton . . . oh, my poor Benton! I've always understood why you are forever so angry with me. How could you be anything different? You heard us fight and later that day you saw your father die. How could you live easily with all that? I'm so sorry for the pain that I have caused you. But you need to know the truth now in order to set your own mind straight about your father and the past.

(Jason starts to interrupt, but Joan stops him.) Please, everyone: wait until I am finished. I must tell you why I am doing all of this now. It's because of Sam and the company, and David and his family. I'm afraid for Sam. He has been trapped all of his life and I don't want him to kill himself with alcohol like your father did . . . or with anything else.

Also . . . I need you all to know that the company really belongs to everyone in the family. We will all now have a say in how it is going to be run.

BENTON: My God, Mom, you sure have dumped a lot on me all of a sudden! What am I supposed to think? Are you kicking me out of having my company?

RUTH: You are correct, Benton, your mother has dumped a lot, but it has been on all of you, not just on you. The information she gave is important for everyone in this room . . . and for all of the family outside of this room.

BENTON: So what am I supposed to do now? What happens to me? I'm the only one who deserves to run this company when Uncle Sam leaves. After all, my father gave his life for it.

RUTH: I know you are feeling hurt and scared now, Benton. You have just been surprised by a lot of information—information that should not have been kept secret from you or anyone else for so long. What you and everyone else do with it is your own choice and your own responsibility.

And I should say this to all of you: Now that the silence is broken and the truth is out, consider how you want to handle this, and what kind of a person you want to be with yourself and your family. Your mother has carefully given you the gift of truth. Please ponder these questions as we take a brief break and return in fifteen minutes.

With the coffee break over, Les joins Ruth for the remainder of the morning.

RUTH: Let's begin. We want to check with everyone to start off. Jason, you had a question before. What are you thinking and feeling right now?

JASON: First, I can't believe all of this! For the first time in my life I think I understand things and maybe even my brother. It's sad to never know your real dad, but it's much worse to know him, lose him, miss him a lot . . . and then find out that all you held sacred about him was a big lie. I don't know if I could handle that. Benton, I'm sorry for you. And for you, Mom, I think you're even greater than I ever imagined. Marsha, now I understand about you, too. And May . . . I just love you.

LES: Who else will say something about themselves?

MAY: I'm fine, but I'm sad for you, Mom. I think you are great. For you, Benton, I'm starting to know better about you. I just wish that you would value me . . . and especially Randy. He is a fine and competent person, and I love him dearly. Marsha, I don't remember anything about Dad hurting you but not me. And we've never talked about it, have we? Do you remember much?

MARSHA: Not really. After all, we were pretty young. I think I remember he would come in our room at night and say I'd been bad. Then he'd take me out somewhere. I know I was always scared of him. I want to say something else, though. (Turning to Joan.) I don't want to keep secrets anymore, either. I am a lesbian; Sophie and I have been lovers for the past four years. I want her to be part of the family, too—like Randy is. I don't want to say anything else right now. And about what happens with the company, I want to talk first to Sam.

JOAN (reaching out): I've known that about you for a long time, honey. And I want Sophie to be part of the family too.

RUTH: And you, Benton—what are you thinking and feeling?

BENTON (in a quiet and almost gentle way): I just don't know. Or maybe I just won't say. But . . . whatever, I'm just not ready yet.

RUTH: It has been a heavy and startling morning. Let's take a break for lunch. Les and I will let everyone know then what's going to happen next. And Joan, thank you again for having the courage to be yourself.

DAY TWO: AFTERNOON

When we arrive for lunch, the first thing we notice is that Bill is present and actually chatting in a lively way with Robert and Randy. He has followed through with Sam's dictate. Marsha, May, and Jason are sitting close together and engaged in serious conversation. Benton, Sam, and David are sitting together and actively talking. Rose and Joan have filled their plates and are heading to the patio. The fabric of the family is beginning to change. We sit off together, talking about the morning and planning for the afternoon.

It's decided that we will meet for a while with the second generation, including Rose, and then finish up the day meeting with everyone together. There's a lot of unfinished business to attend to, and right now our first concern is with Sam and the transition within the business. What does he really want and need to do for himself, and how will the management of the business be taken care of?

Meeting with the Second Generation

We begin by asking Joan to report on what had happened in the Bennington family meeting. In a clear and concise way she summarizes their meeting, sharing her own story of living with Jason and the truth about his death. Both Sam and David respond with a new awareness of their sister and a never-before-experienced respect. Rose is sensitive, caring, and supportive.

Next, we turn to Sam and ask him to begin by briefly reporting on his morning meeting with his son and then to share what he is currently thinking about himself and the future—his and the company's.

SAM: I'm not quite sure what I am thinking about my own future, I just know I want to go somewhere. And oh . . . my meeting with Bill went fine. He's just a kid, that's all.

LES: Okay, let's start with your future. A lot of your family members are concerned about you. Have you heard those concerns?

SAM: Yeah, but they are concerned about me hurting myself and drinking too much, and those really aren't a problem at all. What I want to hear about is how others can help me get out of managing the company.

DAVID: How can Joan and I help you? Do you have anything specific in mind?

SAM: No, not really. But I have been thinking about Benton taking over; that's as far as I've gotten, though. I'm not really sure that he's ready to do it yet. And I also think he might instantly get rid of Marsha and Randy, once I'm not around to protect them. Certainly he's said as much. But it feels urgent to me that I get out of there. The only alternative to Benton seems to be bringing someone in from outside.

JOAN: I'm glad to hear that you have concerns about Benton. Even though he is my son, I have deep concerns about him, too. A big problem is that he thinks he is perfectly qualified; also you have already told him he will take over when you go.

SAM: You know, Joan, when feeling pressured I probably have said that. But I've never confronted him about the way he behaves sometimes. You, of all people, know how hard it is to always speak the truth.

JOAN: You are right; I do.

DAVID: Sam, would you ever consider that maybe I and some of my kids could help a bit? All of us who are here talked about it this morning, and we agreed that it would be possible for me to free up some time. And Robert too would be very interested in this. I think that the younger boys wouldn't have much to offer at this time, but certainly they could get acquainted with Sampson Seed. Unfortunately, Renee is extremely busy with her own business at this point. . . . So what do you think? (Sam and Joan are both totally taken aback with David's offer and show their surprise.)

SAM: I don't know what to say. I just never even considered this possibility. It will take a lot of thought and planning, but let's talk some more.

JOAN: I am very grateful for your interest, David. And I want to say to the two of you that I would like to be in on this planning, too.

RUTH: This sounds like a great opportunity for all of you. Let's stop now, and when we meet a bit later with everyone it will be time for you, Sam, to talk with all of the family members who actually work in the business with you. Everyone else will simply be observers for a while.

Meeting with the Entire Family

Chairs are placed in a small inner circle and a larger outer circle. Ruth will work with Sam, Benton, Marsha, and Randy in the inner circle while Les observes both the inside participants and the outside observers.

RUTH (talking directly to the inner circle): Before we began this weekend, everyone in the room specifically agreed to the overall contract of working together, to the best of your ability, to repair the damaged relationships among family members, and to build new relationships and new family-business teams.

We've been successfully working on the first two for the past two days. Now it's time to turn to the third one, the business. And since you four are the only family members currently working in the company, we are beginning with you. As you know, Sam is planning to leave his CEO post, at least for a while.

Sam, will you begin by sharing your thoughts about the new leadership?

SAM (with his head lowered): Well, I don't know . . .

BENTON (loudly interrupting and glaring at Ruth): There should be no question here. It has been planned for a long time that I will be taking over!

SAM (slowly and quietly): I'm not so sure, Benton. Maybe you are not quite ready for that yet.

MARSHA: Benton, if you become the CEO would you keep Randy and me at the company? And if so, what positions would we have?

RUTH: Really a good question, Marsha, and a good beginning to a discussion.

BENTON: Since this has been a meeting of terrible surprises, I at least will tell you the truth. The answer is a resounding NO. I especially wouldn't keep a weird one like you around.

MARSHA: Yes, it's true that I am a lesbian. But that doesn't have anything to do with my working life or my abilities.

BENTON (sarcastically): Well, then, I should just say that I won't really need you around. You're Sam's helper, but you'll never be mine. You and our little brother can just hang out together.

SAM (standing and in a commanding voice): Benton, that's enough! You have just demonstrated to all of us exactly why you are not ready to lead the company. Your sister is a hardworking and highly valued employee, and your brother is a talented artist who always pitches in to come up with graphic designs whenever we need them . . . and doesn't charge a nickel. Also, he has given your mother a lot more care and attention than you ever have. But in any case, that's no way to talk to *anyone!* I have put many years of honesty, caring, and expertise into Sampson Seeds and I won't permit you to go around abusing people. That ended with my father and your father. I've led this company in a different way than they did, and we will not return to the Dark Ages.

Your mother, your uncle, and I, who are the major shareholders, after all, will decide on what will happen when I leave. There will be a place for everyone, including you. And you too, Marsha and Randy, if you still want to be around there.

And as for you, Benton, you're an intelligent, extremely talented man who acts like an arrogant ass most of the time. Get yourself in hand and maybe you *will* be CEO someday. But not now.

(Everyone in the entire room is stunned yet clearly relieved by Sam's strong remarks.)

BENTON: But—

RUTH: Benton, I think enough has been said for right now. It is clearly time for you to think and to take stock of yourself and consider the changes you're willing to make. Randy, Marsha, is there anything either of you wants to say?

RANDY: I want to say thank you, Sam. And what you say about yourself is correct. You have been an honest and caring leader, and a brilliant one, too. I wish you were going to be around much longer.

MARSHA: The same for me to you, Sam. And thank you also for being like a father to us all these years. You have always made life better for us.

RUTH (after catching Les's nodded agreement): I think we are finished now for the afternoon. We'll all meet together again in the morning.

DAY THREE: MORNING

When we convene, Sam is notably missing. In the previous afternoon, he, Joan, and David had successfully rebonded and were beginning a totally new relationship team: that was the good part of things. However, Marsha had called our room early in the morning to inform us about the bad part. Last night Sam went out alone, had gotten very drunk, and took a fall. Apparently this was his way of undermining himself. We decide that today Ruth will begin with the morning rounds and then work with the third generation. Meanwhile, Les will meet privately with Sam.

Everyone in the big room is buzzing about Sam's mishaps last night. Ruth quickly moves to quiet the conversation by assuring everyone that he is safe and will be meeting this morning alone with Les. She then asks the third-generation members to seat themselves in a circle so they can talk together, while Joan, David, and Rose are to sit together in the back and just look on.

The morning agenda is to talk about the open issues which are looming: first, Bill and his reaction to his father's activities last night; second, the confrontation of Benton yesterday afternoon. Then we will do some structured interactions, designed to help family members all get to know more about one another in the present. The morning is certainly stuffed full.

RUTH: Bill, it was a rough night for your father. What are you thinking and feeling about all of it?

BILL: Well, I'm glad it happened here, where everybody could see and maybe help him. I go through this all the time with him, and that's why I can never really go away for very long . . . and why I can't stay home either. I don't know what he would do to himself if someone's not looking out for him. Which is, I guess, what Marsha does for him at the company. (Bill and Marsha exchange understanding looks.)

RUTH: I agree with you, both about us seeing him and his getting help. That's what Les will be trying to do with him this morning—finding out if Sam will accept the expert help he really needs, beyond the family's support. But . . . Bill, what do you need for yourself? It is a difficult job to take care of a parent who is unwilling or unable to take care of himself.

BILL: You've got it there! I don't even much like or respect Dad anymore. Basically, I really don't want to talk about it, if you don't mind. It's just okay to be here right now.

RUTH (deciding not to push): I'm glad you are here. And thank you for sharing some of your feelings.

This interchange clearly indicates a major change in the way Bill presents himself. He is opening up and revealing a different part of himself. Instead of acting so spoiled, angry, and defiant, he appears to be a concerned and burdened young man, beneath all the bravado. The rest of the group responds to him in a caring way, and we eventually move on.

MAY (in a very nurturing but forthright voice): Benton, you are my brother and I love you very much. But I also hate you for the way you treat Randy, Marsha, Jason, and our mother, too. (She turns to Ruth.) Is it okay to be bringing this up?

RUTH: Yes, go ahead.

MAY: Well, I don't understand why you treat everyone the way you do—and not just family members. You act as if you think you're infinitely superior to all the rest of us mortals. But you're not, you know. I can't even remember you ever being any different than this. I sure hope it gets better in the future. I guess that's all for me right now. I'd like to hear from you now, Benton.

BENTON (in a subdued manner): I don't know what to say. Almost everything has changed for me from the way it was before this meeting started. I don't know if I hate it or if I am grateful. Funny thing, isn't it? What I do know, though, is that besides my wife and kids, the only thing in my life that ever mattered to me was becoming chief of Sampson Seeds. But now I find out that I can't have it unless I change who I am. That's huge! And then on top of that, I'm seeing all of you, and particularly my mother, as very different than I ever thought. It's like an earthquake has hit and upset the whole foundation of my life.

RUTH: I really appreciate your truthfulness and vulnerability in saying all of this, Benton. Just remember that an upset foundation can present an opportunity to build a sturdy and updated structure, which will better meet the needs of everyone both now and in the future. So if you decide you want to rebuild yourself, just let Les and me know. We can probably help you locate the best resources.

ROBERT: Benton, I like knowing you and having a cousin about my age. And I really like being part of this family . . . so if I can help you, I'd like to. Maybe we could even talk tonight.

BENTON: That might be good. Thanks . . . I'll probably take you up on it. Right now, however, I have something I want to say to Marsha and Jason. I won't say this very well (his voice is cracking) . . . but

I'm really sorry for what I've said about you both, and for how I've treated you. That's all.

RUTH (looking around and noticing that there is hardly a dry eye in the room): Thank you, Benton, for showing courage and caring.

At this point Ruth decides that the group will best be served by taking a long break, to allow individuals to connect and support one another in their own ways, which has clearly occurred for everyone. We resume the session somewhat later and continue with an exercise in which each person must come up with an unanswered question and then ask it of the appropriate person. This results in a lively exchange of information, which at times is even quite funny. The group is developing a personality of its own. May and Renee are both wonderfully cohesive forces, and they keep things going in a positive direction.

Meeting with Sam

Sam gets himself downstairs over an hour later than the scheduled group meeting time, so he is clearly relieved to be intercepted by Les and asked to go off and meet privately with him.

SAM: I really blew it, didn't I? You know, Les . . . I just can't keep it together very well anymore.

LES: Yes, you did blow it. But I'm glad that you know it and are concerned about yourself. I think Ruth and I can help, if you are willing to consider our suggestions. Can we talk about you personally now?

SAM: Okay. I'm ready.

LES: We believe that you have a serious problem with both alcohol abuse and depression. We can get you into an excellent treatment program if you'll give us the go-ahead. We also believe that the business will be fine, in your absence, however long that might be, if you will develop a plan that includes using the newfound family resources of David and his family. What would you like to do?

SAM (after some long moments of silence and holding his head in his hands): I agree to both of the things you have proposed. I don't know how to do either one of them myself.

LES: Let's start right now and make the plans.

DAY THREE: AFTERNOON

Sam has seen no one in the family since last night, before he got himself into trouble. Now, as the afternoon begins with everyone present, he feels horrible, looks terrible, and acts ashamed. He and Les are sitting together in the circle, while Ruth has placed herself across from them and close to Bill. The room is quiet and expectant.

LES: As you already know, Sam and I spent this morning working together. He wants to begin this afternoon by saying something to all of you.

SAM (in a halting but clear manner): Last night I again put myself in harm's way. I say it that way because I now know that if I do not stop drinking and get some help, I will end up killing myself. This morning Les has helped me realize that killing myself is a choice that I do not have to make—that good help is available.

I will be leaving the company in exactly two weeks to begin a forty-five-day treatment program in the Midwest. Until then I will work diligently to get everything in order for my absence, which may carry on for much longer than those six weeks. (People begin to respond, but Sam stops them, wanting to continue himself.) Please . . . I have several more things to say.

First, to you, Bill: I want you to be your own person and live your own life. I never did that. I always thought I had to do just what my parents expected of me. I never had the guts to take my own road, like David did. I want life to go differently for you. I think, in some ways, these last years of your wildness was you doing what I really wanted to do myself, which is why I encouraged it all and paid for your good times. That wasn't fair to you. Now things will change—in some ways you'll like and in others you won't. But you'll end up, I hope, being a stronger man someday than I've been.

Second, to you, David: Welcome home. I have treated you unfairly, and I am very grateful for your willingness to join us again, in a different way. I need your help and advice and look forward to it.

And Benton: Don't wait as long as I did to make your changes. You are at risk for losing too much of value to you.

Joan, you are much more than I ever gave you credit for. I am sorry for putting you down so many times. I really don't know how you managed when Jason died, and I greatly respect you for taking care of your four kids and trying to protect them all from an ugly truth. I also need your help . . . so will you help me now?

And, finally, to my daughter, Betty . . . who isn't here but whom I have tried to reach on the phone but haven't yet connected with: I am sorry for the bitterness you feel toward me, and I hope we can soon put all the ugly things behind us.

That's all I have to say right now. This has been an exhausting time. And thank you, Les, thank you all.

Everyone is stunned and touched. This family is forever changed. Still, many choices and plans have to be made. Since it is already after 4:00 p.m., we decide to end the formal meeting for the day and instruct people to "just be together, think, talk, and plan."

DAY FOUR: MORNING

Everyone is up early, meeting in small groups and buzzing around. Some tensions clearly remain, as between Benton, Marsha, and Randy. All the while a new third-generation Sampson Seed group has been evolving. Robert and Bill have both signed in with their interest. David, Joan, and Sam have been talking, talking, talking. Jason, as usual, is quiet. Now, however, instead of guarding his mother, he has his sketch pad out and is sketching the scene outside the window. May and Renee seem to be available to take care of anything anyone needs, and they both often check in with Marsha.

Today will be a shorter day as most of the family members must prepare to leave and make the journey back home tonight. However, many things still need to be done by us before the meeting's end. It is always incredibly exciting and rewarding for us when we reach this point. With this family, we have again successfully walked the road from estrangement to reconciliation. Everyone's life will be different from now on, regardless of whatever happens following today. But the family's next moves and decisions should truly shape and solidify their future together.

We have carefully outlined the unfinished business of the day and the steps that we know must be taken to allow for the best possible outcome.

First, we need to make sure that family members are ready to completely support Sam and his decision to go into treatment. It is easy in the crisis to commit to changing; it is a different story to actually follow through when the time comes. It takes inner strength and family support to ensure a full commitment, from start to finish.

Second, Benton needs to further define himself and his intentions. Hopefully he will begin a new way of connecting with his entire family, both at work and socially.

Third, the family needs to have at least the beginnings of a new leadership plan for the Sampson Seed Company.

We write the three action items on the flip chart and announce that we will be moving through the outline one step at a time; then in the afternoon we'll simply finish up and not deal with anything new.

BILL: I can help with the first item. I will be staying home until Dad leaves. Then I will be flying with him to his treatment program. I am so glad he is going.

RUTH: That sounds great, Bill. What would you like from the rest of your family to support you? And then what will you be doing afterward? I am sure that it will help your father tremendously to know that you have plans.

BILL: May and Randy said that they would be there for me if I need anything. But mostly I think people need to help Dad with the business so he can just go, and I can't do any of that. And yeah . . . I do have plans. After I drop Dad off I'm going to Hawaii for a week. They say the surf is really big this time of year. Then I'll visit Robert for a while and see what goes on there in Phoenix. And finally maybe I'll even go to that family week stuff at Dad's program—I don't know yet.

Several other family members pipe in with their support for Sam. At least at the moment those arrangements seem secure. Les plans to be in touch with Sam on a regular basis, and that's simply all that can be done.

Next, we turn to the second item on the morning's agenda.

RUTH: Benton . . . what about you?

BENTON: I don't know what about me—that's the problem. Always before I've been real certain. But now everything is uncertain . . . maybe just like it was when my dad died.

LES: You know, Benton, I can understand that. So many things have changed during these four days, and for you it is rather like a death. Your pictures of your family, yourself, and your future have all been destroyed, and they've been replaced by something new. You are grieving the loss and needing to get acquainted with something very different from what you knew before. That takes time and is sometimes very difficult.

RUTH: I agree with Les and wonder if there's anything we can do to support you? Also, is there anything you want to say to anyone to finish up?

BENTON: I'd like to be able to call either or both of you if I need to talk. And I just want to say to Marsha and Randy that I'm really going to try to make it much better between us, and I hope you will too. To you, Joan . . . Mom . . . I just don't know what will happen between us.

We spend the rest of the morning on the third action item—developing the outline of an interim plan for Sampson Seeds and beginning to put together a structure for family governance in the future. Joan, David, and Sam have already arranged for David to spend time with Sam before he leaves to catch up on whatever he needs to know. David seems perfect to fill in for Sam until some more permanent decisions can be made. He is family and a principal shareholder, and he also brings a wealth of executive expertise with him. In addition, Robert has developed an uncanny interest in the family and the company and will sometimes be joining his father in California. Everyone is on board with these plans, and although Benton is understandably reluctant and reserved, he too is cooperating.

DAY FOUR: AFTERNOON

For a family with some members who thought they would never speak to one another in a civil tone again or even speak at all, or who were total strangers, the closing atmosphere is electric with enthusiasm and new connections. The vast crevasse between them has been successfully bridged and traversed, with everyone ending up safely together on the same side. The Sampson family certainly still has miles to go, but at least they are now all traveling together in the same direction and on the same road.

In this, our last session with the family, we elect to finish up in a traditional way for us. An underlying tenet in reconciliation is that tremendous personal power and healing comes with speaking freely and speaking your own truth. Our final exercise is a game, which goes like this: Each person has a time to be "it," and when you are "it" everyone in the family shares their appreciations with you. "Its" responsibility is to accept each appreciation and then finally to request two more that have not already been given. This simple game sets the foundation for future interactions and gives people permission and practice to give, receive, and ask for what they want and need. Healthy family systems are built on this positive interface and the mutual positive regard that develops.

We end after two hours of heartfelt exchange. People say their good-byes and go off to pack and head toward their homes. We will remain available to them all for the next months for whatever support and advice they may need from us. Our initial contract with the Sampson family now has been completed.

Chapter 8

Stage III: Rebuild

The family we came from sure is different than the family we are going to be now that we are all together and going ahead.

A client

Achieving reconciliation in a family business beset by hostile or distanced relationships is rather like remodeling a home. It is done in stages, over time. In Stage III of the Reconciliation Model we rebuild family relationships, reconstruct a family "home" for the next generations, and plan for the future. As with remodeling an actual house, doing this usually takes more time, effort, patience, and resources than were originally anticipated. The work is challenging—sometimes tedious and frustrating but always exciting, creative, and, in the end, immensely rewarding. When the remodeled family home is completed, it will be comfortable and strong, accommodating the needs of the present members while carrying the family itself into the future.

This final chapter on our model for achieving reconciliation in ruptured or distanced family relationships considers the process of rebuilding relationships. Equally important, it also provides tools to help guide the business-owning family in future daily interactions, whether in the workplace or in personal lives.

Over the past several years many well-respected family business professionals have focused on finding an answer to this question: What properties most influence the longevity of the family business? This endeavor has led to defining such characteristics as achievable strategies, common vision, appropriate governance institutions, effective conflict-management mechanisms, developing enlightened owners, and building family cohesion (Lank, 2001).

As this chapter develops, our particular conclusions about the specific relational characteristics necessary for family business success will unfold. Before going there, however, we want to highlight what we believe is the most critical relational ingredient contributing to success, without which, indeed, nothing else can be sustained: *an affirming family environment.* Much like the roof on a newly remodeled home, such an environment protects the entire family and all its possessions from the bitter elements, while at the same time allows for the development of other structures and processes that determine success.

An affirming family environment frequently and consistently validates all family members' private and interpersonal experiences, at any age. When someone says that he or she is concerned about something, it is taken into account. It is not discounted by saying, "Oh, you don't know what you're talking about!" If people say they are hurting, other family members supply comfort or try to find out what's wrong, instead of scolding, "Stop being a baby!" When a family member expresses anger or frustration, others listen rather than dismissing this individual as a troublemaker. Whenever a person says that he or she is doing his or her best, others understand and, when necessary, help find resources to further support getting the job done—rather than treating him or her as incompetent. An affirming environment is the best possible family business situation. In this environment each family member's beliefs and thoughts are asked for and responded to seriously, and each person's emotions are also considered important.

By contrast, in a *nonaffirming family environment,* people's verbal and nonverbal communications—their thoughts, feelings, ideas, and desires—are either ignored and not responded to or responded to with no interest, devaluing, or negative consequences. Such persistent and negative reactions to a family member's personal experience, or marked differences between a person's personal experience and other people's experience and treatment of him or her, provide the fundamental ingredients for individual distress and relationship ruptures.

Furthermore, a nonaffirming family environment undermines an individual's ability to trust his or her own thoughts and ideas and, consequently, the ability to regulate his or her own emotions. People then begin to question themselves about whether or not they are able to make valid interpretations of events. This questioning interferes with the development and maintenance of a positive sense of self. It is not surprising, then, that many family members under the stress and demands of the family business develop chaotic and unstable relationships with their parents and children, siblings and cousins.

The development of self-regulatory behaviors, especially the ability to control emotion, is a most important and necessary ingredient in rebuilding relationships. Without self-regulation, identity is insecure and goal-directed behaviors and problem-solving activities are disrupted. An affirming family environment supports each of its family business members in developing and maintaining a stable sense of self. It breeds sturdy interpersonal relationships and allows the family to develop the processes and structures integral to creating and sustaining family cohesion and ensuring the family business's longevity. As we have noted previously, family cohesion—the experience of being part of a stable and productive unit—is believed to be the single most important factor that defines a healthy business-owning family. *Family cohesion can only develop within an affirming family environment,* an environment of mutual respect and positive regard that is generated and maintained by positive interpersonal practices.

At this stage of the Reconciliation Model we work to attain four crucial goals. Attaining them will put into place the four solid cornerstones of an affirmative family environment and allow for the development of cohesion in a family that owns a business together. These goals are: (1) building and preserving trust; (2) fostering collaboration; (3) establishing reconciliation policies and procedures; and (4) growing healthy-interacting families. These are the cornerstones of both family quality and business success and reaching them will make quality family relationships the dominant cultural value of the family business.

GOAL #1: BUILD AND PRESERVE TRUST

The word "trust," the first cornerstone of an affirming family environment, is often and easily used. As a concept it is frequently talked about, but in fact trust is very difficult to actually understand . . . and it is certainly hard to achieve, especially when relationships have been injured.

So what exactly is trust? We consider trust to be a firm belief in the reliability, truth, or strength of a person or thing. We apply this in two different ways: trust is a phenomenon that has relevance first to the individual, and then interpersonally. Trust as an individual issue means that "I can rely on myself and my abilities to think clearly and manage my feelings in whatever situation I am facing." Trust as an interpersonal issue means that "I can rely on someone else to say what they mean and mean what they say; and follow through in caring ways."

Achieving a trusting relationship in family business needs an affirming family environment, individuals who are internally validating of themselves and externally validating of others, and a commitment to reciprocal participation between the giver and the receiver of trust. Therefore, repairing relationships and restoring trust in a conflicted family business is truly a family affair. Rebuilding trust when relationships have been wounded, or building trust when it was never there to begin with, is a matter of behavioral change on one person's part and the acknowledgment and acceptance of that change on another person's part.

Is rebuilding trust really possible in some business-owning families when relationships have gone so badly awry that they seem irreparable? The answer is yes, but only if its members are willing to commit to the goal and do the necessary work. Restoring trust, or building trustworthiness when it has been absent entirely, requires great courage—courage to face oneself, change, and to accept others.

A new state of trust among family members must be earned, for ruptured relationships are not automatically repaired just because there is increased understanding and transformed perceptions. Trust can only really be restored, or formed satisfactorily, when specific and necessary changes in behavior are sustained over time, which involves reciprocal and ongoing efforts made by all family members. A general principle in the field of marital and family therapy states that behavioral change precedes relationship change and establishing mutual trust. This principle very much applies also to family members who work together as managers and/or owners of a family business.

The conversations that people have with themselves are the best indicators of whether or not they can trust themselves because "self-talk" is really what drives behavior. When people's internal conversations are mostly affirming, motivating, and realistic, people are ready to challenge themselves with behavioral changes, new roles, and responsibilities in the family business. However, when people's internal conversations are based in fear or anger at themselves and/or others, behavioral changes will most likely be impossible to accomplish.

With this information in mind, our work in the relationship-rebuilding phase frequently involves individual and family group meetings that focus on helping people take charge of their own minds by recognizing what they really think and feel about themselves and others. We explore such topics as their myths about their own interpersonal effectiveness, and we assist family members in developing "cheerleader" statements for themselves regarding how effective they will be in the family business environment. People are asked to prepare lists of the things they like about themselves as a manager and/or owner in a family business, actual or future, and of the things they need to learn to like about themselves in order to succeed as a family business member and leader. We also help family members learn to positively reinforce desired behaviors in others—always remembering, of course, that positive reinforcement works best when feedback is immediate and repeated many times.

Four interpersonal characteristics have been identified as being related to rebuilding trust in family businesses: character, competency, predictability, and caring (LaChapelle and Barnes, 1998). When there is a willingness to see the truth, both competency and predictability are fairly easy to measure. It soon becomes clear whether or not people are ready, willing, and capable of doing the job they are assigned or privileged to do. On the other hand, character and caring are more difficult to determine, especially if family members wish to disguise and hide themselves.

So what happens when some family members are unwilling or unable to change their discord-producing behaviors? What happens when family members operate in a nonaffirming way and are unwilling to see others either as competent or as improving their skills in critical areas? When people present blocks to making positive changes, either in themselves or in other persons, the persistent family will return again to scrutinizing the antecedents of these behaviors: developing knowledge and understanding, improving open and honest communication, and committing anew to a commonly held vision. As mentioned earlier, the Reconciliation Model is not linear; it allows for moving back and forth between the stages as needed for successfully reconciling troubled relationships.

Finally, whenever a family member is obviously unwilling to change and he or she has little or no capacity for self-criticism and compassion for others, he or she should simply not be permitted to occupy a position of power in the family business, either at the present time or in the future. This decision must be made regardless of how competent this individual appears to be or how many academic degrees have been earned. Why is this? Because the longevity of the business depends on having respectful and caring family relationships that nurture trust. If trust either cannot be built or restored through reconciliation and maintained thereafter, both the family and its business will suffer. Family members will become further estranged, with their relationships probably never repaired.

When the family operates within an affirming environment, people are more apt to learn new trustworthy behaviors and to perceive and be perceived by others as becoming trustworthy.

Trust increases decision-making ability, problem-solving skills, productivity, and energy to devote to the company's present and future activities. With mutual trust present among them, family members are able to focus their individual talents and abilities on the company, confident that information, knowledge, and resources will be utilized and shared for the common good. Families working together in this way can produce interpersonal magic; anything seems to become possible.

GOAL #2: FOSTER COLLABORATION

The second cornerstone of an affirming environment is collaboration. The word collaborate has two main meanings: either to labor as an associate of others, or to cooperate with the enemy. Family business actually has a place for both possibilities, and reconciliation can succeed from either position. Whether working as compatible associates or cooperating as truce-abiding enemies, collaboration can happen, allowing the business to go ahead.

Collaboration is about people working together toward a common purpose and clear values and goals. Each person knows and utilizes his or her skills, operates as an independent and unique individual, yet frequently subordinates his or her own wants to the greater good. This is *interdependence*. Each family member is willing to give and receive and to lead and follow.

What capacities are needed to develop collaboration? The same capacities needed to develop an intimate marriage (Kelly, 1996) can be easily transferred to the realm of collaboration in family business.

- Maintain a high level of devotion to the common goal.
- Mutually work to maximize positive interactions.
- Mutually work to minimize negative interactions.
- Support all programs that work to achieve these first three processes.
- Challenge anything that interferes with pursuing these processes.

The ability to maintain a collaborative relationship over time is directly related to a person's level of commitment—a commitment, expressed in both attitude and actions, to the development of the family and the business. In his recent book on creating commitment, Michael O'Malley (2000) explored the components of high commitment. When adapted to family businesses they are as follows:

- Cohesiveness: Individuals are bonded by common values, goals, and mutual positive regard.
- Pride: Family members feel proud of themselves and their family.
- Mutuality: Family members feel that their interests will be taken into account regardless of their position in management or as a shareholder.
- Fulfilled: Family members feel fulfilled in their jobs, supported in their work, and positively regarded by one another.
- Rewarded: Family members understand the special benefits that result from being part of the family company.

In addition to a commitment to positive processes, the family, and its company, collaboration requires that the partners have the ability to skillfully regulate their emotions and control their behaviors within the stressful and affect-laden workplace. Here again we see the importance of an affirming environment that helps people manage themselves in the moment-to-moment interactions of family business—a mix of cognitive, affective, and behavioral components.

Most people are able to keep negative or extreme emotions under control much of the time so as to maintain social equilibrium. Some people, though, need help in learning to manage themselves differently. Being a successful partner in a life journey, whether it is one of marriage or family business, takes a sustained effort. Many people give up too soon, especially if they have not developed the resilience needed to work through the inevitable relationship ruptures.

Following is a case example of a family business in which collaboration was being adversely affected by the struggle of one family member to regulate himself. Fortunately, we were able to step in and help out.

Commitment was strong among the third-generation members of the Rauch family, who were equal owners of a large California winery. The seven cousins had grown up side by side, getting to know one another well as they played and then worked together in the vineyard and at the winery. They lived in the same community and had spent their early school years together. They loved and respected their grandparents, the land, and the family traditions. Their fathers had done well, treated each other fairly, and even figured out how to pass their ownership on equitably to the seven children in the next generation.

Problems in collaboration arose, however, because not all of the seven cousins proved equally able to manage their emotions and relationships. We were approached by a representative of the cousins because they desperately needed to learn how to communicate better when dealing with current problems and planning for the coming years. In particular, Bruce, the head of winery production and transportation, was the center of everyone's concern—even to himself. Although he had been struggling mightily to control his anger it nonetheless erupted whenever he was with his older cousin, Paul, who headed field operations. Moreover, because of his anxiety about managing himself, he could barely sit in the same room with his sister.

Since affect is contagious, Bruce's difficulties frequently triggered family uproars, bringing many business meetings to an abrupt end. Bruce recognized that his problem, emotional instability, was impacting everyone. He regretted his lack of control and told us, "I just don't know what's wrong with me . . . or what to do about it."

We began our consultation by teaching all family members, including Bruce, some handy little tools to help contain themselves, and therefore also contain the contagious affect that often afflicted them in their interpersonal relations. These were simple techniques to help them "manage their minds" in better ways so that they were better able to regulate their responses in the business environment. Basically, they were cognitive tools for recognizing what is going on internally, accepting oneself as is, assessing the situation of the moment, and then deciding how best to respond.

Bruce, of course, had already recognized and accepted that his behavior was adversely affecting the others and he swiftly learned some of the mind-management tactics, along with several self-calming techniques. Actually, the entire group also benefited from learning and using these tools. They were quickly able to cooperate in minimizing negative interactions and maximizing positive interactions. Thus effective collaboration was readily established among the winery firm's seven owner-cousins.

Our work with the Rauch family was both easy and quick. The cousins all knew and cared about one another, and they respected one another's abilities. In addition, they all had a strong commitment to the business and a common underlying value system. Regarding the Sampson family and their very different situation, it was only after many years of estrangement and considerable effort at reconciling relationships that the family reached a collaborative relationship. With new understanding and commitment their results were eventually phenomenal.

GOAL #3: ESTABLISH RECONCILIATION PRACTICES

Numerous elements have been considered important in governing the business-owning family. Each family, of course, must personally craft its own unique approach to governing itself, based on its particular needs and relational style. All families, however, need to include some mechanism for repairing damaged family relationships. In this our third goal—the third cornerstone of an affirmative environment—we focus on practices essential for reconciling relationships.

Our aim here is to define the particular elements most important in a restorative philosophy and an affirmative family environment. Our focus is on validating decision-making practices; creating conflict-resolution strategies; viewing the family as a helping community; and developing capable people.

Validating Decision-Making Practices

Governing the family is different from governing the business. Governing the family is about establishing policies and procedures that protect family relationships and give the people of the family equal relationship power. Honoring this, of course, can present monumental difficulties, but doing everything possible to overcome those difficulties has proven well worth the effort.

Families have been making decisions together since Mom and Dad first met, decisions such as where to go, what to eat, when to have children, where to live, what college to go to, and what kind of a business to found. In the best family situations even a child's preferences have been taken into account. The child's beliefs and thoughts have been asked for and responded to seriously and the child's feelings have been considered as important communications. This is an affirming family environment.

The business-owning family that continues in this "best" way and maintains an affirming family environment will provide fertile ground for its members to grow, develop, and collaborate, regardless of the problems they face.

In many cases, family members may live far away, be widespread, and extremely busy, but the best policy is to validate each family member by asking for his or her input, ideas, and feelings. Take everyone into account even when the family is so large that different subgroups have chosen representatives to come to meetings. Weigh everyone's contributions—even when you know you won't like the answers. Why do this? Because an unwillingness to share relationship power in the family can ultimately have serious strategic and financial consequences for the family that owns and operates a business together.

In affirming family environments, as we indicated earlier, every family member is supported in contributing his or her competencies and interests to the family. Validating decision-making practices empowers family members and supports development of mutual interests. When families operate in this way, they create the probability that the younger members raised in this equitable and individual-affirming familial system can someday become a real "team at the top" (Katzenbach, 1998) because they have been encouraged to develop their complementary and diverse skills and to hold themselves mutually accountable for the decisions that are made.

When it comes to actually sitting down together and helping business-owning families work through a problem or make plans for the future, we find that the "six thinking hats" method (De Bono, 1999) is a particularly helpful decision-making tool. This is a structured method for solving problems, large and small, in which everyone's participation is encouraged and considered important, and everyone's individual identity, experience, and contributions to the family are taken into account. Another virtue of this method is that each person has an opportunity to lead the process, whenever his or her particular skills are called for.

In a recent consultation situation, for example, the youngest sister, a psychologist, and the only family member not working in the company, discounted her contributions to the board of directors, and in turn was discounted by other family members. Through using the "six thinking hats" method, the exceptional value of her intuition and feeling was finally recognized. From then on she held herself in higher regard, participated differently as a shareholder, and was welcomed at last as an important contributor to the family board. In addition, the family conflict that had always arisen because of her pushing to be heard and counted was greatly diminished.

Conflict-Resolution Strategies

Families have different discord-tolerance levels. Some families fragment over seemingly small matters, while others remain speaking and working together after large violations. In governing the business-owning family it is most important that a conflict-resolution process be in place for whenever ruptures occur, whether large or small. The Reconciliation Model is obviously our favored approach. But whatever the family's chosen way of resolving intrafamilial disagreements, some mechanism must be in place that does the following:

- Makes the relationship rupture, rather than any person, the problem
- Requires all family members to take relevant responsibility for resolving the conflict
- Protects family members against damaging personal exposure and shame
- Shows equal respect for all family members
- Results in a resolution that everyone can embrace

Business-owning families, similar to all families and all businesses, have different alternatives for resolving serious conflicts among their members. Reconciliation, as presented in this book, negotiation, mediation, and litigation, are all possibilities. Each approach has different uses and impacts the family in different ways. Our choice is reconciliation because of its focus on relationship repair.

Negotiation, a general approach, involves a structured discussion that sometimes is facilitated by an outsider. Hopefully it leads to a specific agreement that settles the conflict between the disputants. Negotiations can be very successful, especially when working to create concrete solutions regarding amounts of money or who gets what possessions. In a family business dispute, however, if the relationship is not kept in central focus, the personal styles of the family negotiators themselves can create new relationship wounds that lead to further problems and escalation of the conflict.

Mediation is a controlled negotiation wherein the parties are protected from further wounding by the operations of a third party, a neutral person with full authority to act on behalf of both sides in the dispute. The focus is on resolution of the concrete problem through keeping the parties apart, frequently even in separate rooms. This approach prevents personal styles and problems from mutually escalating the misunderstandings and dispute. Again, however, no consideration is given to reconciling the parties' relationships and preparing them to move forward as collaborating members of the same family business team. If the mediated solution is accepted as fair and mutually advantageous, then and only then does the possibility exist for the parties to reconcile and only after considerable effort.

Litigation, of course, is adversarial and retributive, passes judgment, and does not attend directly to any relationship restoration. It is time-consuming and costly, and can go on for years, every minute of which presents opportunity for new harm to individual family members, the family itself, and the family business.

As we mentioned previously, having some nonlitigious conflict-resolution practice in place is one of the most important determinants of longevity in family enterprise (Lank, 2001). Whatever the specific form, the particular practices of successful families place emphasis on restoring relationships.

Family As a Helping Community

An affirming family environment uses all family members as part of a helping community and everyone from an early age onward is invited to be a caring part of the family community. Therefore, each individual, regardless of generation, skill, or position in the family or its business, is regarded as equal, worthwhile, and important. The focus of the family community is to help bring out the best in each family member. Ideally, of course, this means listening to, nurturing, and empowering one another within an environment of trust, respect, and accountability.

This kind of family peer support facilitates decision making, problem solving, conflict resolution, and reconciliation. To help in rebuilding trust, for instance, members of a helping family community might point out "behavioral mistakes" in the interest of promoting self-awareness and self-correcting; or they might root for those who are striving to make changes. In the family constellation everyone is a peer. For example, often a grandchild can understand, motivate, encourage, and get the best out of a grandparent when others cannot. In-laws in their own group can understand and support one another in the challenges of being "unofficial" family members.

In the Sampson family, Rose, David's wife, who before the reconciliation had never even met most of her husband's family members because she shared her husband's estrangement from his birth family, became critically important and a powerful influence within the family community. She encouraged David to take part in the family reconciliation process, and then joined him at the meeting. She supported Joan and therefore helped her make her very important disclosures, which ultimately affected and changed the entire family. Without Rose, reconciliation would have been much more difficult.

May had never worked in the business or even been interested in or concerned about it, except for her husband Randy's uncertain future there. May was essentially a leader in creating family cohesion. She never forgot about anyone, or, it should be said, she always remembered everyone. She relentlessly pursued the vision of a united family, yet never expected or competed for recognition of her efforts. Although Sam and Benton had often claimed that they held the family business together, it was May who held the entire extended family together with her heart.

Let's look at a case example of the value of a mutually supportive familial association on a small scale. Bonnie and Melinda along with their brother, Jake, had decided to divide and then sell some of the family land holdings as a way of diversifying their interests and paying their taxes. Soon after this decision was made, however, Jake backed out and began hassling each of his sisters to change her mind about the sale.

We had participated in the initial decision making and were on call to help the family stay on track and implement their decision. So when Jake became frightened and ambivalent about letting go of properties that had been in the family for over a century, we helped Bonnie and Melinda respond to him in a caring way by understanding and acknowledging his dilemma and also reconfirming their own resolve to continue on task.

Most important, though, Bonnie and Melinda talked daily and supported each other every step of the way. The affirming environment of this family finally helped Jake come back into agreement so that the three siblings were able to complete the multimillion-dollar sale.

Developing Capable People

Successful family businesses start early and never give up on developing the human and intellectual capital of their family. Truly their most unique resource, it differentiates any family business from its competitors and sustains the enterprise over time.

An affirming family environment naturally supports the development of capable people. It helps every family member identify and develop the prerequisite skills needed to participate as an affirming family member and be a significant contributor to the helping community—and someday, if he or she chooses, an effective leader of the family business.

Roberts (1987) recognized that people who have the foundation of human esteem believe that both they and others are capable, powerful, lovable, and valuable. These beliefs come about over time, as people recognize that they contribute personally to the well-being of family members and family relationships, have the power to influence what happens to them, can manage their emotions, are effective interpersonally, and can trust their own judgment (Glenn and Nelson, 1988).

Families who continuously focus on developing the younger generations into capable people will have the opportunity to found or retain highly successful family businesses.

GOAL #4: GROW HEALTHY-INTERACTING FAMILIES

Business-owning families with a vision of beating the odds and extending into subsequent generations need to form and maintain outstanding interpersonal habits to carry them and their enterprise into the future. An important part of an advisor's role in this final stage of the Reconciliation Model is to aid the client family in adopting a set of rules and practices that will guide their future interactions—the fourth cornerstone. Affirming family environments and healthy relationships don't just happen, nor do they just automatically go on and on. To maintain through the generations, they need rules for operating, constant attention, care, and the support of every family member.

Throughout the many years of our professional experience we have been particularly interested in the relational rules that support healthy interactions in the highly volatile environment of the business-owning family. Surprisingly, the same rules that help businesses run better, with some modification will help families run better as well. The following highly important rules for healthy family business relationships are derived from T. J. Rodgers' "no excuses" management principles (Rodgers et al., 1999). These six rules support a family's restorative practices on a daily basis. They also support business-owning families in achieving and sustaining healthy interpersonal relationships and business success. As family business relationship advisors, we focus ardently on helping families integrate these rules into their everyday operations.

- *No Secrets.* Secrets, by definition, exist without the knowledge of others. Designed for escaping notice or observation, secrets undermine trust and collaboration. Secrets promote doubt and suspiciousness, and run contrary to the collective wisdom regarding the openness necessary to successfully govern the business-owning family. Secrets turn family members against one another and are the fertile ground for oppressive environments, fragmented families, and litigated conflicts.
- *No surprises.* Surprises are unexpected events or circumstances that can undermine relationships and the business. Because of their tendency to shock, dumbfound, dismay, and even horrify others, they run counter to predictability and reliability—both important components of trustworthiness.
- *No lies.* Lies are false statements made with the deliberate intent to deceive. When family members and business partners lie, they destroy any chance for actually knowing or trusting one another. Lies create false pictures by making things look better or at least different than they really are. They manipulate. A pattern of lies usually builds, one lie upon another, and then the conflict produced by the lies can easily escalate out of control.
- *No distractions.* Distractions divide attention, prevent concentration, and interfere with problem solving. Dysfunctional systems are made up of distractions. They undermine the competencies of individuals, prevent opportunities to learn and grow,

destroy the predictability of the relationship, and inhibit collaboration.

- *No excuses.* Excuses are pleas offered as a reason for being pardoned or exempted from responsibility. Self-justifications, which are in fact rationalizations, undermine taking individual responsibility for one's actions and the impact of one's behavior on others in the relationship system. Accepting excuses supports secrets, lies, and family illusions.
- *No illusions.* Illusions deceive by producing false impressions. Illusions eventually bring down companies and destroy lives. Healthy family business systems deal with truths regardless of the perceived immediate consequences—even hard truths such as a son's abuse of power, a sibling's substance addiction, or a father's failing ability to manage himself and the company.

When families and companies follow these six rules, they are less vulnerable to both the normal and unexpected adversities of daily life, whether at the office or at home. By using these rules individuals are better able to develop the specific skills, social competencies, and attitudes that help them handle themselves and their interpersonal relationships. Businesses are better able to chart the marketplace and develop achievable strategies for success.

Our Reconciliation Model also uses a set of research-based criteria that aid families in creating and maintaining new and healthy relationship systems. Jerry Lewis (1998) and others in the field of marriage and family therapy have greatly contributed to the following recommendations for well-functioning business-owning families. Again, the focus of our efforts as advisors is to help families adopt restorative practices that promote relationship healing:

- *Share relationship power.* All family members, no matter what their involvement in the business or how many shares they control, must be allowed to hold significant and equal relationship influence. Where family relationships are concerned, CEOs must not have more relationship influence than siblings who do not work in the business. After all, they are all children of the same parents, and one does not become a more valuable or worthy person just because he or she attained a bigger position in the business. Many years of family struggles and estrangement, and even many companies themselves, can be saved if family members are given equivalent relationship power and respected influential places in the family relationship circle, regardless of the circumstances of their business involvement.

- *Respect individual differences.* Each family member has a distinctive set of innate abilities (determined by variable biological and developmental factors), as well as different experiences, interests, strengths, and skills. Each person also has a unique personality. These diversities manifest themselves as differing needs for closeness and independence where the family and the family business are concerned; as differing styles in interpersonal relationships; and as different levels of personal investment in the company. Each person in the family needs to be considered as valuable as all the others, and just as capable of bringing a distinctive richness to the family and its business. In other words, every family business has something of value to gain from every family member; it only needs to be discovered and then encouraged.

- *Contain the conflicts.* Conflict between people comes naturally, because people are different from one another. Conflict can be healthy and supply opportunities for growth and learning or, if allowed to broaden in scope and increase in intensity, can escalate and disable the usual mechanisms of individual and relationship repair—sometimes even beyond the possibility of reconciliation. Recognize conflicts early and repair the relationships quickly.

- *Stay active and involved.* The biggest obstacle to reconciliation in family business is nonparticipation of family members in efforts to reconcile broken relationships. In healthy relationships people contribute, stay active, and are involved. Family members who are passive, or who refuse to connect with or participate in problem-solving processes, should be immediately challenged.

- *Keep the focus positive.* Excellence in both personal and business arenas requires being supportive and accepting of others and oneself in all endeavors. Research on relationships (Gottman and Silver, 2000) reveals that a partnership is best able to achieve optimal levels of performance when at least a 5 to1 ratio exists between positive and negative interactions. As we have emphasized over and over again in this chapter, an affirming environment fosters results that can be amazing.

- *Be grateful.* In every family, showing gratitude is important and appropriate. People who are grateful see the good in every situation. They look for what is going right and hold onto the kindness and advantages that have come their way. Every generation of a successful family business treats the next generations of family members with charity and kindheartedness when they pass along opportunities and wealth. Each new generation that receives the gifts of a business and family members to work with benefits from others' actions, courage, and foresight. Being grateful is recognizing that someone has deliberately given you something of value just because you are a family member—and you are you. Gratitude keeps individuals, families, and businesses healthy, so express it often!

MOVING ON

In our work with the owners of Sampson Seed Company, this third stage of our model, rebuilding relationships and preparing for the future, began during the last day of the intensive family meeting and concluded nearly two years later. This is similar in any family business we work with because putting needed changes into action and building new relationships are developments that only happen when the family spends an extended amount of "ordinary" time working and being together.

In the first and second stages of the Reconciliation Model, the role of the relationship advisor is one of intense involvement and actively directing the reconciliation process. In these two stages the consultant is necessary and integral in the family's life and in bringing about changes within it and the family business. Because families have been put off balance by relationship conflicts, they trust their advisors and in many ways depend on them to help rebalance themselves and their business management in healthier and more productive ways. It is an advisor's job to be present in Stages I and II, when individual wounds and relational ruptures are exposed and in need of repair, and to be active in directing the family members in safely recognizing and reconsidering their manner of functioning, including how they conduct their relationships.

In the third stage of our model, though, the role of the advisor dramatically changes to quietly helping the family put into place the four cornerstones of an affirmative family environment. As advisors, our most critical assignment now is actually to make ourselves nonessential to the family by simply guiding them, as necessary, in ways that will help them take over and carry themselves into the future, finally without our assistance. As ethical and competent professionals we pull back and move on, which is sometimes a difficult task when we have become particularly fond of a family and are interested in whatever has been going on with them. Also, there can be attractive emotional and even financial perks for staying involved as consultants. But in the third stage of the model, saying a final good-bye confirms a relationship-consulting job well done.

The role of the advisor in family business is discussed in more detail in Chapter 9, where we consider the various professional and ethical conundrums resulting from the dilemmas that arise when advising business-owning families.

Interlude 4: Moving into the Future

It is the week following the conclusion of the Sampson family reconciliation meeting in Carmel, and we've been working to ensure that the family follows through and finishes with their commitments. During the meeting itself the family had completed plans for remodeling the management of Sampson Seed Company. These were passed with unanimous—although hesitant for some—approval.

Since Sam certainly represents the center beam in this family business, we have committed ourselves to do whatever we can to make sure he enters the alcohol treatment program. Les provides the main background support, and begins each day with a phone call to Sam.

Meanwhile, Bill, Benton, David, and Marsha, the family members who have daily direct contact with Sam, call us with any concerns or questions about how they can best help out. On the Monday of the second week after our meeting we'll hold a conference call to include all of these key support people plus Joan, and Sam himself. Things seem to go well for Sam until the first weekend, when he predictably wavers and Bill once more has to deal with his father's self-destructive behavior.

By the time our Monday conference call actually takes place, everyone is itching to talk, notably Bill and David. There are two important items on the agenda for our call, Sam and the arrangements to help him and the management of the company during his absence.

It seems as if Sam is attempting in various ways to wiggle out of his commitment to treatment, so our first focus is to help the family all work together to keep Sam on track—a great accomplishment for people who had formerly been so resentful, antagonistic, and divided against one another. Sam is told not to worry about anything except healing himself, since final determinations about his future and that of the family business can easily wait. Bill restates his intention to personally accompany his father to the treatment program, while Marsha announces that she will also be joining them on the trip, and from there she will meet Sophie and take a long-deserved vacation.

Next, David wonders how he can arrange to be more available during Sam's anticipated six-week absence; he also expresses concern about plans for the future of the business, especially if Sam really decides not to return at all to Sampson Seed Company. Amidst strongly voiced objections from Benton and much support from Joan and Sam, David agrees to be present at Sampson Seed three days a week while Sam is involved in treatment. Officially, he will be the interim CEO, giving special attention to mentoring Benton.

BUILDING TRUST AND COLLABORATION: BENTON

Our next few months with the family are spent assisting family members in building trust and collaboration. We're pleased that Sam has made it into the treatment program. However, in several phone contacts we have heard that with Sam gone, Benton has resumed his arrogant, controlling posture.

Marsha shared with us that her older brother's need to be right automatically puts him above everyone, and he constantly implies that anyone not agreeing with him is wrong and inadequate. In addition, an angry May and Randy say that Benton still acts as if he knows best about who other people are and what they think and also he doesn't listen to anyone. Whenever he's questioned about anything Benton behaves as if he's just been attacked and then he attacks.

It's true that some of Benton's behavior is understandable, especially considering his experiences in the past: the trauma over the circumstances of his father's death and his grandiose expectations based on verbal promises of one day leading the family company. However, Benton's way of interacting with people subverts his skills and administrative talent, and also makes it impossible for others to like, respect, or trust him—or wish ever to include him as a member of a collaborative team.

Both Joan and David have expressed their interest in giving Benton the chance to succeed at the helm of the company since that's his cherished goal and no one else has his intense interest or potential to lead. But all three of the second-generation family members entrusted with the company, though pledged to help Benton succeed, have already agreed to remove him if need be. It's obvious now that a difficult family course lies ahead, especially for Joan, who will need to draw many hard lines with her son. Benton must soon be confronted with a choice: either change his way of behaving toward others, or else give up his lifelong dream of running the Sampson Seed Company.

Our next direct contact with the family, coming two weeks after Sam is settled into treatment, is a four-hour in-person meeting with Joan and David, with the understanding that eventually Benton will be asked in. Our assigned task, in short, is to help them take the last steps in breaking the spell of oppression which has hung over this family and its business for years, carried down from its founder, Bill Sampson, from one generation to the next.

We first work with Joan and David so that they will understand and agree to what needs to be done. There must be no more secrets, excuses, or illusions controlling the future. Benton has to summon up the determination and courage to change himself. He will be asked to undertake several tasks: to obtain outside professional assistance in changing his intolerable attitudes and behavior; to accept David as a family and company mentor; and to establish a trustworthy and respectful relationship with employees and with family members working in the company. It will be made clear to Benton that if he doesn't willingly participate in these and other change-producing actions, he will not become CEO and he will never hold a controlling interest in Sampson Seed Company.

JOAN: Wow! I don't know if I can do all of that to my son. He's going to be furious and may never speak to me again.

RUTH: It is time . . .

JOAN: Oh, you don't need to say anything more! I know that I really need to do this because I have to finally take a stand . . . and protect my family. I even see this as protecting Benton from himself.

DAVID: We have to act. Sam is behind us in this, too, you know. . . . Joan, I was never there for you after Jason died. But now I'm here and finally ready to do my part. I will support you and the rest of our family all the way. You can't even imagine how important all of this involvement is to me. It's like I've been given another chance in life. Since the day I was born, I never believed I could have this with my family: to be included, respected, and cared for.

LES: Okay, it sounds like there is agreement between you. (Joan and David both nod affirmatively.) So let's go!

After the four of us have a brief stretch, we invite Benton to join our meeting. He first expresses surprise at seeing his mother present, and then sits down somewhat separate from the rest of us, who are at the other end of the conference table. David begins by again offering Benton his support in a mentoring relationship. He then outlines the major shareholders' requirements for changes that Benton will have to make if he is ever to become the company's chief executive officer.

BENTON (in a loud, sharp tone): You can't do this to me! Joan, you're not going to let this happen, are you?

JOAN: Yes, Son. I agree with all that your uncle David has said, and I am in full support of everything on that agenda for you. And, by the way, I am also in full control of how many shares you will eventually hold in this company.

BENTON: You'll probably throw everything away by giving it all to Jason, anyway!

JOAN: That has never been my intention, and you can be assured it won't happen. I have always wanted to honor your grandfather's and your father's wishes that you head this company someday. However, this simply will never happen if you don't learn to treat other people in a very different way than both your dad and your granddad did. Change your ways and you shall receive . . . that will be my gift to you.

BENTON (quite subdued): I guess I have to believe you, don't I?

JOAN and DAVID (in unison): Yes, you do.

When the meeting concludes, Benton's back is still up. He is unwilling to make any commitment to change, and at one point he even angrily declares that he will leave the company. His mother and uncle both tell him that whatever he decides to do will be *his* choice. A meeting for Benton to bring his final decision to the table is set for three weeks hence.

In the intervening weeks we hear that Benton is taking a lot of time off from the company; he's clearly considering his options. Not only is he spending time conferring with his wife, Barbara, but he's also gone hiking in the High Sierras with Robert. The cousins had become fast friends during the Carmel meeting.

For the follow-up meeting with Benton, everyone, including Benton, arrives punctually. Immediately we get to the main issue: What is Benton's decision?

BENTON: Simply said, I have decided to accept and try to do all that you require of me, and I'm ready to proceed at any time.

RUTH: Benton, that's really good to hear! But I'm interested in knowing how you reached your decision. It's important for the rest of us to understand just what you're thinking about.

BENTON: Several things were very important to me. First, Barbara doesn't want to move away from here—under any circumstances. She also said she knew that she and the kids would also benefit from my "betterment" program. Second, Robert was an immense help to me. (David smiles.) He really helped me see the value of staying—of not throwing my life's dreams away just because I am angry and scared. He also thinks I can accomplish whatever you've asked me to do. I guess Robert has had his own experiences with doing some of these things himself.

The four of us then lay out a program for Benton. We refer him to a therapist in his own community who we know can help him understand his feelings and behavior and make the necessary changes both in the company and with his family.

David arranges for weekly phone contacts with Benton, and says he'll soon be recommending that Benton take specific and intensive management-training courses elsewhere. In addition, Benton will spend some time each month in David's and Robert's office in Phoenix.

This current core group, which hopefully will someday include Sam, is going to be checking regularly to explore ongoing experiences with Benton. A date is set in six months to reconvene. When we end the meeting, Joan says tearfully to us: "My children and I have so much to look forward to now . . . and so *very* much to thank you for."

FINISHING WITH THE FAMILY

Following the family meeting in Carmel, we knew that many loose ends in relationships would need some tying-up help from us before the Sampson clan would be ready to pull back from this intense level of work. During the months afterward we've been able to follow through with almost everything. Following is a summary of what has happened in several nuclear family units.

Sam, Betty, and Bill

Sam successfully completed his treatment program. During the course of that program Bill joined his father for the family week. Unfortunately, Betty was unable to participate because of a difficult pregnancy—although we don't know if she would have actually gone had her health allowed it. However, when making her decision not to go, Betty had promised us that she'd meet with us and her father some time in the near future. Eight months went by before we were actually able to arrange that meeting.

When that meeting time arrived Sam was well into his recovery—and was a different person. He had finally ended the contentious divorce settlement and was treating his children's mother fairly. These two factors, plus his willingness to make amends to his daughter, helped immensely in bringing about the reconciliation scene.

SAM: I want to begin, Betty, by saying how very sorry I am that I hurt you and treated both you and your mother in abusive ways. I am at fault. I did mean and unthinking things to you both, which neither one of you in any way deserved. I have missed having you in my life. Please forgive me. And then let's see if there is a way we can go ahead. I want to be your friend, and I also want to get to know my son-in-law and my grandchildren.

BETTY (overwhelmed with tears): I have been waiting and hoping for so long for this. Thank you, Dad.

We helped them talk about many things. Then Sam and Bill accepted Betty's invitation to join her and her family for the Sunday after Thanksgiving. Bill and his sister and her family would be spending Thanksgiving Day together at their mother's home.

At present, Sam and Betty maintain a distant but considerate connection. They are friendly with each other at family meetings. In addition, Sam plans to continue to see his grandchildren several times a year. Bill and Betty have a growing sibling relationship, and both are looking forward to when Bill settles down and Betty's children have cousins to play with. Sam and Bill remain very close.

What a long way to have come for people who were at one time determined to never speak to one another again! (We'll tell you later about what Sam decided to do about his work and his life.)

Joan, Benton, May, Marsha, and Jason

The Bennington family has been transformed. Benton has accomplished much of what was required of him. He now treats his family members with both caring and respect and the difference has reverberated throughout the entire family relationship system. Believe it or not, the Bennington family plans to spend Thanksgiving together for the first time since Jason Sr.'s death. (Beginning at age eight, Benton had always found somewhere else to go to attend a family feast, and Joan never stopped him.)

Of particular note is the change in Barbara's relationship with her husband's family. As soon as Benton was willing to allow this, Barbara seemed eager to get to know everyone. Her children now get together with May and Randy's children, and she has little hesitation about letting them visit their grandmother at her home. In fact, the girl cousins, who soon will include Betty's daughter, love to meet for tea at Joan's place. Moreover, Marsha and Sophie have recently adopted a six-year-old girl, and she's currently the center of attention for all the third-generation girl cousins. It's as if they are replaying the happy get-togethers of long ago that were arranged by their grandmother, Marsha.

David and the Entire Phoenix Bunch

This part of the Sampson family proceeds as usual—though, paradoxically, usual is in an entirely different way, for their extended family now includes twenty new blood relatives, an addition that happened almost overnight. Unbelievably, the total count now of the entire Sampson family clan numbers forty persons, which includes spouses, domestic partners, and adopted children.

Of special significance is the close and sometimes inseparable relationship that has developed between Robert and Benton. Barbara says that they are like twins who have finally found each other after separate but very similar experiences in life.

Renee visits May and Marsha often. Rose and Joan have become good friends. Although both Randall and Richard are interested in the larger, newfound Sampson family, they are mostly occupied with their own young families, attending graduate school programs, and finding their way as junior members in their father's company, SS&S Development Services.

Christmas this year will be an incredible event. Rose and David have invited the entire family to Phoenix, and everyone, even Betty and her family, will be coming. The entire hotel where they'll be staying, which is owned by Smithly, Sampson, and Sons, will be occupied with family members.

SAMPSON SEED COMPANY: AN EPILOGUE

Needless to say, things are very different in the family business since the first family meeting in Carmel. The second family business meeting is planned for late spring in New Mexico.

Sam never returned to management at Sampson Seed Company after undergoing the treatment program. However, he still retains all his shares (he didn't insist on being bought out) and is now the president of the board of directors. Having moved his residence to San Francisco, he is currently affiliated with a respected firm of management consultants, and working with family firms is his specialty. He reports that he is happy and sober . . . and will be remarried soon.

Sam redecided about his life, made personal and professional changes for himself, and still is never more than a phone call away from his family and the family company.

With everyone's approval, the CEO torch has recently been passed to Benton. After the intense "rebuilding" period, Joan, David, and

Sam all agreed that Benton was ready to take over. He will now lead Sampson Seed Company energetically and competently, having persuaded the rest of the family that he is truly a changed man. A detailed employment contract was devised that included safeguards for Benton and the other family members working in the firm.

The board of directors now includes Joan, David, Sam, Benton, Robert, and three outside directors. The shareholders are set up to meet twice yearly, and a family business meeting, to which all Sampson family adults will be invited, is to occur on an annual basis.

Several other new and very exciting changes have occurred within the Sampson Seed Company itself.

Randy has been promoted to Benton's old position and is now vice president of operations. He and May are highly pleased. "That's all we ever wanted," they say; "just to be treated fair and square and to raise our kids here in this town."

Marsha, who now heads new business development, is shepherding two new projects. The first one, which is the more exciting for her personally, is a joint venture with Renee and Jason. They are packaging and marketing gourmet seeds. Renee, who for some years has owned several high-end retail establishments, decided to include brightly packaged seeds among her gourmet items. They took off quickly, and now, because of her customer base, are gaining much wider recognition. Jason is kept busy designing new packaging, and recently he actually created something that can be framed: enlarged and framed pictures of the seed packets. Extravagantly priced, they are so extraordinarily popular that Jason has hired creative help and is moving into a new and larger studio space. Exhilarated, he says he's surprised at himself, for he never even imagined he'd ever succeed at commercial art.

The second new project comes from Benton and Robert and their constant interface. SS&S and Sampson Seeds are jointly developing some acreage for the production of unusual nursery plants. Sam's son Bill, who might always be best known for his love of traveling, is now on the payroll for this new horticultural venture: he is exploring different places in the world and bringing back possible new items for this experimental agricultural project. He is learning a lot and loving it, and has even developed university connections to help him with the scientific part of his work.

In telling the tale of the Sampson Seed Company, we can supply no conclusion. With many family members involved now, and surely more to come in the fourth generation, it is a vibrant and developing entity. An end to this successful family business is nowhere in sight.

We continue to be available to the Sampson family on an on-call basis, and we are sure to be present at the next family meeting.

In concluding their story we simply want to thank all family members for letting us become part of their lives and for sharing so much of themselves with us. In a team effort over time, we all contributed to bringing about a family reconciliation and a family business transition to a very successful future.

Chapter 9

Being the Best We Can Be

You saved his life and you saved our business for them. I can't even begin to say thank you.

A client

The job of consulting with family-owned businesses is a complex and complicated assignment that involves a multitude of variables. Doing one's best requires combining the expertise and ethics of a particular profession with an appreciation of family dynamics, plus an understanding of the ultimate challenge of any business—economic survival.

In this final chapter we consider some noteworthy professional and ethical issues that each advisor faces when working with families who own a business together and most likely have one or more members actively engaged in running it. The questions that we address here have important implications for the conduct, and in some cases the outcome, of any consultation.

People who work with family-owned businesses enter the field from many different professional backgrounds. They are called, and call themselves, by many different names: consultants, advisors, coaches, change agents or change managers, and facilitators—to name a few. This diversity in nomenclature demonstrates that there are many different approaches to helping family businesses accomplish their goals. But no matter what background orientation or current approach to problem solving, every professional who consults to families in business, in whatever capacity and context, must be sensitive to and understand the ins and outs of the multiple relationship issues that are likely to confront them as they proceed in their work.

To a large extent, the accountant, the attorney, and the management specialist are all relationship advisors, because many times their clients are people in conflict. When clients have hurts that run deep, the logic they use to manage their behavior is not always immediately apparent; more often than not it is internally or personally driven. To facilitate needed change, family business consultants must understand this internal logic and use it to help guide clients in the direction they wish to go.

In the field of family business consulting, various professional viewpoints and ethical codes interface and sometimes clash. This point makes it important to consider some of the overriding questions that each of us must ponder in situations in which intrinsic values may differ. In ethics, the systematic approach to understanding right and wrong, it is much easier to pose these questions than to resolve them, because often there are many answers to what is "right." In keeping with this irony, we don't try to provide answers to the ethical questions raised in the situations specific to working with business-owning families. In this chapter, we merely want to raise some important considerations and share our own way of approaching some quandaries.

When following the Reconciliation Model, it is always important to think about and openly discuss the ever-present difficult issues that each of us must face. As advisors we serve as models to our clients for actively seeking the truth and dealing with the difficult problems confronting them. Therefore, a failure to discuss the ethical dilemmas confronting us could leave us vulnerable to our own prejudices. We intend to consider the following questions.

- Who, exactly, is the client?
- How does an advisor keep confidentiality?
- How does an advisor maintain neutrality?
- When is a team approach called for, and what is its value?
- When is it time to say good-bye and move on?

WHO IS THE CLIENT?

Since it is not always possible to advance the welfare of the business and the family at the same time, much less the welfare of each of the subgroups or individuals seeking a consultant's assistance, the question of who we are working for is central to planning our approach. Different family business advisors, depending on their profession of origin, who has engaged them, or who pays their fees, could rightfully regard as clients any or all of the following: the business itself; the family; any or all of the different subsystems that make up the family or the business; any or all of the individuals involved; or a specific person (usually the one who called in the consultant to begin with).

Certainly part of the answer to who is the client has more to do with an advisor's professional values and training than it does with the situation itself. Thus a management background leads the advisor in one direction, a relationship focus leads in another. As relationship advisors, we take a very specific focus: we regard the entire business-owning family as our client. But we must also account for other avenues. In considering the family as our client, our challenges are to balance individual, family, and business perspectives; to factor in cultural considerations; and to make ethical decisions.

Balancing Individual, Family, and Business Interests

Balancing individual and family interests can create a predicament. For instance, how does one decide which is more important: the desire of parents to hold their family together through ownership of the business they or their ancestors founded; or their children's strong wish to separate from the business and invest their shares in other ways? Does the advisor help facilitate an amicable "divorce" or at least a "divorce" in which the two sides are able to preserve rational communication and mutual consideration? Or does the advisor opt for helping this "marriage" continue, even though it comes at the cost of individuals sacrificing their chances for self-fulfillment in other, sometimes preferred careers?

Succession usually matters a great deal in family businesses, so this and other issues of sudden or abiding concern frequently bedevil families and advisors. Such large questions are certainly answered differently depending on who the advisor considers to be the client, or the solution that the advisor himself or herself personally values.

We also need to consider the balance between family well-being and business prosperity. In a collision between the individual and the business, most consultants would consider the business to be their client and therefore help the family resolve the issues on behalf of the business. But what happens when family and business management collide? Perhaps the family itself feels threatened if a family member is no longer wanted in the business, or if it is decided that he or she is not capable of becoming or remaining as CEO. How do people choose between their various options: their children and maintaining good family connections on the personal side, and the success, sale, or maybe even the failure on the business side? How do parents with different preferred positions resolve the issue among them?

All of these situations and questions are extremely difficult to resolve. It requires a creative, thoughtful, and well-informed advisor to navigate the troubled waters in the interests of whomever is their client.

Factoring in a Family's Culture

What exactly is culture? There are many definitions of culture but the defining factor of any culture is that its members solve problems in similar ways (Hofstede et al., 1990; Schein, 1992; Trompenaars et al., 1997). This designation serves to guide us in our work with clients, because for us culture is about behavior rather than about beliefs, which are attached to values. True, behavior and values overlap, but they aren't the same thing. From our perspective the most important aspect when factoring in a family's culture is whether or not it promotes an affirming environment.

Regardless of a specific cultural pattern or its origin, it is crucial for family business advisors, of whatever professional orientation, to acknowledge the central role that culture plays in organizing people's lives. Each family has its own culture, including their unique set of values, expectations, and rules, plus the values of their particular ethnic or national culture. Thus culture obviously impacts the consultation relationship, the process of the consultation, and the advisor. To work effectively with people whose practices and values are different from our own, it is important to understand each family's own culture in order to both honor and respect it.

It is easy to see how a failure to account for a particular family's style or lived values (i.e., culture) would seriously hamper an advisor's ability to work with a family business. For example, those families who value the family's "we-ness" over the individual's "I-ness" will very likely resist any advisor's attempts to encourage individual autonomy. Similarly, expecting and asking people to evoke feelings in a family culture that does not support this practice will probably meet the same fate, as will other strategies, such as promoting either emotional closeness or individual achievement when these are not part of the culture (Trompenaars and Hampden-Turner, 1997).

Communication styles, conflict-resolution styles, the structure of the organization, and openness to outsiders are also part of the family culture, as are patterns of management and ownership succession, and the degree of members' involvement with the business (McGoldrick and Toast, 1993). As a result, important issues such as role definition, performance criteria, and compensation for family members have cultural loading.

Cultural considerations definitely factor into decisions about how and to which family members the management of a family's business will ultimately be transferred. Most notably, they are often directly related to how a family traditionally perceives and feels about birth order and gender, for instance, firstborn sons versus younger male siblings and females. Another crucial matter seen from a similar cultural and ethnic perspective is who will own major and possibly controlling shares of company stock. Such decisions may also involve issues such as fairness and equity, in-laws, and even divorce and adoption.

One key to success of the family business is how adaptable its unique culture is to the changing dictates of life and business cycles, and to the changing environment in which either organization, whether family or business, must function. The family's culture, the way in which it goes about solving problems, must be sufficiently flexible so that beneficial changes can be implemented as the family goes through the various stages of its life cycle. Many businesses, like the people who run them, tend to continue behaving in routine-set, nonproductive ways, discounting and turning deaf ears to crucially helpful new information. The consequences may be dismal if the company's operating style remains out of sync with the changing times, thereby risking becoming outdated.

Each family also has its own set of rules, usually unwritten, that guide family members as they make their way in the world. The set of rules that make each family unique can also be thought of as *that family's culture*. In both families and in businesses, for example, some family cultures clearly promote competitiveness and a permissive atmosphere that allow oppression and the sidelining of certain groups or persons from full participation. One ingrained attitude feeds into another. Competitiveness without limits becomes the breeding ground for intrafamilial aggressiveness (Sperry, 1998).

Understanding culture is one thing; changing a culture that facilitates unwanted behavior is another. In a family business the culture is often set by the founder, whose force of character determines how things are to be done (Schein, 1992). This tells us where to focus our attention. It also helps us to know that cultural patterns are quite entrenched and it reminds us to be patient, facilitate small changes, and reinforce them frequently and regularly.

WHAT ABOUT CONFIDENTIALITY?

Confidentiality in the advisor-client relationship is one of the most fundamental principles of professional ethics and successful consultation. But how can confidentiality be respected and maintained in a consultation situation that is apt to have so many variables, including the people involved? This is a major issue to be addressed generally and with each new consultation situation.

Establishing and maintaining a policy of confidentiality is a linchpin in setting and keeping trust between family members and advisors, and among family members themselves. Significant and needed attitudinal, behavioral, and relationship changes depend on confidentiality.

Concerns about confidentiality are evident from the very beginning of the engagement. Before hiring advisors prospective clients are likely to ask for their references. Understandably, new clients want to be able to call a few previous clients and ask whatever they need to know in order to feel assured that a particular advisor will be right for them. This, of course, is standard practice in business, and some business advisors actually list former and current clients and other contacts on their Web sites.

As relationship advisors, we look upon our consults with family businesses as different in this regard. Professionals working with relationships, frequently psychotherapists, must work at the other end of the reference-giving spectrum. Revealing clients' names is a breach of professional confidentiality. In fact, it is improper even to ask a client for permission to release his or her name, since the close nature of the therapist-client relationship might make it hard for the client to say no to such a request.

Bridging the gap between a prospective client's need for information and a past client's right for privacy is even more complicated. To ask owners for permission to use their names and the family businesses' names as references also means that we are asking for permission to publicly identify the other family members. This is a permission one person cannot grant for another person.

Using case examples in this book, even for teaching purposes, is another example of the confidentiality conundrum. We have addressed this issue in the preface, where we noted that we not only disguised family businesses to the point in which the business could not be identified, but we also combined case material from different families and circumstances. Our commitment is to keep to the sense of the situation rather than the actuality. Such is the need for relationship advisors to preserve confidentiality.

Confidentiality is perhaps the most tender tenet in all of family business advising. Easily agreed to, it is far more easily broken. Emanuel Rosen (2000) in his recent book *The Anatomy of Buzz* shows how utilizing the invisible social communication networks of society can be incredibly successful in marketing products, via "word-of-mouth" marketing. Unfortunately these same networks that are so useful to today's companies also operate in every family in the form of gossip, which undermines confidentiality. Therefore, it is imperative for advisors to establish a specific policy of confidentiality and request that family members respect one another enough to honor it; and of course it is important for advisors to stick to it themselves, without fail.

Holding confidences means that family members and advisors must always be willing to protect others from exposure and shame. In other words, the essence of confidentiality is the protection it offers to the family.

Maintaining confidentiality is different from keeping secrets. When there are secrets among certain family members, the secret keepers, which may include an advisor, although they have formed an alliance for self-protection, they are, in effect, acting against the best interests of the family. Thus as relationship advisors we follow the rule of *no secrets*. In working with a family, we are clear from the outset that we do not keep or support secrets from other family members.

Whenever we learn something important and possibly problematic about a family member—something important that other family members do not know, and which would likely impact them negatively if it were not disclosed, we always encourage and help family members to reveal that information in a safe and caring way. Most often the energy behind the secret is the fear of shame and retribution that would follow disclosure to the others. When we focus on the ultimate impact of discovering the secrets, usually emotional distance and anger, disclosure becomes the lesser of the evils. When we help everyone deal with the consequences of some revelation, we often find that the processes of relationship repair and behavior transformation are actually accelerated.

MAINTAINING NEUTRALITY—IS IT POSSIBLE?

Like confidentiality, an advisor's neutral and nonjudgmental stance contributes to clients feeling safe enough to be able to reveal themselves openly and give the appropriate information that will aid in the change process, especially when it is personal information. Yet neutrality is extremely difficult to achieve when working with business-owning families in which there is a constant pull to take sides. Neutrality is also difficult to achieve given an advisor's own inherent personal biases. But no matter what the issue, when family business advisors maintain constancy, impartiality, and distance, they are in the best position to do their job well.

We want to be clear, though, that this principle of neutrality does not preclude taking a stand when it is necessary to do so. For example, we are scarcely neutral about oppressive behavior patterns. Oppression hurts people and oppressive behaviors need to be stopped. In such family circumstances, as in many others, we maintain neutrality by being on the side of the family as a unit.

Our work with the Sampson family demonstrated another extremely important aspect of the principle of neutrality—that of *multidirected partiality* (Boszormenyi-Nagy and Spark, 1973). By achieving a positive connection with everyone, each family member gains support and confidence through experiencing us as in his or her "corner" rather than everyone experiencing us in nobody's corner.

The principle of neutrality is well established in some aspects of the practice of law: a lawyer cannot represent two members of the same family because the individuals may have conflicting interests. Likewise, in the medical profession, doctors may not treat members of their own family who have serious medical conditions. In the behavioral health field a psychotherapist may not be someone's therapist and a business partner at the same time.

This brings us to the important consideration of dual relationships—relationships in which there is overlap and ambiguity in roles and responsibilities. Dual relationships make it extremely difficult for the advisor to separate his or her personal interest from the interest of the client.

Family business advisors frequently face the situation of dual relationships. For instance, they are often asked to be "double agents" and sit on a client company's board of directors, or offered stock in lieu of cash payments for services, or given gifts and other perks that go with being part of the inner circle. Accepting any of these offers compromises an advisor's ability to remain independent and maintain neutrality. The advisor must be clear about his or her own boundaries, which translates into knowing the limits of the advisory role, understanding the danger of shifting from the outside advisor to the inside "friend," and recognizing when that shift is happening. Keeping neutrality is what assures all of us that we are following the ethics of our profession.

In the field of family business advising, which includes all the professionals who are engaged in consulting services, an overall tradition of professional ethics has developed. These service agents are expected to:

- Exhibit strong self-discipline
- Have a high degree of knowledge and the ability to apply that special knowledge
- Show primary commitment to the client, setting aside self-interests and concerns
- Be devoted to service rather than financial or status rewards for the self

THE TEAM APPROACH TO ADVISING

Serving the needs of people who live, love, and work together is a complex and exciting challenge for professionals from many backgrounds. Each discipline supplies ample useful knowledge to the family business arena. However, no one person or profession can bring all of the outside help that may be needed, sometimes quite urgently.

Advising a family business is usually a team effort, just as being a member of a business-owning family is a team effort. Each professional advisor, regardless of his or her specific area of expertise, has something special to offer. Yet to do the best job, experts must depend on one another. All professional advisors need to be experts in their own field, and they should also know some of the basics of the other fields that make up an existing consulting team. Also, everyone on the team needs to know what he or she does not know, and when to call in the special expertise of other colleagues.

Teams of advisors, often uncoordinated, are a fact of life for family-owned businesses because several disciplines are typically employed by them. Not surprisingly, professionals see their clients from their own special perspectives. At times, a profusion of experts can be confusing, since many different solutions for any particular problem are often proposed. Each consultant is, of course, likely to have his or her own preferred methodology, thereby demonstrating the need for a coordinated effort. The field of advising family businesses has taken a large first step toward promoting this kind of teamwork.

Although the theory of consulting teams is sound, in practice the team approach is not without its problems. Building a team when diverse professionals have often staked out their territory and frequently guard it with a passion takes a strong commitment. Maintaining a team takes considerable time, energy, and innumerable meetings. There is a steep learning curve during which team members must become reasonably knowledgeable about what each of the other team members do. Also, trust has to be built so that the others can rest easy whenever another team member is working with the family firm. Moreover, the team approach is apt to be more expensive for the client.

Psychological factors present challenges as well. When consultants operate in a team tensions tend to develop among them that actually mirror those in the business-owning family itself (Smith and Zane, 1999). Managing these tensions requires considerable self-awareness and skill, and often the help of an outside facilitator as well.

To make matters more difficult, the environment in which the family firm operates presents a moving target. Everything is constantly changing—the market, the legal environment, and the people involved. Those changes supply feedback information that the team must integrate into their overall approach (Dickson et al., 2001). On the one hand, a group finds it more of a task to integrate this feedback than an individual would; but on the other, sometimes a group can see problems, solutions, and outcomes better than an individual.

Despite such difficulties and drawbacks, though, the team approach offers many benefits to the client: multiple views and skills, a broader knowledge base, and the ability to improve the fit between the advisor and the client. Multidisciplinary teams work best when someone assumes the leadership role and is ultimately accountable. However, some models that provide for interdependence and joint accountability, even when outside one's particular discipline, also appear to work (Rawlings, 2000).

As an alternative to maintaining an always-available team, many family business consultants consider themselves to be a team captain who calls in the specialists as they are needed. This approach may better serve the needs of the business, the family, and the professionals themselves. In our role as relationship consultants we are frequently called in specifically to bring about reconciliation among members of the family-owned business; when the reconciliation is complete, we transition the family back to the ongoing consulting team.

Professionals also frequently operate conjointly in subgroups of the multidisciplinary team. By "conjointly" we mean two or more team members working together with the family to resolve particular issues. A conjoint approach is especially helpful in dealing with relationship problems among contending parties or estranged members in a family business. To get the job done right, a consulting partnership is absolutely essential in handling a complex reconciliation effort with a number of family members involved. Relationship consultants working conjointly are better able to:

- Provide safety so that all family members can get the individual help they need to successfully manage themselves in difficult discussions and reveal themselves in difficult circumstances.
- Track the process and help the family stay on task. Often this can be a challenge when there are strong emotional reactions that make it hard for advisors and family members to keep their focus.
- Help contain the conflicts and manage emotions. Advisors must notice and respond to emotions in family members including those who may not be central to the current concern of the moment. Conjoint teams allow one person to track the issue and the other to track the emotions.
- Provide reality testing. It is easy for the advisor to become so involved in the family's web that he or she loses perspective. A co-leader, standing outside, can often help regain perspective and move the family along.

In this book we have demonstrated the conjoint approach in our work with the Sampson family. For instance, during the third day of the three-day group meeting our strategy of dividing the family and working individually with Sam served a dual purpose—taking care of Sam and moving the group along. Working as a team allowed Les to work individually with Sam and help protect him from the shame of exposure to the family while he was collecting himself and moving from feeling to thinking about important decisions he needed to make. This approach also allowed Ruth to work with other key players by helping them prepare for the meeting with Sam and continue with the business at hand. Other segments of the work clearly showed the tracking process in action: as partners each of us followed a line of thinking that the other had started, to either a conclusion or a turning point.

SAYING GOOD-BYE AND MOVING ON

Often advisors need assistance in saying good-bye to clients and moving on. Just like family members who are unable to let go and move on, advisors may have a hard time accepting the necessity of changing the guard.

Before getting into the question of when advisors end the consulting connection, let's first look at some important questions that family members must answer when they are readying themselves for retirement from long-held positions with the family company:

- Where do I go from here, and what do I move on to?
- Can I rely on those who are taking over for me?
- What will the future bring financially?
- Will anyone still care about me?
- Will anyone still notice who I am; will I still be important?

Initiating conversations about the issues raised in these questions helps the family address the unfinished business that needs to be taken care of when someone leaves his or her long-held position in the family enterprise. It also sets the stage for the family, with our help, to create a good-bye ceremony, mourn the losses, and say hello to a different present and a brand-new future. Creating good-bye rituals for family members is part of the relationship consultant's job. The traditional "gold watch" ceremony has great significance and is extremely valuable in helping everyone in the family move on.

As advisors, we too must eventually answer a similar set of questions. We must address these same issues, but privately. Giving ourselves the "gold watch" is a reminder that moving on is a symbol of a job well done.

Saying good-bye and moving on, however, is sometimes quite difficult for advisors because they have become stuck in fantasies of their own importance and in the comfortable predictability of the engagement. Advisors often have become an integral part of the family and may have allowed themselves to be enticed with perks to stay around, as often is the case. On the other hand, families themselves usually have a tremendously difficult time letting go of treasured advisors and it is our responsibility to teach them to let go by doing so ourselves.

So, as relationship advisors, we must continuously remind ourselves that we are truly successful only when there is no longer a need for us. Our primary concern and commitment is to the family and getting them ready to be on their own. We know that our goal in helping them has been achieved only when we have become *unimportant* to that business-owning family.

CONCLUSION

Our book has been about the most important relationships of peoples' lives: relationships with parents, children, siblings, cousins, spouses, in-laws, and other connections as they exist and are challenged within a business-owning family. We have shown how as concerned professionals we can help our clients change, heal, and survive into the future when one, some, or even many of these family relationships are currently conflicted, ruptured, or estranged.

As we bring our book to its close, we are aware that most of the stories about family business presented have had successful outcomes in that relationship repair was achieved by using our Reconciliation Model. However, in some difficult situations the relationship hurts had gone too deep for too long, with the ruptures so severe, complex, and far-reaching that family members simply found it impossible to reconcile. In some other situations, family members with a vested interest in maintaining the status quo refused to participate in efforts to reconcile and change. Finally, we have also presented several stories in which reconciliation was never even tried, resulting in circumstances that led to a fragmented family and a failed business. All of these stories represent the realities of the world of family business relationships.

In each of the reconciliation successes in which trust was reestablished there is restored faith in the family and great promise for the future of the business. Even in reconciliation failures, though, prospects for the future can become positive if family members eventually are willing to recognize, accept, and learn from their past. In the families where the opportunities for reconciliation were missed, there is always hope, because it is never too late to end estrangement. Family members, especially those in the next generations, can overcome their differences and distrust of one another to rise above the problems of the past and work together in ways that will guarantee the enduring success of the family business.

Keeping a family together is clearly a difficult task. Keeping a business-owning family together and working collaboratively can be far more daunting; it requires patience, persistence, and care. In writing this book we have particularly wished to help family members and family business advisors in these ways: to understand and appreciate the fragility of the relationships of people who live, love, and work together; to respect the transformational power existing within positive family relationships; and to learn the tools for reconciling relationships that have been ruptured or alienated.

If you are a member of a business-owning family, we hope that you have learned that it is possible to travel through the intense pain of estrangement and arrive at the other side—accepting, caring about, and affirming yourself and others in ways that you never thought were possible.

If you are a business advisor, we hope that we have provided ample evidence that either you or relationship specialists can help client families achieve reconciliation when their relationships have gone awry, thus giving them a new chance to achieve accord and long-term prosperity in the business they own together.

As family business advisors we have the power to help clients heal ruptured family relationships, change their lives, and succeed in their business. How any one of us chooses to use that power is both a professional and a personal decision that is influenced by training and tempered by practical experience.

References

Bader, E. and Pearson, P. (1988). *In Quest of the Mythical Mate*. New York: Brunner/Mazel.

Bader, E. and Pearson, P. (2000). *Tell Me No Lies: How to Face the Truth and Build a Loving Marriage*. New York: St. Martin's Press.

Bandura, A . (1999). Moral disengagement in the perpetration of inhumanities. *Personality & Social Psychology Review*, 3:193-209.

Basch, M. (1988). *Understanding Psychotherapy*. New York: Basic Books.

Berne, E. (1963). *The Structure and Dynamics of Organizations and Groups*. Philadelphia: J.B. Lippincott.

Berne, E. (1964). *Games People Play*. New York: Grove Press.

Biringen, Z., Emde, R., and Pipp-Siegel, S. (1997). Dyssynchrony, conflict, and resolution: Positive contributions to infant development. *American Journal of Orthopsychiatry*, 67:4-19.

Boszormenyi-Nagy, I. and Spark, G. (1973). *Invisible Loyalties: Reciprocity in Intergenerational Family Therapy*. New York: Harper & Row.

Bouraine, A. (2000). *A Country Unmasked*. Oxford: Oxford University Press.

Bowen, M. (1978). *Family Therapy in Clinical Practice*. Northvale, NJ: Jason Aronson.

Boylan, R. (1991). The Bingham Saga. Book Review. *Columbia Journalism Review*. July/August. <http//www.cjr/year/91/4/bingham.asp>.

Buber, M. (1974). *I and Thou*. Translated by W. Kaufman and S.G. Smith. New York: Charles Scribner.

Davis, L. (2002). *I Thought We'd Never Speak Again: The Road from Estrangement to Reconciliation*. New York: HarperCollins.

De Bono, E. (1999). *Six Thinking Hats*. Boston: Little Brown.

Dickson, P., Farris, P., and Verbeke, W. (2001). Dynamic strategic thinking. *Journal of the Academy of Marketing Science*, 29:216-237.

Friedman, D. (1991). Bowen theory and therapy. In G. Gurman and D. Kniskern (Eds.), *Handbook of Family Therapy II* (pp. 134-170). New York: Brunner/Mazel.

Gersick, K., Davis, J., McCollum-Hampton, M., and Lansberg, I. (1997). *Generation to Generation: Life Cycles of the Family Business*. Boston: Harvard Business School Press.

Gersick, K., Lansberg, I., Desjardins, M., and Dunn, B. (1999). Stages and transitions: Managing change in family business. *Family Business Review*, 12:287-297.

Glenn, S. and Nelsen, J. (1988). *Raising Self-Reliant Children in a Self-Indulgent World: Seven Building Blocks for Developing Capable Young People.* Fair Oaks, CA: Sunrise Press.

Gordon, S. and Baucom, D. (1998). Understanding betrayals in marriage: Synthesized model of forgiveness. *Family Process,* 37:425-451.

Gottman, J. and Silver, N. (2000). *The Seven Principles for Making Marriage Work.* New York: Three Rivers Press.

Goulding, M. and Goulding, R. (1995). *Changing Lives through Redecision Therapy* (Third Edition). New York: Grove Press.

Greer, C. (1998). Without Memory There Is No Healing. Without Forgiveness, There Is No Future. Interview with Archbishop Desmond Tutu. *Parade,* January 11:4-6.

Gulbenkian Commission (1996). *Open the Social Sciences: Report on the Restructuring of the Social Sciences.* Stanford, CA: Stanford University Press.

Hofstede, G., Neuijen, B., Ohayv, D., and Sanders, G. (1990). Measuring organizational cultures: A qualitative and quantitative study across twenty cases. *Administrative Science Quarterly,* 35:286-316.

Jacobson, N. and Margolin, G. (1979). *Marital Therapy: Strategies Based on Social Learning and Behavior Exchange Principles.* New York: Brunner/Mazel.

Johnson, H., LaVoie, J., and Mahoney, M. (2001). Interparental conflict and family cohesion: Predictors of loneliness, social anxiety, and social avoidance in late adolescence. *Journal of Adolescent Research,* 16:304-318.

Johnson, S. (1998). Listening to the music. *Journal of Systemic Therapies,* 17:1-17.

Kadis, L. and McClendon, R. (1998). *Concise Guide to Marital and Family Therapy.* Washington, DC: American Psychiatric Press.

Kaslow, F. (1996). Recurrent themes across diagnoses. In F. Kaslow (Ed.), *Handbook of Relational Diagnosis and Dysfunctional Family Patterns* (pp. 523-532). San Francisco: Jossey-Bass.

Katzenbach, J. (1998). *Teams at the Top: Unleashing the Potential of Both Teams and Individual Leaders.* London: McKinsey and Company, Inc.

Kelly, V. (1996). Affect and the redefinition of intimacy. In D. Nathanson (Ed.), *Knowing Feeling: Affect Script and Psychotherapy* (pp. 55-104). New York: Norton.

Kelsh, N. and Quindlen, A. (1998). *Siblings.* New York: Penguin.

Kouzes, J. and Posner, B. (1993). *Credibility: How Leaders Gain and Lose, Why People Demand It.* San Francisco: Jossey-Bass.

LaChapelle, K. and Barnes, L. (1998). The trust catalyst in the family-owned business. *Family Business Review,* 11:1-15.

Lank, A. (2001). Determinants of longevity of the family business. *F.B.N. Newsletter,* 29:15-19.

Laursen, B., Finkelstein, B., and Townsend, B. (2001). A developmental meta-analysis of peer conflict resolution. *Developmental Review,* 21:423-449.

Lawson, D.M. (2001).The development of abusive personality: A trauma response. *Journal of Counseling & Development,* 79:505-509.

Lewis, J. (1998). For better or worse: Interpersonal relationships for individual outcome. *American Journal of Psychiatry,* 155:582-589.

Lewis, J. (2000). Repairing the bond in important relationships: A dynamic for personality maturation. *American Journal of Psychiatry,* 157:1375-1378.

Lewis, J., Beavers, W., Gossett, J., and Phillips, V. (1976). *No Single Thread: Psychological Health in Family Systems.* New York: Brunner/Mazel.

Madanes, C. (1995). *The Violence of Men.* San Francisco: Jossey-Bass.

Maggio, R. (Ed.) (1992). *The Beacon Book of Quotations by Women* (p. 28). Boston: Beacon Press.

McClendon, R. and Kadis, L. (1983). *Chocolate Pudding and Other Approaches to Intensive Multiple Family Therapy.* Palo Alto, CA: Science and Behavior Books.

McGoldrick, M. and Gerson, R. (1985). *Genograms in Family Assessment.* New York: Norton.

McGoldrick, M. and Toast, J. (1993). Ethnicity, families, and family business: Implications for practitioners. *Family Business Review,* 6:283-300.

Moos, R. and Moos, B. (1986). *Family Environment Scale Manual* (Revised Edition). Palo Alto, CA: Consulting Psychologists Press.

Nathanson, D. (1992). *Shame and Pride.* New York: Norton.

Nelson, B. and Wampler, K.S. (2000). Systemic effects of trauma in clinic couples: An exploratory study of secondary trauma resulting from childhood abuse. *Journal of Marital & Family Therapy,* 26:171-184.

Olson, D., Sprenkle, D., and Russell, C. (1979). Circumplex model of marital and family systems. *Family Process,* 18:3-28.

O'Malley, M. (2000). *Creating Commitment.* Hoboken, NJ: John Wiley & Sons.

Penn, P. (1982). Circular questioning. *Family Process,* 21:267-280.

Polster, E. and Polster, M. (1974). *Gestalt Therapy Integrated: Contours of Theory and Practice.* New York: Vintage.

Prochaska, J. and DiClemente, C. (1992). Stages of change in the modification of problem behaviors. *Progress in Behavior Modification,* 28:183-218.

Rawlings, D. (2000). Collaborative leadership teams: Oxymoron or new paradigm? *Consulting Psychology Journal: Practice & Research,* 52:36-48.

Roberts, D. (1987). *Able and Equal: A Gentle Path to Peace and Symbiotic Systems.* Los Angeles: Human Esteem Publishing.

Rodgers, T., Taylor, W., and Foreman, R. (1999). *No Excuses Management.* New York: Currency/Doubleday.

Rosen, E. (2000). *The Anatomy of Buzz: How to Create Word of Mouth Marketing.* New York: Doubleday.

Schatzman, M. (1976). *Soul Murder: Persecution in the Family.* New York: New American Library.

Schein, E.H. (1992). *Organizational Culture and Leadership* (Second Edition). San Francisco: Jossey-Bass.

Schlenker, B., Pontari, B., and Christopher, A. (2001). Excuses and character: Personal and social implications of excuses. *Personality & Social Psychology Review,* 5:15-32.

Senge, P. (1990). *The Fifth Discipline.* New York: Currency/Doubleday.

Shengold, L. (1999). *Soul Murder Revisited: Thoughts About Therapy, Hate, Love, and Memory.* New Haven, CT: Yale University Press.

Smith, D. (1997). *Taking Charge of Change: 10 Principles for Managing People and Performance.* Cambridge, MA: Perseus Publishing.

Smith, K. and Zane, N. (1999). Organizational reflections: Parallel processes at work in a dual consultation. *Journal of Applied Behavioral Science,* 35:145-162.

Sperry, L. (1998). Organizations that foster inappropriate aggression. *Psychiatric Annals,* 28:279-284.

Tomkins, S. (1963). *Affect, Imagery, Consciousness, Volume 2: The Negative Affects.* New York: Springer.

Trompenaars, F. and Hampden-Turner, C. (1997). *Riding the Waves of Culture: Understanding Cultural Diversity in Business* (Second Edition). London: Nicholas Brealy Publishing.

Truth and Reconciliation Commission (TRC). (1998). *Report of the Truth and Reconciliation Commission,* Volumes 1-5. Capetown: Juta.

Walsh, F. (1994). Healthy family functioning: Conceptual and research developments. *Family Business Review,* 7:175-198.

Watkins, R. (1993). *Birthright: Murder, Greed, and Power in the U-Haul Family Dynasty.* New York: Morrow.

Werner, P., Green, R., Greenberg, J., Browne, T., and McKenna, T. (2001). Beyond enmeshment: Evidence for the independence of intrusiveness and closeness-caregiving in married couples. *Journal of Marital & Family Therapy,* 27:459-471.

Index

Page numbers followed by the letter 'i' indicate illustrations.

SPECIAL 25%-OFF DISCOUNT!

Order a copy of this book with this form or online at:
http://www.haworthpress.com/store/product.asp?sku=4920

Reconciling Relationships and Preserving the Family Business
Tools for Success

_____in hardbound at $37.46 (regularly $49.95) (ISBN: 0-7890-1799-7)

_____in softbound at $22.46 (regularly $29.95) (ISBN: 0-7890-1800-4)

Or order online and use special offer code HEC25 in the shopping cart.

COST OF BOOKS_____

OUTSIDE US/CANADA/
MEXICO: ADD 20%_____

POSTAGE & HANDLING_____
*(US: $5.00 for first book & $2.00
for each additional book)*
*(Outside US: $6.00 for first book
& $2.00 for each additional book)*

SUBTOTAL_____

IN CANADA: ADD 7% GST_____

STATE TAX_____
*(NY, OH MN, CA, IN, & SD residents,
add appropriate local sales tax)*

FINAL TOTAL_____
*(If paying in Canadian funds,
convert using the current
exchange rate, UNESCO
coupons welcome)*

☐ **BILL ME LATER:** ($5 service charge will be added)
(Bill-me option is good on US/Canada/Mexico orders only;
not good to jobbers, wholesalers, or subscription agencies.)

☐ Check here if billing address is different from
shipping address and attach purchase order and
billing address information.

Signature_____

☐ **PAYMENT ENCLOSED: $**_____

☐ **PLEASE CHARGE TO MY CREDIT CARD.**

☐ Visa ☐ MasterCard ☐ AmEx ☐ Discover
☐ Diner's Club ☐ Eurocard ☐ JCB

Account # _____

Exp. Date_____

Signature_____

Prices in US dollars and subject to change without notice.

NAME_____

INSTITUTION_____

ADDRESS_____

CITY_____

STATE/ZIP_____

COUNTRY_____ COUNTY (NY residents only)_____

TEL_____ FAX_____

E-MAIL_____

May we use your e-mail address for confirmations and other types of information? ☐ Yes ☐ No
We appreciate receiving your e-mail address and fax number. Haworth would like to e-mail or fax special
discount offers to you, as a preferred customer. **We will never share, rent, or exchange your e-mail address
or fax number.** We regard such actions as an invasion of your privacy.

Order From Your Local Bookstore or Directly From
The Haworth Press, Inc.
10 Alice Street, Binghamton, New York 13904-1580 • USA
TELEPHONE: 1-800-HAWORTH (1-800-429-6784) / Outside US/Canada: (607) 722-5857
FAX: 1-800-895-0582 / Outside US/Canada: (607) 771-0012
E-mailto: orders@haworthpress.com
PLEASE PHOTOCOPY THIS FORM FOR YOUR PERSONAL USE.
http://www.HaworthPress.com   BOF03